TE WAHIPOUNAMU

# SOUTH-WEST NEW ZEALAND

WORLD HERITAGE AREA

PHOTOGRAPHS BY ANDRIS APSE

INTRODUCTION BY ANDY DENNIS

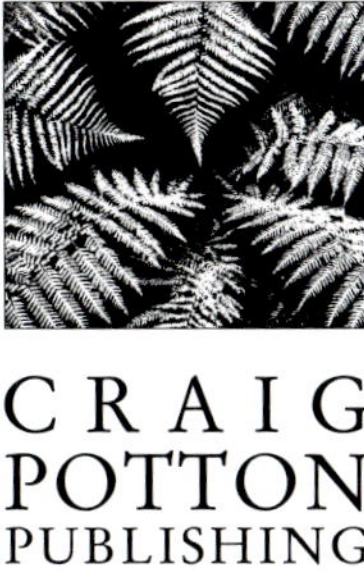

CRAIG
POTTON
PUBLISHING

Acknowledgements
Many of the photographs in this book are the result of years of wandering, some were produced under the pressure of a deadline.

In all situations there were people interested in this project, willing to share
their experience and knowledge. In some cases this help came at their personal expense.

There are many who could be mentioned for their advice and encouragement.
However, the following list is of those who contributed significantly to the project. My sincere thanks go to these people:
Alan Bond, Richard Hayes, Tim Innes, Ian James, Lou Sanson, Dave Saxton, Jeff Shanks, Ken Tustin.

Published by Craig Potton Publishing,
98 Vickerman Street, PO Box 555,
Nelson, New Zealand

Photography: Andris Apse
Introduction and captions: Andy Dennis
Map: One Sky Design
Production: Robbie Burton, Craig Potton and Tina Delceg
Publishing Coordinator: Robbie Burton
Filmwork: Printgroup, Wellington, Ltd
Printed in Hong Kong by Everbest Printing Co. Ltd

First published in 1997



The publishers wish to thank William Heinemann Ltd for permission to reproduce an extract
from Douglas Adams' *Last Chance to See*; and Brian Turner for permission to
reprint an extract from Peter Hooper's *Our Forests Ourselves.*



ISBN 0 908802 40 4

# SOUTH-WEST NEW ZEALAND

Dedicated to the memory of Bondie

*"To die completely, a person must not only forget but be forgotten, and he who is not forgotten is not dead."*

Samuel Butler

# CONTENTS

# FOREWORDS

In this book Andris Apse has captured the stunning beauty of Te Wahipounamu South-West New Zealand. Presented in this way it is easy to understand why the New Zealand government nominated, and UNESCO granted, World Heritage status to this outstanding natural landscape.

I remember, when I was a child, Andris Apse was given the unfortunate task of photographing my family. His skills were sorely tested, but he made us look surprisingly good. He has made his photography into an art form, and, in this fine collection of images, used the raw material in the World Heritage Area to dramatically depict this magnificent area of New Zealand.

At over a million hectares Fiordland National Park is endowed with an amazing variety of landscapes; Mount Aspiring, Westland and Mount Cook national parks too have spectacular scenic qualities, which Andris reflects in this publication. Being one of the first landscape photographers in New Zealand to take panoramic views of the land, Andris has imbued in his work a real sense of space, and in these photographs conveyed the wilderness and isolation that makes South-West New Zealand such an important place to New Zealanders and to the world.

The Department of Conservation and Andris Apse are in a sense working together to preserve New Zealand's natural grandeur forever. This book will communicate to all who look through its pages, including those without ready access to Te Wahipounamu, why it's been worth preserving the World Heritage Area for future generations of New Zealanders.

Dr Nick Smith

Minister of Conservation, 1997

In an increasingly crowded world where wilderness everywhere is being engulfed and displaced by humans, Te Wahipounamu—the South-West New Zealand World Heritage Area—emerges as a special place. A place where nature rules, where penguin footprints trail across beach sands, and where the ancient forests of Gondwanaland live on, yielding only to mountain landscapes as impressive as any on the planet.

It is also a place where the people of New Zealand, Pakeha and Maori, locals and distant city dwellers, and politicians of all persuasions, have embraced the inspirational concepts of the World Heritage Convention and put them into practice. Today, anything other than permanent protection of all the south-west's superlative natural phenomena seems unconscionable. Yet it was the advancing chainsaw fronts in the forests of Okarito and western Southland that triggered the outpouring of popular protest which led to the area's permanent protection in 1989. Forests that had endured storms, floods, earthquakes and glacial advances were seen to be vulnerable to whining chainsaws. An unhappy compromise of a region pockmarked by logging seemed likely until the World Heritage concept took the debate about the future of the region's forests beyond the tenuous needs of the present, and required the decision-makers to consider the true significance of the choices they faced. They chose wisely.

The World Heritage Convention proved to be a powerful ally to the conservationists who sought to have this area dedicated to nature. For the generation ahead the challenge is to safeguard the wonders of Te Wahipounamu from alien species—the biological chainsaws of deer, possums, thar, stoats and rats—and from being overwhelmed by mechanised tourism.

Let the beautiful images and compelling words of this book keep the spirit of Okarito alive. Let them enthuse all of us to ensure this special place suffers neither from neglect or over-use. We must approach this task humbly, and in awe and wonderment at one of nature's finest creations.

Kevin Smith, Director
New Zealand Royal Forest and Bird Protection Society

# INTRODUCTION

*'Fiordland, a vast tract of mountainous terrain that occupies the south-west corner of the South Island, New Zealand, is one of the most astounding pieces of land anywhere on God's earth, and one's first impulse, standing on a cliff top surveying it all, is simply to burst into spontaneous applause.'*

Douglas Adams

The photographs in this book are a celebration of one of the largest remaining areas of pristine wilderness in the temperate zones of the world—Te Wahipounamu, or the South-West New Zealand World Heritage Area. Beyond all else they are a celebration of the elemental forces that have shaped this remote corner of the far-flung islands of New Zealand into landscapes of extraordinary diversity and wild beauty, and endowed them with such effective natural barriers to human penetration and settlement that many of this country's unique native plants and animals, and the ecosystems that support them, have been better able to survive here than anywhere else. They are too a celebration of the wisdom and foresight of those New Zealanders who, from as early as the 1880s, have been aware of the necessity of setting aside large areas of unspoilt wild country both to protect their intrinsic values and for the benefit, use and enjoyment of those who need such places for inspiration, solitude and escape. In this respect they are also a celebration of a maturing conservation ethic that has seen attention increasingly focused on protecting distinctively New Zealand landscapes and ecosystems that were poorly represented in earlier national parks and reserves—in particular coastal and lowland forests and wetlands. And they are, of course, a celebration of the aesthetic spoils of the numerous visits made by Andris Apse into this vast southern wilderness terrain, and of the skill and patience he has devoted to capturing its landscapes and light in these immensely satisfying panoramic images.

The publication of a book celebrating the larger of New Zealand's two World Heritage areas (the other contains the volcanic landscapes of Tongariro National Park in the centre of the North Island) is timely for a number of reasons. In the first place, despite the fact that three of our most prominent national parks have been World Heritage areas since 1986, the concept of 'World Heritage' has not yet received much publicity in New Zealand, and still seems to be little comprehended by the wider public. A second reason is that as this book goes to print, the New Zealand government is in the process of applying for World Heritage status for its wildlife-rich subantarctic islands, and it would therefore seem to be an appropriate occasion for raising the profile of our existing World Heritage areas. And thirdly, its year of publication (1997) marks the twenty-fifth anniversary of the adoption by the United Nations Educational, Scientific and Cultural Organisation (Unesco) of the World Heritage Convention—or, to give it its full title, the 'Convention for the Protection of the World's Cultural and Natural Heritage'—which for the first time provided a framework for nations to work together to protect cultural or natural features, sites or areas that are of such outstanding significance that they are deemed to be part of the common heritage of all peoples.

The World Heritage Convention was drawn up by the General Assembly of Unesco in 1972 with the broad objective of ensuring that the foremost natural and cultural wonders of the modern world would be given the best possible chance of escaping the fate of the Seven Wonders of the ancient world, all of which, with the exception of the pyramids of Egypt, have now vanished. To this end nations participating in the convention undertake to work together to preserve outstanding cultural sites and natural areas as key components of a common global heritage. New Zealand adopted the convention in 1984, and two years later Mount Cook, Westland and Fiordland national parks were together added to Unesco's list of World Heritage sites and areas. Then, in 1990, largely as a result of the advocacy of the Royal Forest and Bird Protection Society, these along with Mount Aspiring National Park and most other significant intervening and adjacent protected natural areas were incorporated into a single vast South-West New Zealand World Heritage Area (Te Wahipounamu) containing 2.6 million hectares or about ten per cent of New Zealand's total land area. The name Te Wahipounamu (which means 'The Place of Greenstone') was chosen in recognition of the great cultural signifi-

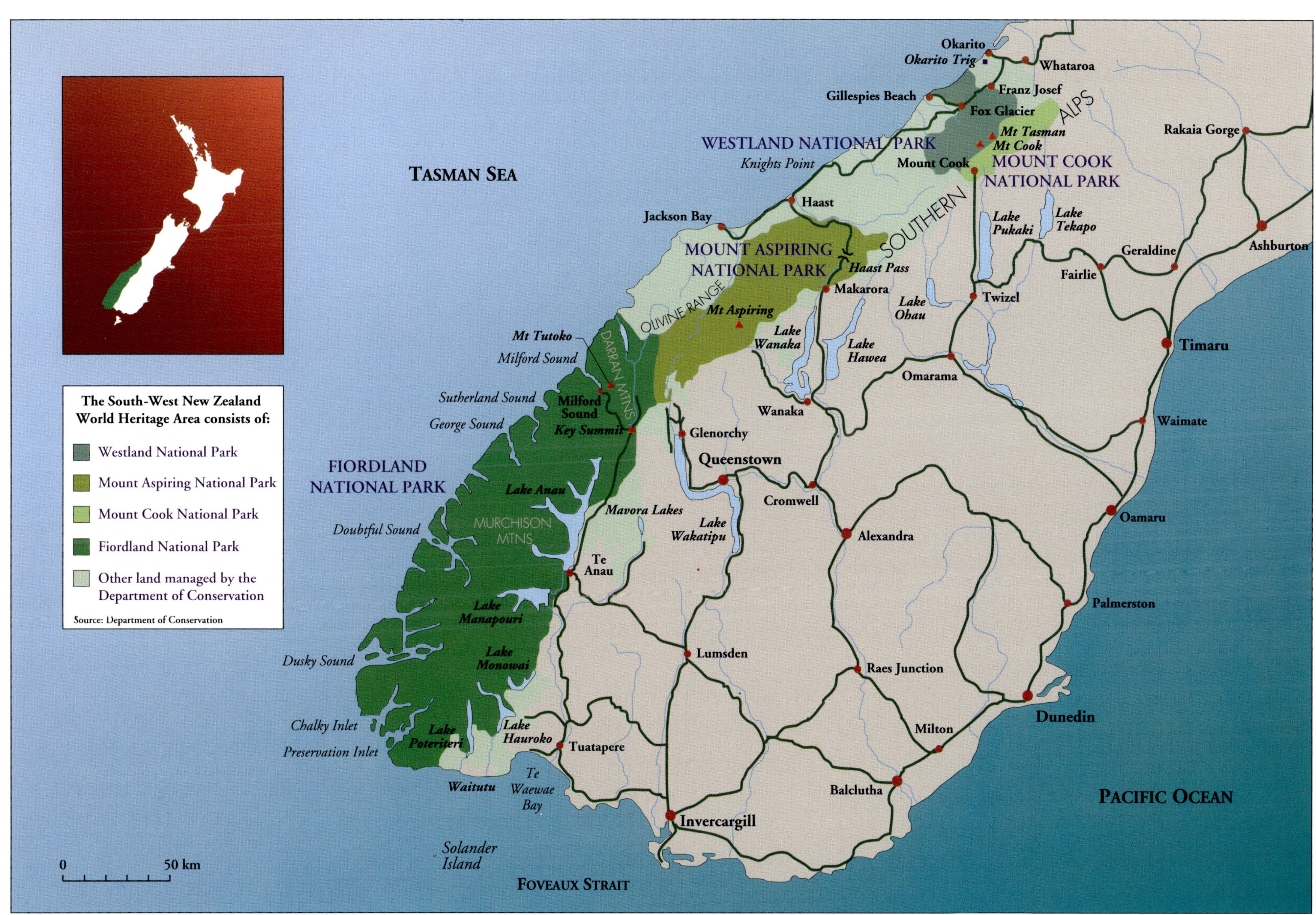


Te Wahipounamu South-West New Zealand World Heritage Area

cance of the area to Maori, especially as an ancient source of the prized pounamu (greenstone), and of the support given to the application for World Heritage status by the Ngai Tahu tribe, which represents the great majority of Maori with manawhenua (customary rights and authority over land) in this part of the country.

To date there are 506 World Heritage sites or areas, about three-quarters of them cultural monuments like the pyramids of Egypt, Britain's Stonehenge, the historic centre of Rome or the Inca city of Machu Picchu. The remainder include many of the world's most outstanding natural areas, including Serengeti National Park and Ngorongoro crater in Tanzania, Yellowstone, Grand Canyon and Yosemite national parks in the United States, Sagamartha (Everest) National Park in Nepal, Ecuador's Galapagos Islands, and Australia's Great Barrier Reef and Kakadu and Western Tasmania national parks. No surrender of sovereignty is involved when a country becomes a party to the World Heritage Convention, or when it has its cultural sites or natural areas added to the World Heritage list. Management remains in the hands of the host nation, and the only influence the international community can have is through encouragement and persuasion, the provision of technical and financial assistance, or by revocation of World Heritage status if such changes occur that a site or area no longer meets the qualifying criteria. The international prestige of being added to the World Heritage list has often resulted in significant increases in tourist interest, as has occurred in South Westland after the opening of the World Heritage Visitor Centre at Haast in 1991 and the associated publication of a World Heritage highway guide for the route through South Westland and across the Haast Pass.

To qualify for addition to the World Heritage list, natural sites or areas must constitute 'outstanding examples of the major stages in the earth's evolutionary history', or provide 'outstanding examples of ongoing geological process or biological evolution', or qualify as 'superlative natural phenomena, formations or features' (by virtue of their being sites containing 'the most important ecosystems' or areas of 'exceptional natural beauty'), or they must encompass 'the most significant natural habitats where threatened species of animals or plants of outstanding universal value still survive'. These are complex and overlapping criteria, and while the photographic component of this book provides adequate testimony of the presence in Te Wahipounamu of 'superlative natural phenomena' (at least in as much as these are areas of 'exceptional natural beauty'), the rest depend on deeper layers of significance woven into these wild south-west landscapes which probably need some further explanation.

For example, the whole of Te Wahipounamu provides an outstanding record of the Pleistocene epoch (the past two million years) and its series of ice ages and warmer inter-glacial periods. Virtually every mountain, valley, lake and fiord is a legacy of the sculpting work of ice age glaciers, while much of the lowland landscape of South Westland and vast Mackenzie Basin south of Mt Cook have been constructed by the massive transporting and dumping operations of these same glaciers. Inter-glacial episodes have also left their record in the landforms, most notably in the Waitutu region on the south coast of Fiordland where a remarkable sequence of thirteen raised marine terraces has created one of the best records anywhere in the world of the widely fluctuating sea levels that occurred during the Pleistocene epoch. There are too outstanding examples of the impacts of the Pleistocene ice ages on the region's plants and animals, most strikingly shown by the absence of otherwise ubiquitous beech forest from a 160-kilometre section of central Westland.

Much further back in time—somewhere about eighty million years ago—ancestral New Zealand finally broke away from the primeval southern super-continent of Gondwanaland (which for hundreds of millions of years had included Antarctica, South America, Africa, India and Australia) and began its long era of separate evolution. Loaded with Gondwana plants and animals that continued to evolve free from the diluting influences which subsequently affected all other pieces of this ancient tectonic jigsaw, it was, in a very real sense a 'Southern Ark'. Subsequent plants and animals that managed to migrate to New Zealand were mainly of tropical origin, and thus unsuited to the cooler southern parts of their new home. The net result has been that the south-west region of New Zealand today provides the best modern preservation of the ancient biota of Gondwanaland—and hence of this major primeval phase in the earth's evolutionary history. Foremost among the surviving Gondwana links are the beech and podocarp families of trees, and a range of unique animals that includes kiwi, large carnivorous land snails, and many other invertebrate groups.

As well as its remarkable record of the imprint of the Pleistocene ice ages, Te Wahipounamu also provides numerous outstanding examples of ongoing geological processes. These include evidence of the rapid rate at which the Southern Alps are continuing to rise along the Alpine Fault (indicated by displaced terraces either side of the fault in Westland National Park), and rather more obvious evidence of the equally rapid rate at which these rising mountains are being knocked back down by wind and water and ice. Dramatic examples abound of the way in which the glaciers and rivers of the region continue to shift vast volumes of shattered mountains down to lower altitudes, assisted by regular cataclysmic events such as the huge landslip that

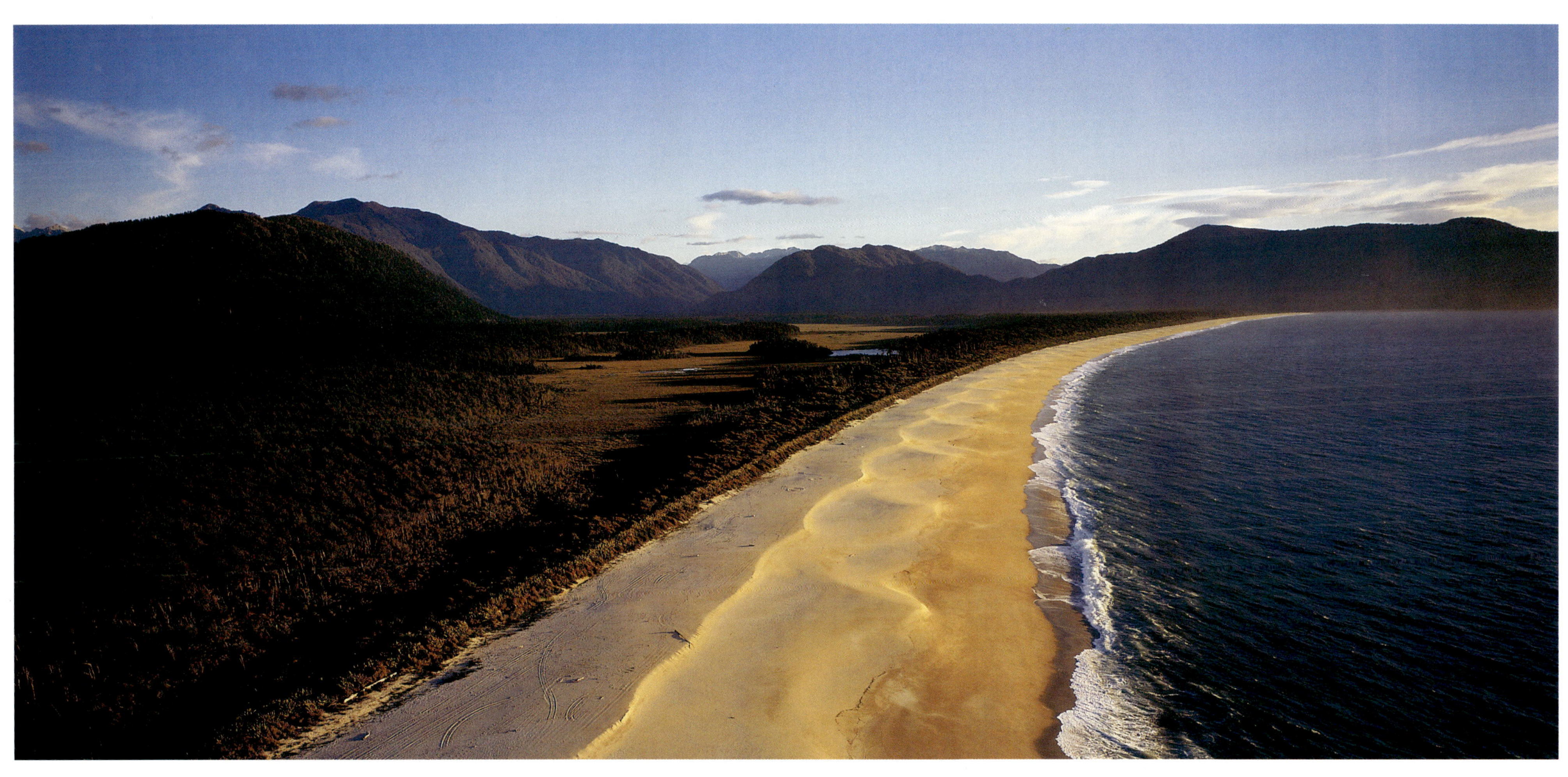

South Westland: Ohinemaka beach, coastal forest and wetlands, just south of Bruce Bay.

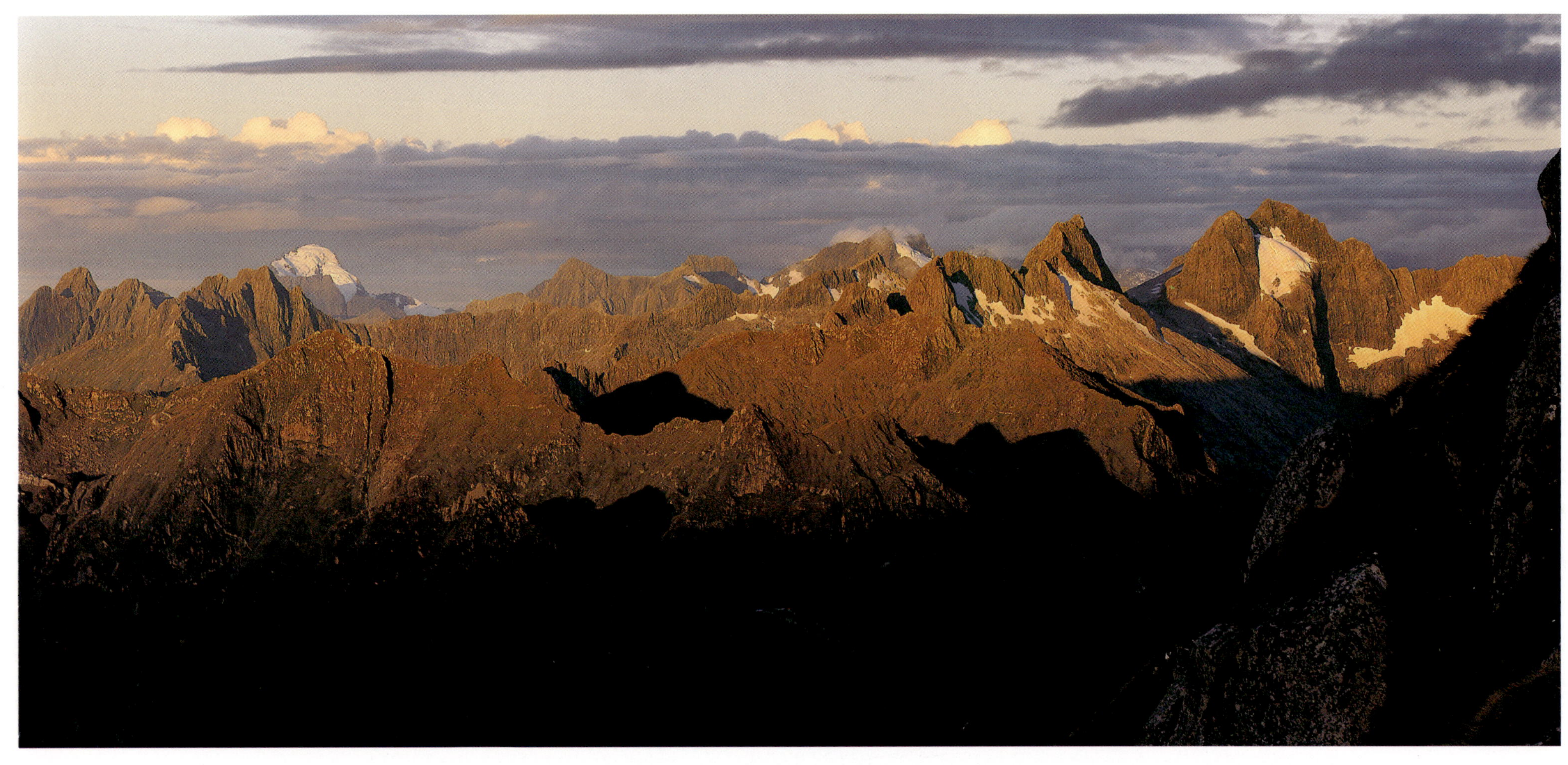

Fiordland National Park: Glaciated ridges and summits at the head of Sutherland Sound, looking north to the snowcapped Mt Pembroke.

detached from the summit of Mt Cook in 1991, lowering the height of the mountain by ten metres and delivering millions of tonnes of rock rubble down onto the surface of the Tasman Glacier. Spectacular landscape rearrangements are constantly taking place at the terminal regions of the larger glaciers, with the main West Coast glaciers at present rapidly re-advancing down valley while across the Alps in Mount Cook National Park large lakes are forming in the lower reaches of the Tasman and Godley glaciers as more ice melts in summer than is replaced by winter snows.

Te Wahipounamu also contains the most significant natural habitats for a wide range of threatened indigenous plants and animals, some of which are very clearly of 'outstanding universal value'. More than forty species of birds, all unique to New Zealand, have become extinct over the past 1,000 years since humans first landed on these shores, and many more now are today threatened with a similar fate. Birds in this predicament whose last strongholds are within the World Heritage Area include South Island brown kiwi, takahe, yellowhead, yellow-crowned parakeet and Fiordland crested penguin. Of these, South Island brown kiwi are confined to this south-west corner of New Zealand where they survive in three isolated populations (Okarito, Haast and Fiordland) which are now thought to be genetically distinct, and two of which have very low numbers. Fiordland crested penguins are probably the rarest penguins in the world with a population of less than 5,000 scattered around the coasts of South Westland, Fiordland and Stewart Island. And takahe, which excited worldwide interest when rediscovered in Fiordland in 1948 fifty years after having been thought to be extinct, are confined to the Murchison and Stuart mountains west of Lake Te Anau, where the present wild population is believed to number less than 200 birds.

Efforts to protect the values now encompassed in the World Heritage criteria began with sizeable tracts of mountain lands in the Mount Cook region being reserved in 1885 and 1887 (the first significant reserves anywhere in the South Island mountains), and continued with the setting aside of a huge area of Fiordland in 1905 (905,000 hectares) and a series of reserves created in the region of the West Coast glaciers and nearby scenic lakes from 1911. Although the early reserves at both Mount Cook and Fiordland were set aside 'for national park purposes' with the aim of providing South Island counterparts for New Zealand's first two national parks at Tongariro (in 1894) and Mt Egmont (in 1901), no national parks were created in the southern half of the South Island prior to the 1950s. The principal reason for this was the absence of a general legislative framework and agreed criteria for creating national parks, which meant that a separate Act of Parliament was required in each instance. Things became easier after the passage of the first National Parks Act in 1952, and within little more than a decade the four national parks now gathered together in Te Wahipounamu had been established. The first of these was Fiordland in 1952, followed by Mount Cook in 1953, Westland in 1960, and Mount Aspiring in 1964. In their original form each of these parks was significantly smaller than they are today, most notably Mount Aspiring which has increased by over seventy-five per cent from an original area of just on 200,000 hectares to its present 355,546 hectares.

The fact that by 1964 there were four large national parks spread along the ranges of south-western New Zealand was magnificent testimony to the foresight and dedication of those responsible for their creation, but the task of protecting the natural integrity of this wildest and most remote part of the country was by no means completed, and over the next twenty-five years a number of the most prominent conservation campaigns in New Zealand history were mounted to protect key landscapes and ecosystems of areas that are now included in Te Wahipounamu. The first of these resulted from a proposal in the early 1960s to raise the levels of lakes Manapouri and Te Anau in Fiordland National Park for hydro-electricity generation, a scheme which, had it gone ahead, would have caused major desecration of two of the country's most pristine larger lakes. The scheme provoked the biggest environmental controversy in New Zealand history (and one that almost certainly affected the outcome of the 1972 general election) before the natural level of these lakes was finally given statutory protection. A decade later another major confrontation took place, this time in South Westland, as conservationists battled to protect the last great tracts of lowland podocarp forest in the country and bring some ecological balance to a network of national parks and reserves which, up to that time, had been heavily biased towards the protection of mountain regions. The resulting addition of around 20,000 hectares of coastal and lowland forest to Westland National Park in 1982, and the subsequent protection of all remaining publicly owned forests south of the Cook River in 1989 (which included 300,000 hectares of lowland forest), were of huge national and international significance for conservation. Indeed, if the creation of Te Wahipounamu had achieved nothing more than providing a political catalyst for securing the long-term protection of these South Westland lowland forests and their extensive areas of associated freshwater and coastal wetlands, this alone justifies the effort involved many times over.

The granting of World Heritage status is thus another significant step in more than a century of conserva-

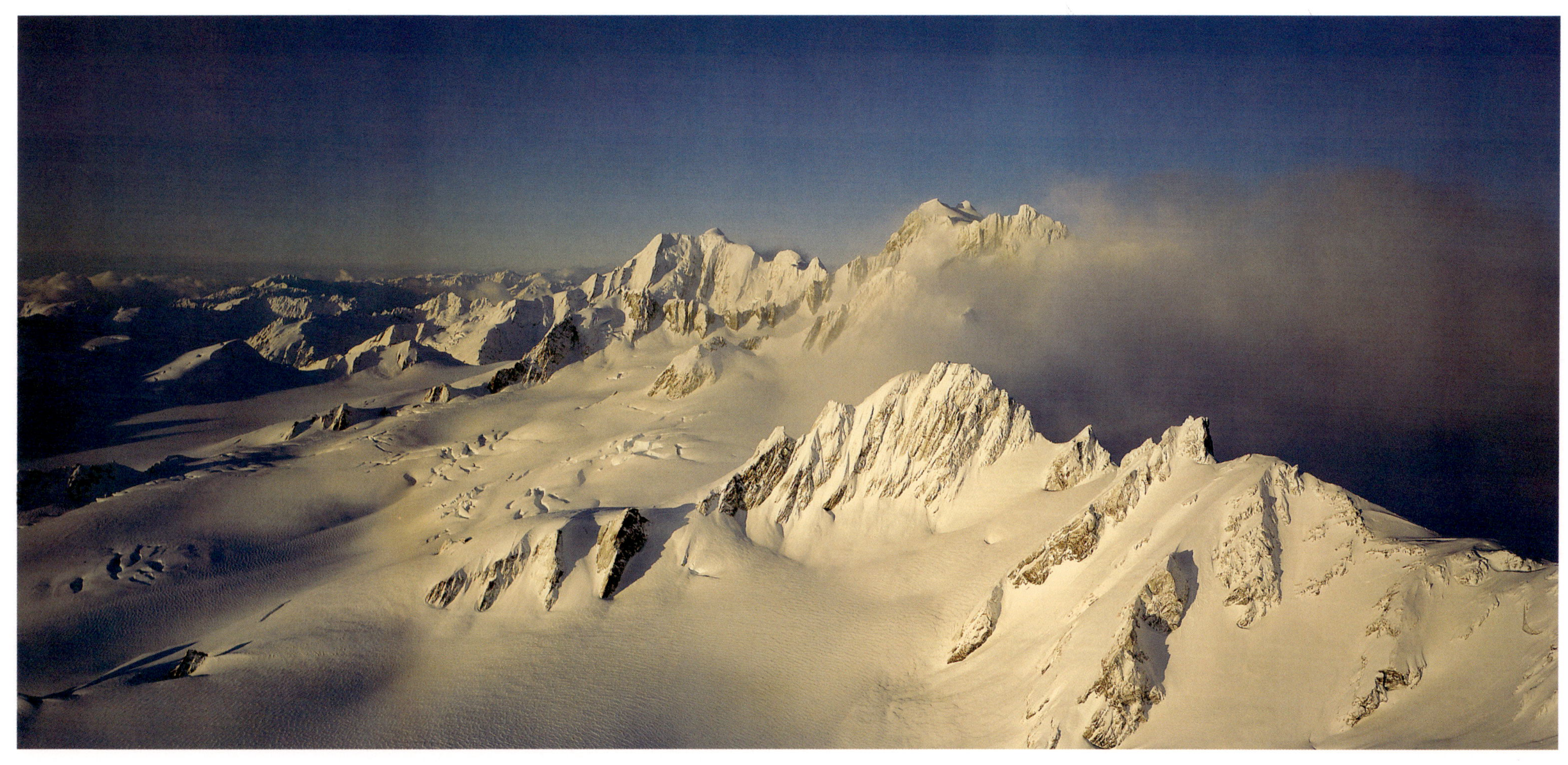

Westland National Park: The Main Divide of the Southern Alps from snowfields above the Franz Josef Glacier.

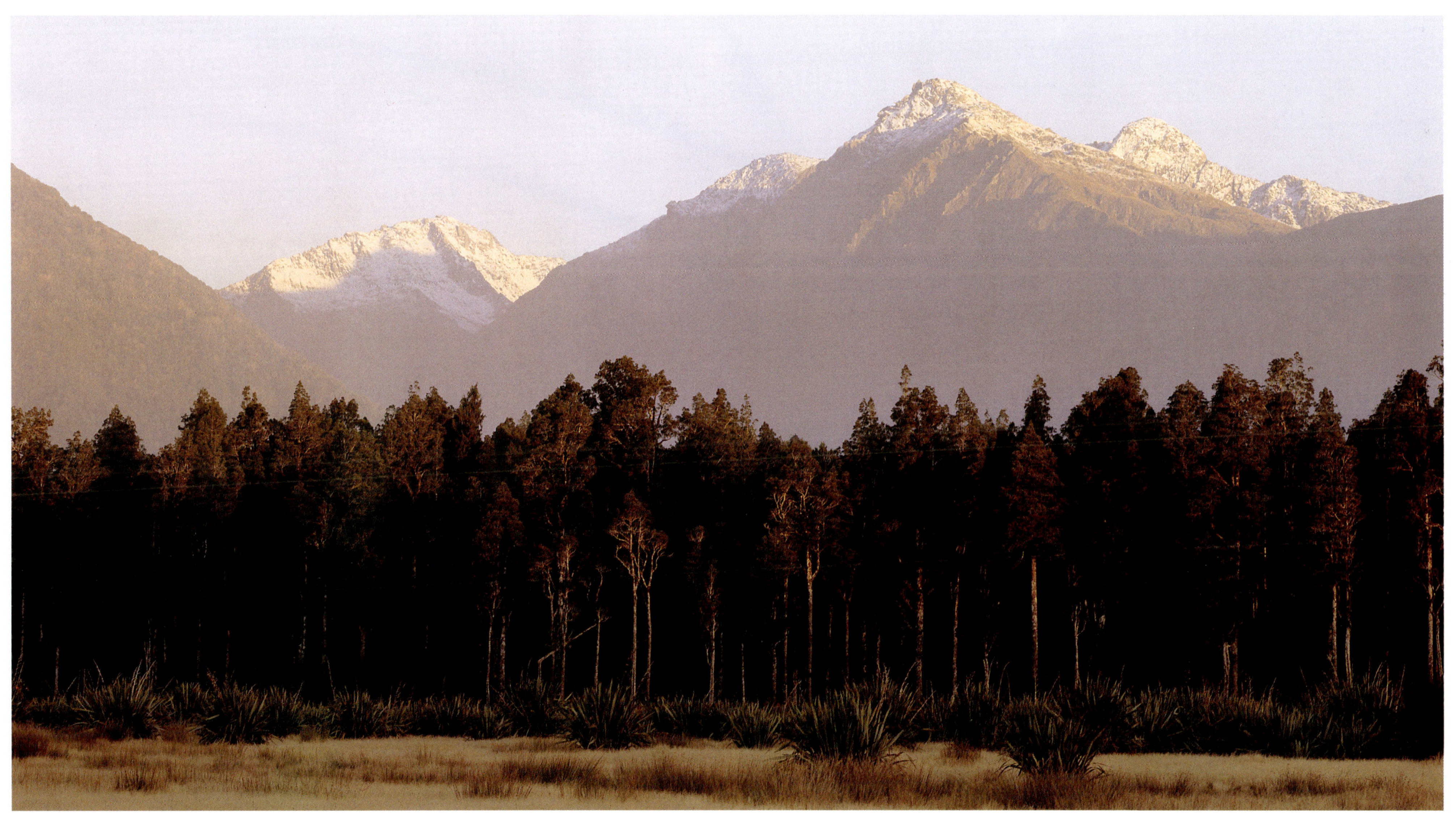

South Westland: Southern Alps foothills rise above forested coastal plains near the mouth of Makawhio River.

tion effort in south-west New Zealand, but there still a number of major tasks confronting those who care deeply about the preservation of wild places and their naturally occurring communities of plants and animals before it can be truly said that adequate protection has been provided for all significant landforms and ecosystems in this part of the country. These include a much greater commitment to marine protection and to extending the range of protected landscapes and ecosystems on the drier eastern flanks of the Southern Alps, and also to improving the quality of important ecological areas already protected, especially in their role as habitat for rare and threatened native wildlife. There are as well pressing issues related to human use and enjoyment of some parts of Te Wahipounamu, and although examination of these lies beyond the scope of this book it is worth remembering that elsewhere in the world outstanding natural areas have often seen much of their elemental character eroded by excessive and/or inappropriate visitor use. Yosemite and Grand Canyon national parks in the United States are obvious examples of World Heritage sites whose value as places of escape and inspiration has been hugely compromised by crowds, concrete, commerce, noisy machines and a philosophy of visitor use that has more to do with profit than with the preservation of natural integrity. Similar trends are becoming apparent at the main tourist attractions in Te Wahipounamu (Milford Sound, Mount Cook and the Fox and Franz Josef glaciers) and in this context we would do well to heed the words of the great American photographer of wild landscapes, Ansel Adams, whose lifelong association with Yosemite Valley led him to warn as far back as 1945 that tourism would ultimately pose a greater threat to national park values than the degradations of the oil, logging, mining and cattle ranching industries combined.

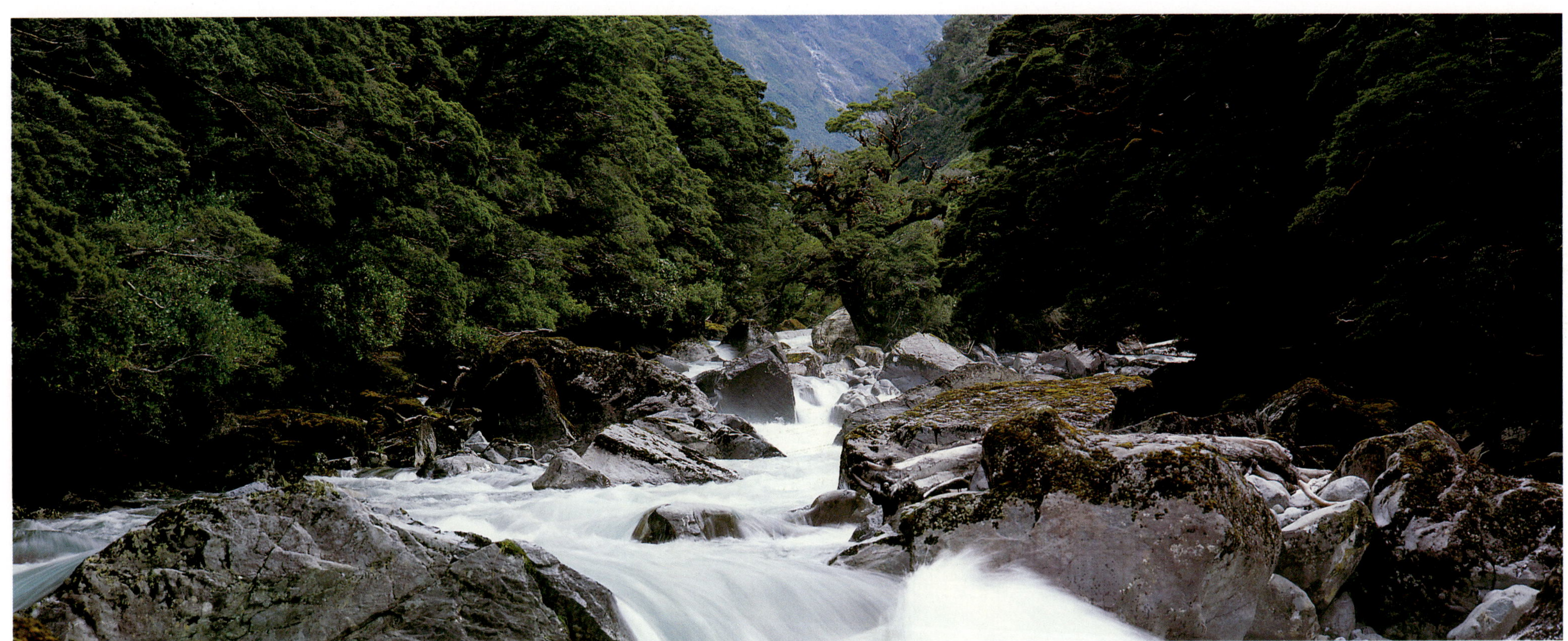

Fiordland National Park: Flanked by beech forest, the upper Hollyford River cascades between boulders on its way to the Tasman Sea.

The most fundamental deficiency at present is that the western and southern boundaries of the national parks and other protected lands gathered together in Te Wahipounamu end at the mean high water mark, and except for a couple of small marine reserves in Milford and Doubtful sounds give no protection to the sea, seabed or inter-tidal areas. The fact that over the past 100 years New Zealand has managed to protect 2.6 million hectares of land in this part of the country but only 783 hectares of its coastal marine environment supports the assertion that in protecting its marine environment New Zealand lags a century behind its considerable achievements in protecting land areas. In this context it is worth noting that the proposal to seek World Heritage status for New Zealand's subantarctic islands is expected to include a twelve nautical mile zone of coastal marine environment, and there is thus surely also a good case for taking urgent steps to protect a zone of similar size around significant parts of the coast of Te Wahipounamu. Among their many outstanding natural values, these south-western coasts provide the main stronghold of the world's rarest penguin (Fiordland crested penguin), a major component of the habitat range of the world's rarest dolphin (Hector's dolphin) and unique ecological conditions in the Fiordland fiords where a peaty-brown surface layer of freshwater created by the very high rainfall restricts light and enables marine plants and animals usually found at much greater depths to establish in shallow water.

Substantial additions are also needed to increase the range of protected lands on the eastern side of the present World Heritage Area. West of the ranges protection usually extends from the mountains to the sea, but on the drier eastern side of the alps high-country sheep runs regularly extend to within a few kilometres of the Main Divide. The net result of this is that eastern landforms and ecosystems are nothing like as adequately protected as their western counterparts, despite their often having outstanding value for conservation. Things are however now changing as these eastern high-country pastoral lands become involved in a process of tenure review, a major outcome of which should be that large areas on the eastern side of the Southern Alps are retired from grazing and given permanent protection.

A third major task concerns the way we manage lands which have already been set aside to protect their intrinsic values and the extent to which our concept of protection also involves the goal of restoration. The most obvious example of this task is the quality of wildlife habitat that we are today able to provide in our national parks and other protected natural areas. When Europeans began settling in New Zealand 150 years ago forests everywhere were filled with the song of innumerable birds, but today there is an eerie silence in much of our native forest, even in places as seemingly pristine as South Westland and Fiordland. The principal cause of this has been introduced predators like rats, cats, stoats, ferrets and possums, and the main hope today for recreating something of the older natural order of things, and providing secure sanctuary for a long list of threatened species, is on predator-free offshore islands.

There are about twenty islands around the coast of Fiordland and South Westland that are already providing sanctuary conditions, or have the potential to do so, and in this respect Te Wahipounamu has an important role to play in ecosystem restoration and threatened species recovery. But the longer term goal must be to recreate conditions in which birds and other exiled native wildlife can once again thrive in mainland habitats. To this end plans are being made for intensive control of predators in some mainland parts of Te Wahipounamu (and elsewhere) and the creation of what are sometimes described as 'mainland habitat islands'. If these experiments succeed, and can be sustained, then the value of Te Wahipounamu as a World Heritage Area will be immeasurably increased, and visitors will not only be able to gaze in awe at its magnificent scenery but may again hear a continual chatter of yellowheads and parakeets in the beech forests of the Eglinton Valley, the calling of kiwi at night throughout South Westland, and the haunting booming of kakapo echoing from the fortress-like ramparts of the Fiordland valleys.

Andy Dennis

# MOUNT COOK NATIONAL PARK

Mount Cook National Park is New Zealand's foremost high alpine national park, extending along a sixty-five kilometre section of the Main Divide between the head of the Godley Glacier in the north and the upper icefields of the Mueller Glacier in the south. Two-thirds of the park's western edge is a shared high mountain boundary with Westland National Park. Created in 1953 from a series of reserves dating as far back as 1885, the park contains twenty-two of the twenty-six named mountains in New Zealand over 3,000 metres in height, and the five largest glaciers on the eastern flanks of the Southern Alps. In all, about forty per cent of the park's 94,422 hectares is occupied by a permanent covering of snow and ice, with much of the rest being bare rock, scree, gravel riverbed and tawny tussock grassland. Outstanding features include Mt Cook/Aoraki, which soars above the surrounding lofty mountains, and at 3,754 metres is easily the highest mountain in Australasia, and the twenty-nine kilometre Tasman Glacier, which is the longest glacier in mid-temperate regions of the world. For more than 100 years the Mount Cook region has been the principal arena for mountaineering in New Zealand, and for much the same period the broad open valleys of the Tasman and Hooker rivers have provided visitors with easy access deep into this sanctuary of towering mountains and large slow-moving valley glaciers.

In addition to its stunning alpine scenery, Mount Cook National Park also provides numerous graphic illustrations of the geological processes that have created the Southern Alps, and which are still constantly rearranging the landscapes of this rapidly rising and deeply fractured chain of mountains. The large areas of the park occupied by scree, moraine and gravels (which in the Tasman riverbed are up to five kilometres wide and 500 metres deep) bear witness to the vast amounts of shattered rock continually being stripped from the park's mountains, and of the key role the major glaciers have in transporting this eroded rock to lower altitudes. Most of this relentless erosion occurs at a rate too slow to observe, but there are notable exceptions. In periodic high intensity floods large boulders can be heard tumbling down the beds of sediment-laden glacial rivers. And from time to time huge rock avalanches deliver millions of tonnes of rubble into the valleys—like the one that detached from the east face of Mount Cook in 1991, lowering its summit by about ten metres.

Compared with other parts of Te Wahipounamu, plant cover in Mount Cook National Park often appears sparse, with forest in particular being confined to a few small scattered remnants. But despite the barren appearance of many areas, a remarkably diverse range of resilient alpine plants has spread across much of the park, and where habitats are reasonably stable and soils have been able to form, there are shrublands and herbfields as rich as anywhere in the New Zealand mountains. In addition to the numerous mosses, lichens and liverworts, over 550 species of higher plants occur within the park, of which some 420 are native New Zealand species. And while many of these are inconspicuous or spread thinly across riverbeds, moraines, screes and fellfields, in places like the Hooker valley or Blue Stream near the terminal of the Tasman Glacier, large mountain buttercups, foxgloves, daisies and gentians flower prolifically among tall tussocks and russet-green shrubs, creating exquisite alpine gardens whose beauty is enhanced by the stark landscapes of rock, snow and ice with which they are surrounded.

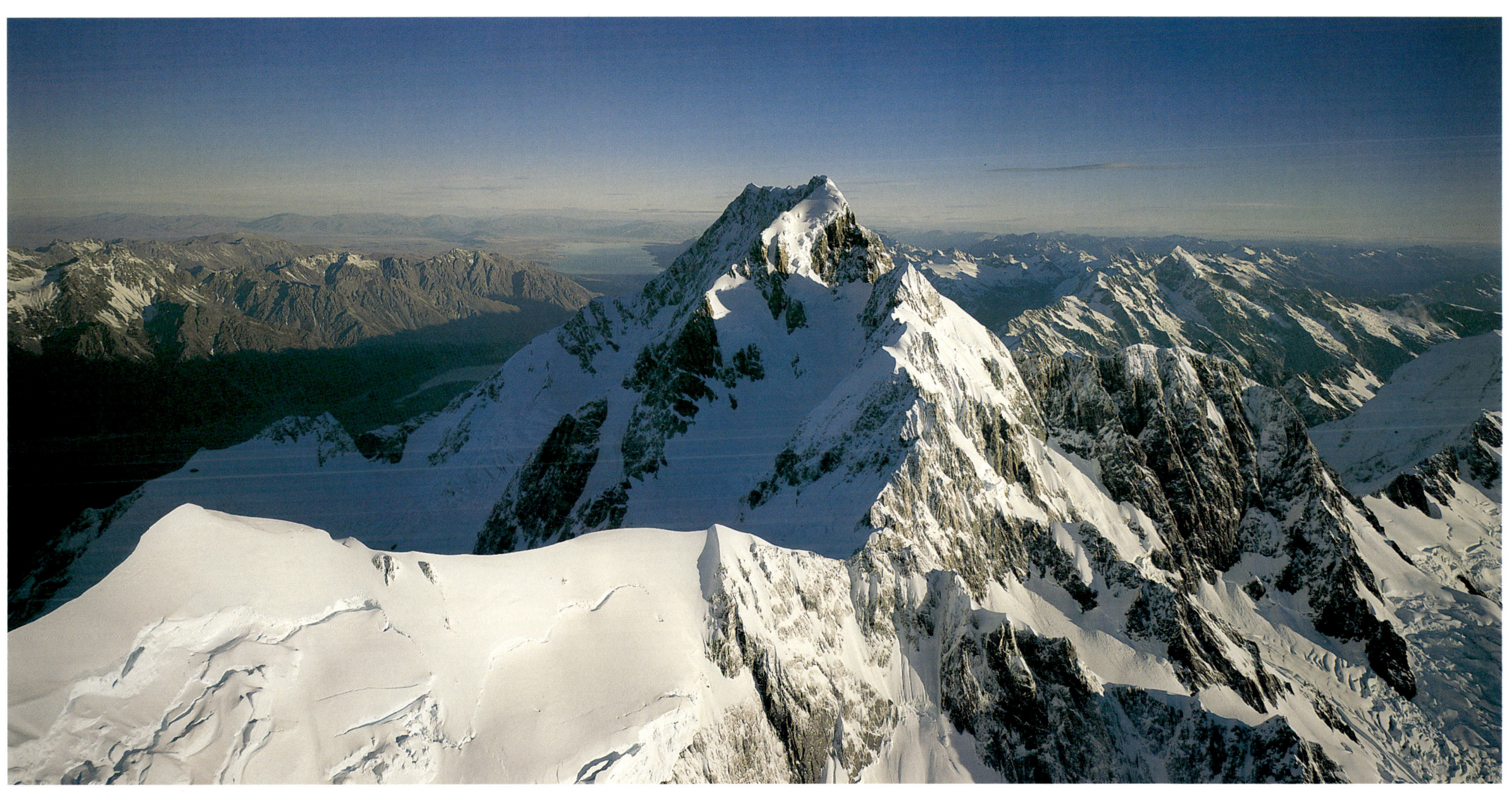

Ice ridges and summits lead to Aoraki/Mt Cook (3,754 metres), viewed from the north above the Main Divide.

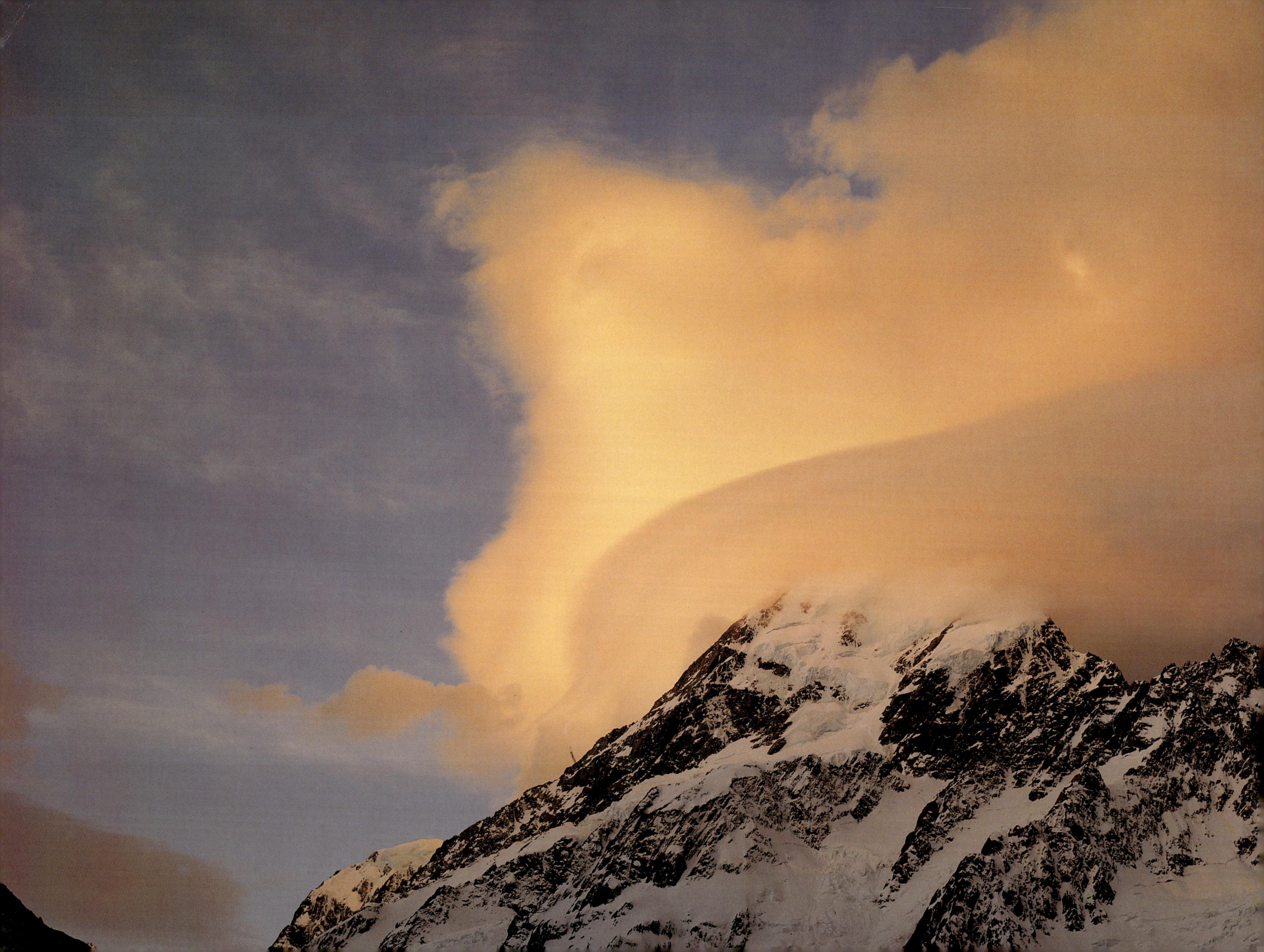

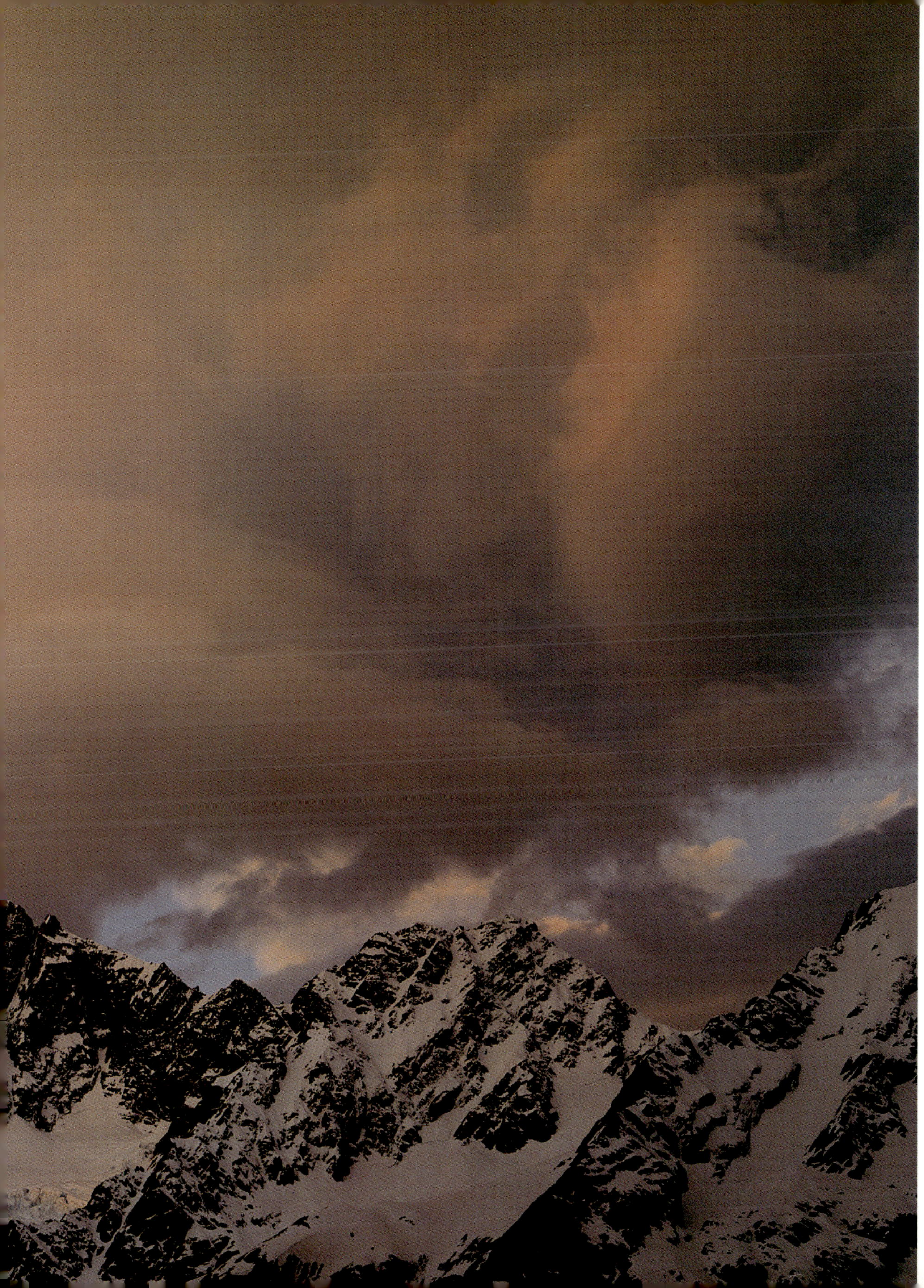

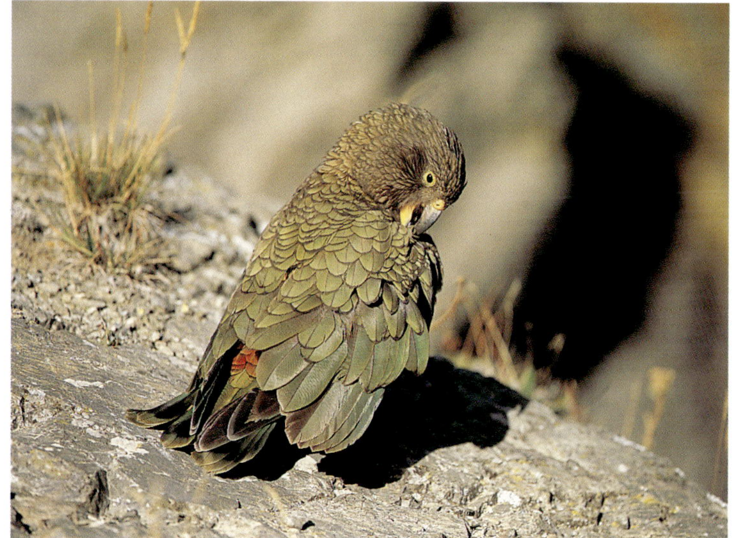

The only mountain parrot in the world, kea occur throughout the mountains of Te Wahipounamu, and are common at places like Mount Cook Village and the terminal regions of the Fox and Franz Josef glaciers.

LEFT: Clouds billowing across the summit of Mt Cook catch the last of the evening sun.

OVERLEAF: Skiers on a day trip to the head of the Tasman Glacier enjoy some fine wilderness skiing below Tasman Saddle hut, a mountain refuge for climbers and ski-tourers. Scenic flights and glacier landings are a major tourist attraction at Mount Cook and with helicopters now also servicing this expanding market the disruption of 'natural quiet' by incessant mechanical noise has become a major conservation issue at Mount Cook as well as at other popular locations in Te Wahipounamu like Milford Sound and the Fox and Franz Josef glaciers.

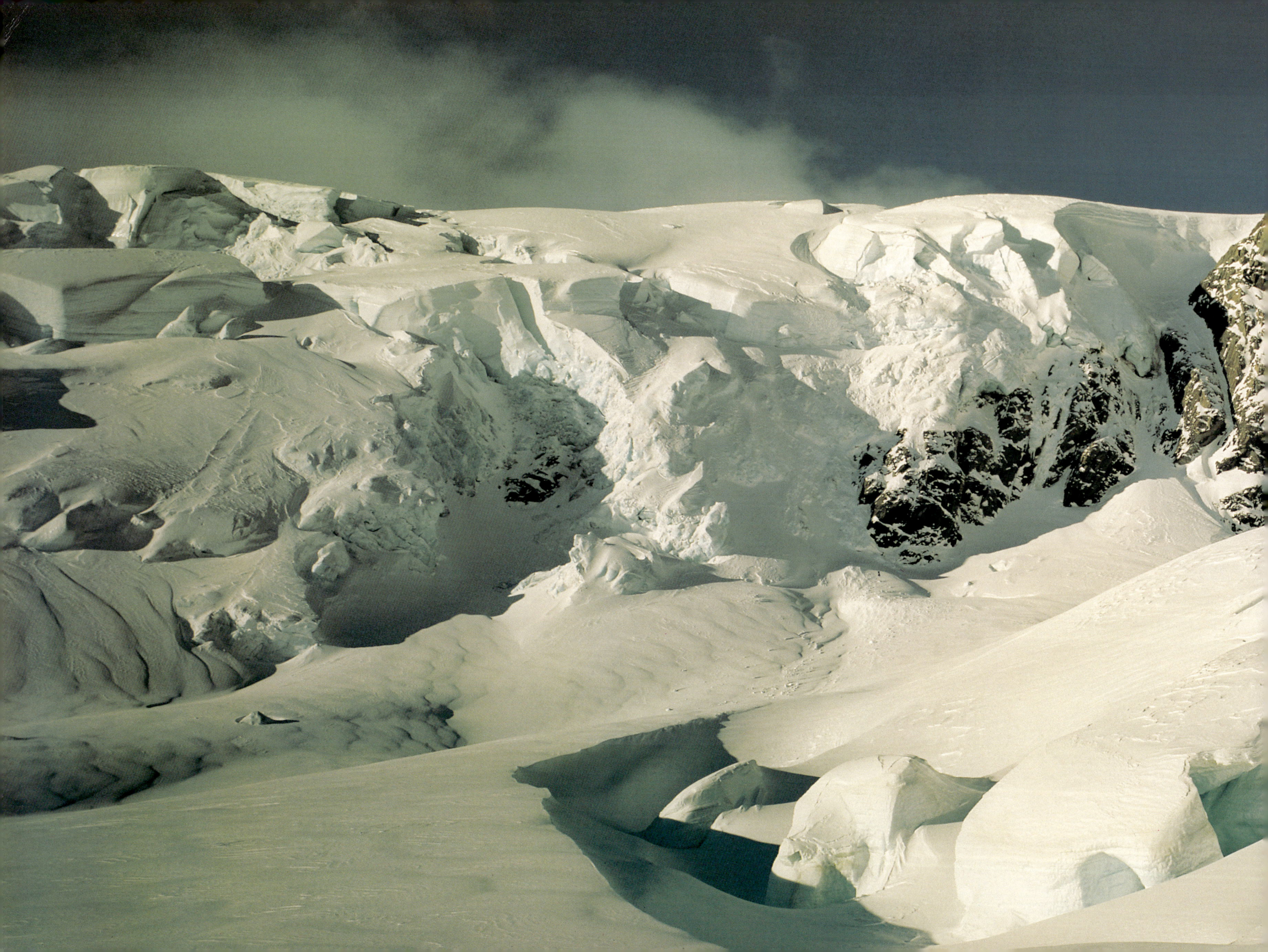

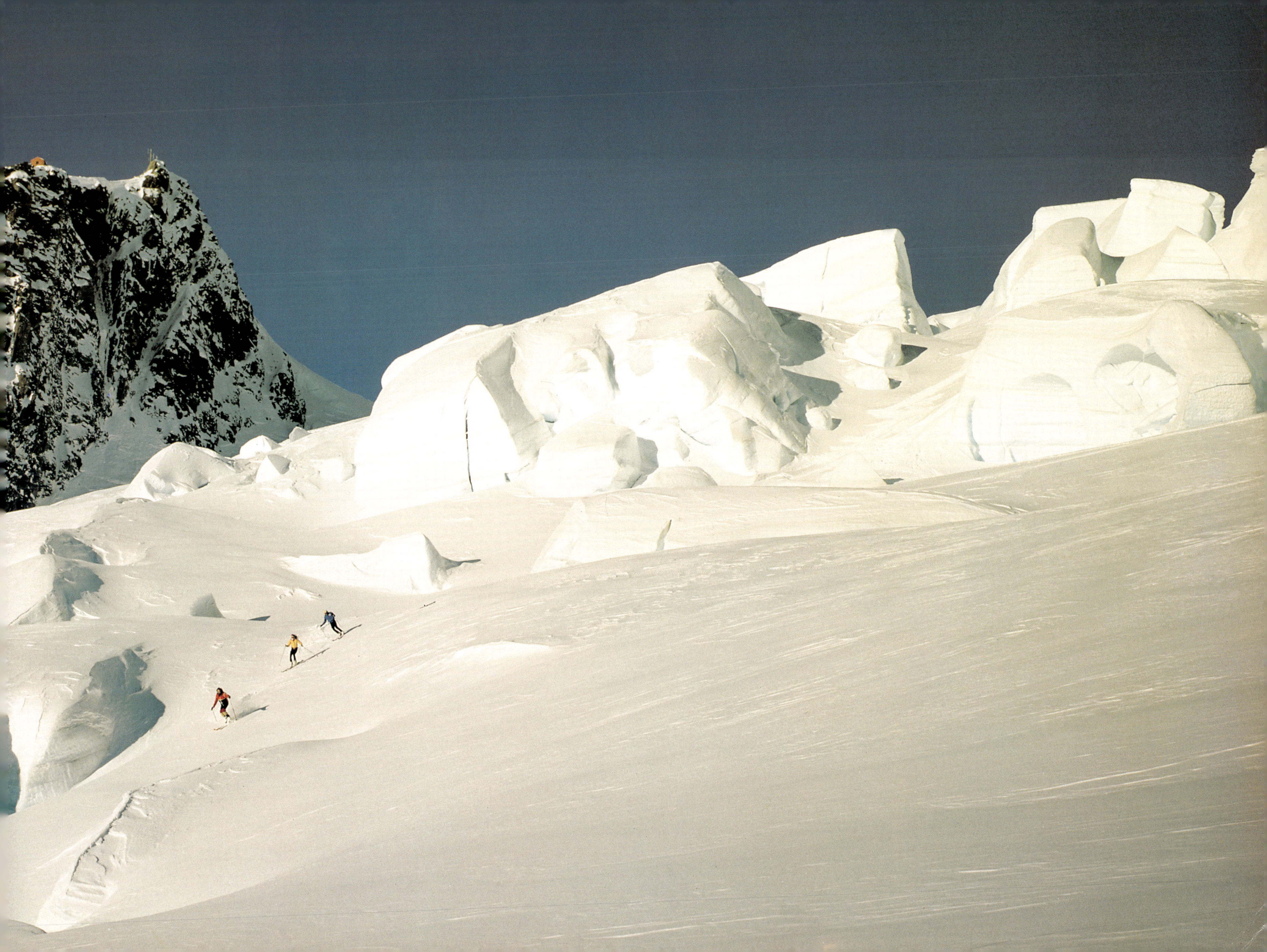

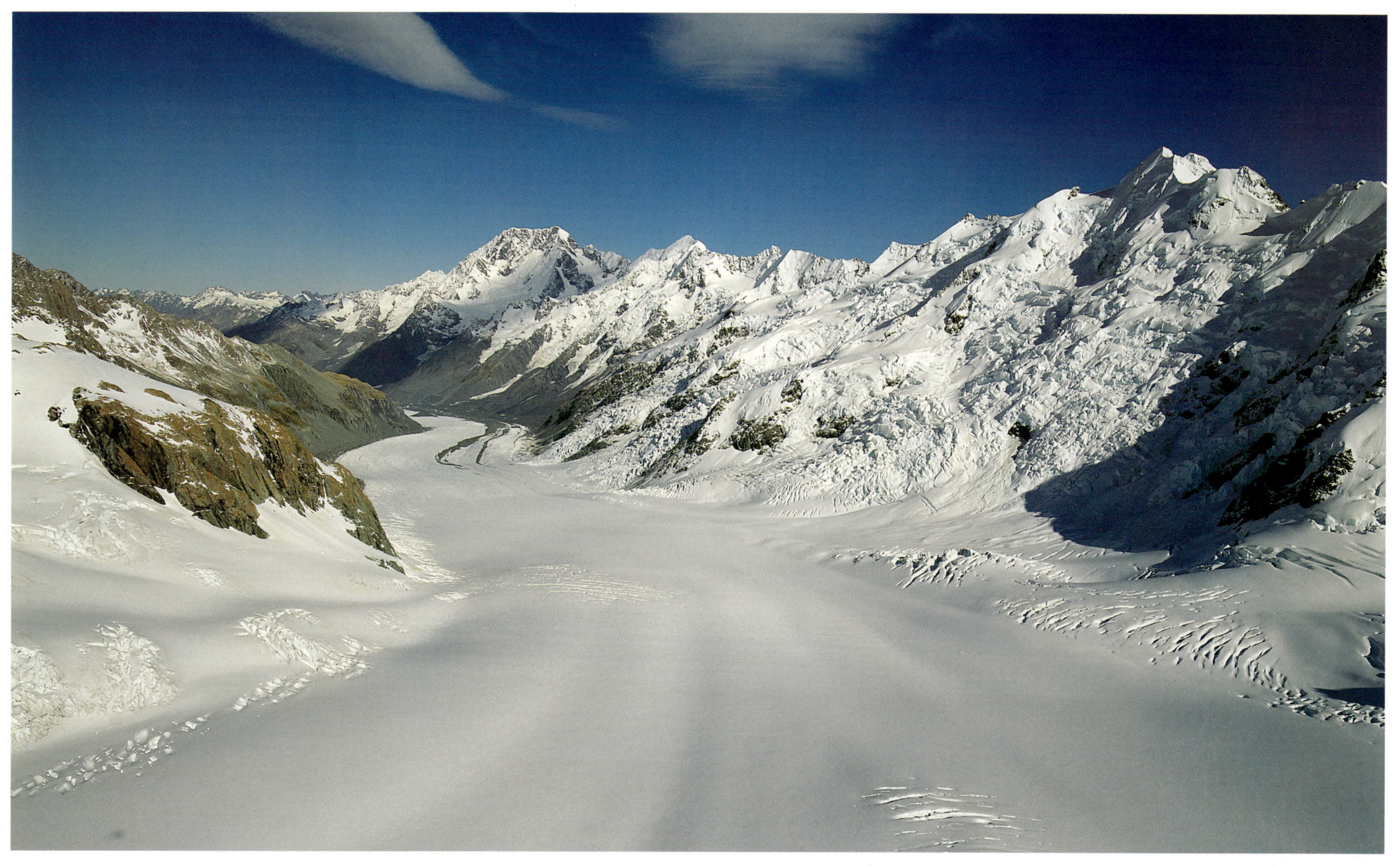

The upper half of the twenty-nine kilometre Tasman Glacier (the longest glacier in mid-temperate regions of the world), looking down-valley from near Tasman Saddle to the east face and long summit ridge of Aoraki/Mt Cook (3,754 metres).

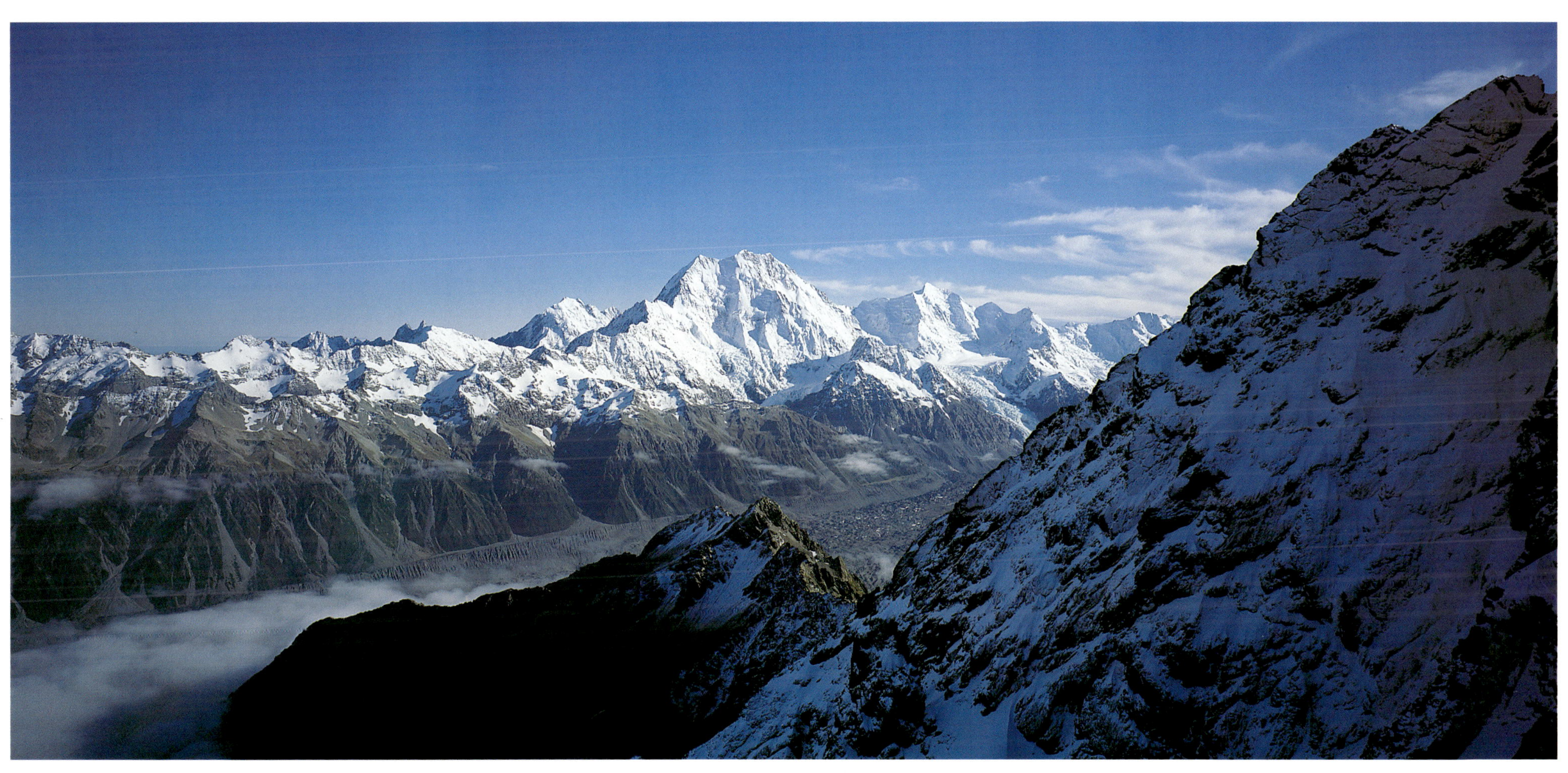

Morning light on the eastern faces of Aoraki/Mt Cook with La Perouse (3,079 metres) to the left and Mt Tasman (3,498 metres) to the right, photographed from near The Nuns Veil on the Liebig Range. Between Mt Cook and Mt Tasman the broad ice-shelf of the Grand Plateau ponds glacial ice fed from higher up these mountains from where it cascades down the Hochstetter Icefall to join the Tasman Glacier.

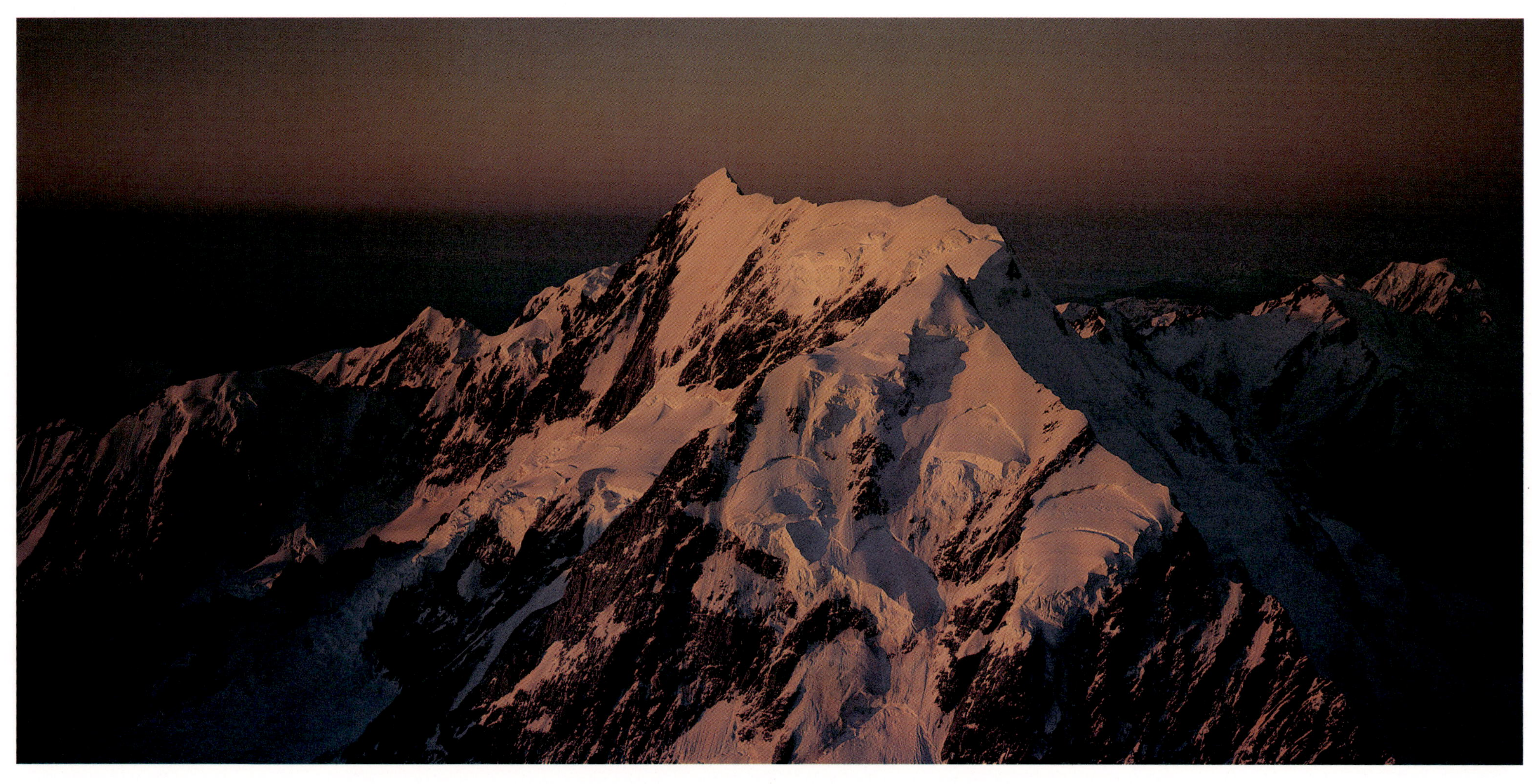

*Mehemea ka tuoho ahau me maunga tei tei—If I should bow my head let it be to a high mountain* (Maori proverb).
Last light on the western (Hooker) face of Aoraki/Mt Cook.

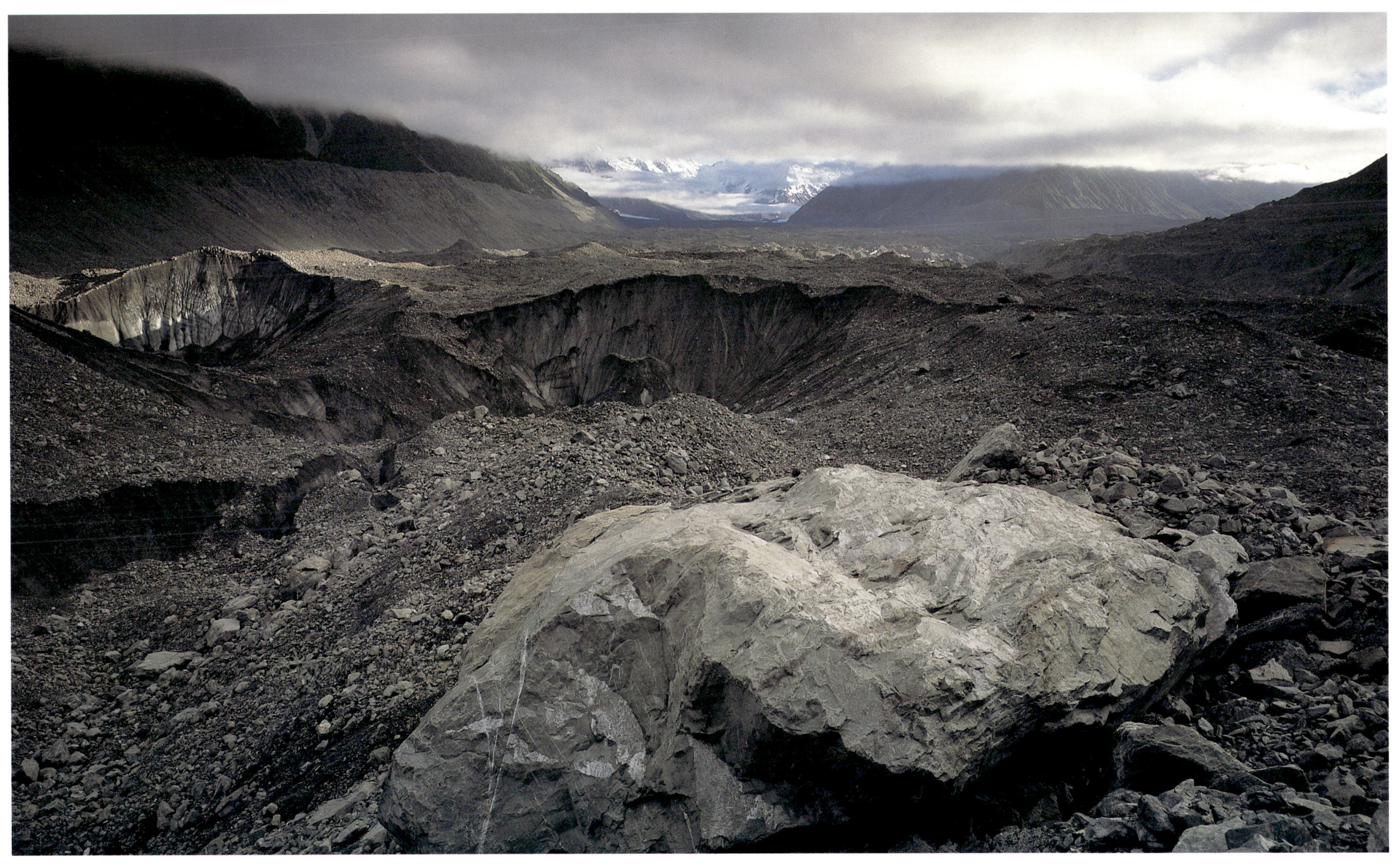

The moraine-covered lower reaches of the Tasman Glacier, looking northwards towards the feeder glaciers at the head of the Tasman valley. Under this thin covering of moraine the ice is 400 metres thick at this point on the glacier.

# WESTLAND NATIONAL PARK

Westland National Park is located on the western side of the Southern Alps adjacent to Mount Cook National Park, extending from a common boundary along the crest of the Main Divide to the coast of the Tasman Sea thirty kilometres distant. The park has distinct upland and lowland sectors separated by the line of the Alpine Fault, which defines the western edge of the Southern Alps from Nelson Lakes to the mouth of Milford Sound. The park was created in 1960 as part of celebrations marking 100 years of European settlement on the West Coast, although much of the lowland sector was not added until 1982 after widespread public opposition to plans to allow large tracts of pristine forest in these areas to be milled. As a result of these additions the park today protects an outstanding range of natural landforms and ecosystems, from coastal and lowland forests and wetlands to the summits of the highest mountains in the country. The park is the main northern entry point to Te Wahipounamu, and although of relatively modest size (117,547 hectares), it offers unparalleled opportunities to encounter many of the kind of features that make the whole south-west corner of the South Island a region of international significance.

Along the high alpine barrier that constitutes the park's inland boundary are nineteen of the twenty-six peaks in New Zealand that exceed 3,000 metres in height, as well as a number of large icefields. In these high altitude realms Westland and Mount Cook national parks have much in common. Away from their higher peaks and icefields, however, their subalpine regions are vastly different. The major valley glaciers west of the Alps drop more steeply, more swiftly and with very much cleaner faces than their counterparts in the east, and the valleys into which they drain are much narrower, with gorges being as common in the west as broad open river flats are in the east. But the most striking difference is that the flanks of the western side of the Alps are covered in a dense mantle of forest and shrublands, whereas east of the Divide the mountainsides consist mainly of tawny tussock grasslands and barren grey screes.

Virtually the entire lowland landscape of the park was created during a succession of glacial advances that saw glaciers advance to about twenty kilometres beyond the present shoreline. The timelines of these chillier periods can be reconstructed from the sinuous moraine ridges that extend seawards from the base of the Alps. In the mosaic of forest covering these ancient moraines, and on the intervening floodplains of the major rivers, are many outstanding features, including the best surviving areas of dense rimu forest in the country, the best examples of matai/totara forest, and the habitat of the rarest subspecies of kiwi (Okarito brown kiwi). These lowland areas are also much more readily accessible than the park's alpine regions and provide visitors with an outstanding range of chances to experience fine West Coast lowland scenery, forest walks, the reflective serenity of lakes Wahapo, Mapourika, and Matheson, and superb coastal explorations at Okarito and Gillespies Beach, both of which provide elevated lookouts with panoramic mountains-to-sea vistas unmatched anywhere else in New Zealand.

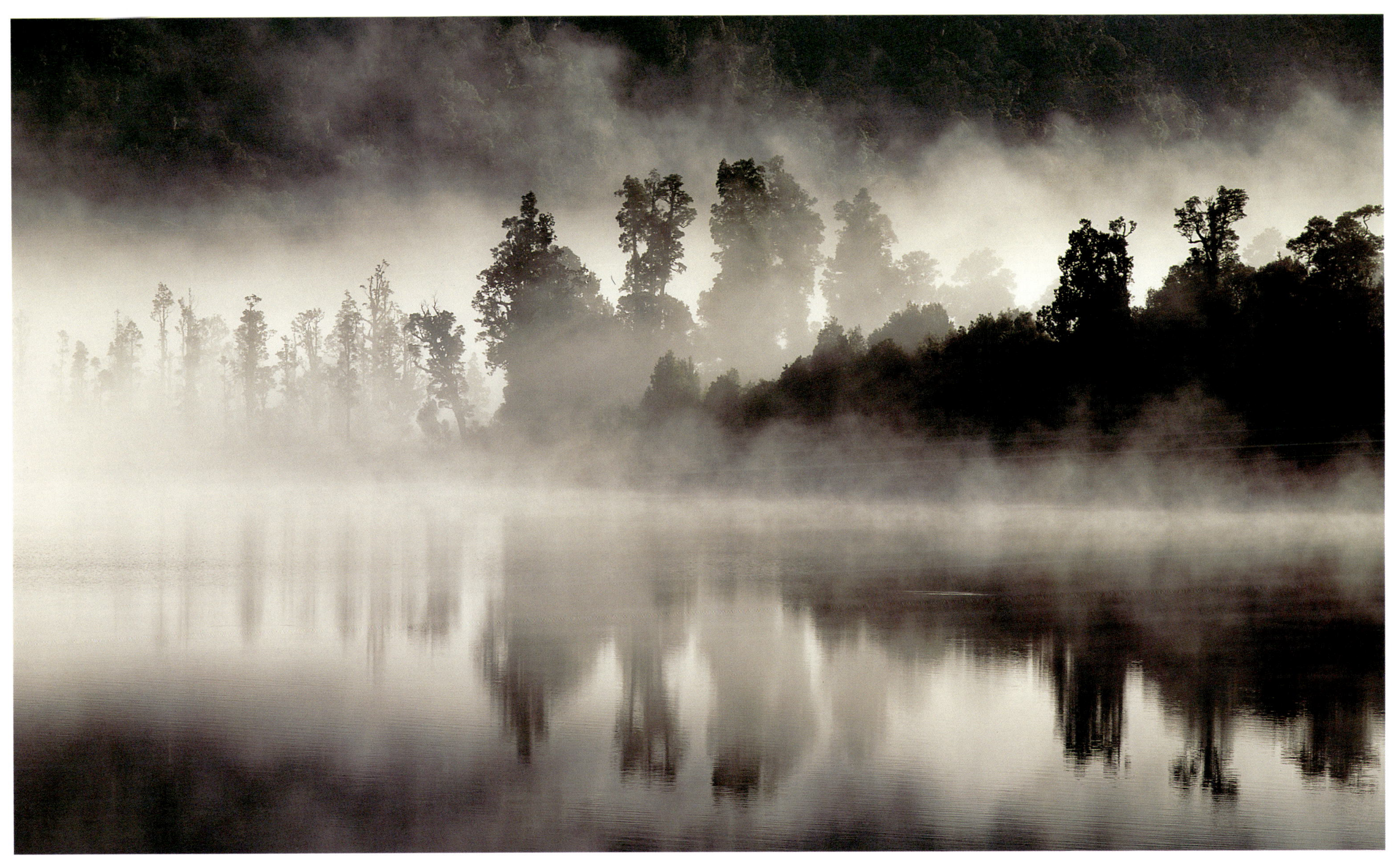

Morning sun slowly dissolves mist ponded over Lake Mapourika, gradually bringing the kahikatea forest on its eastern shore into sharper focus.

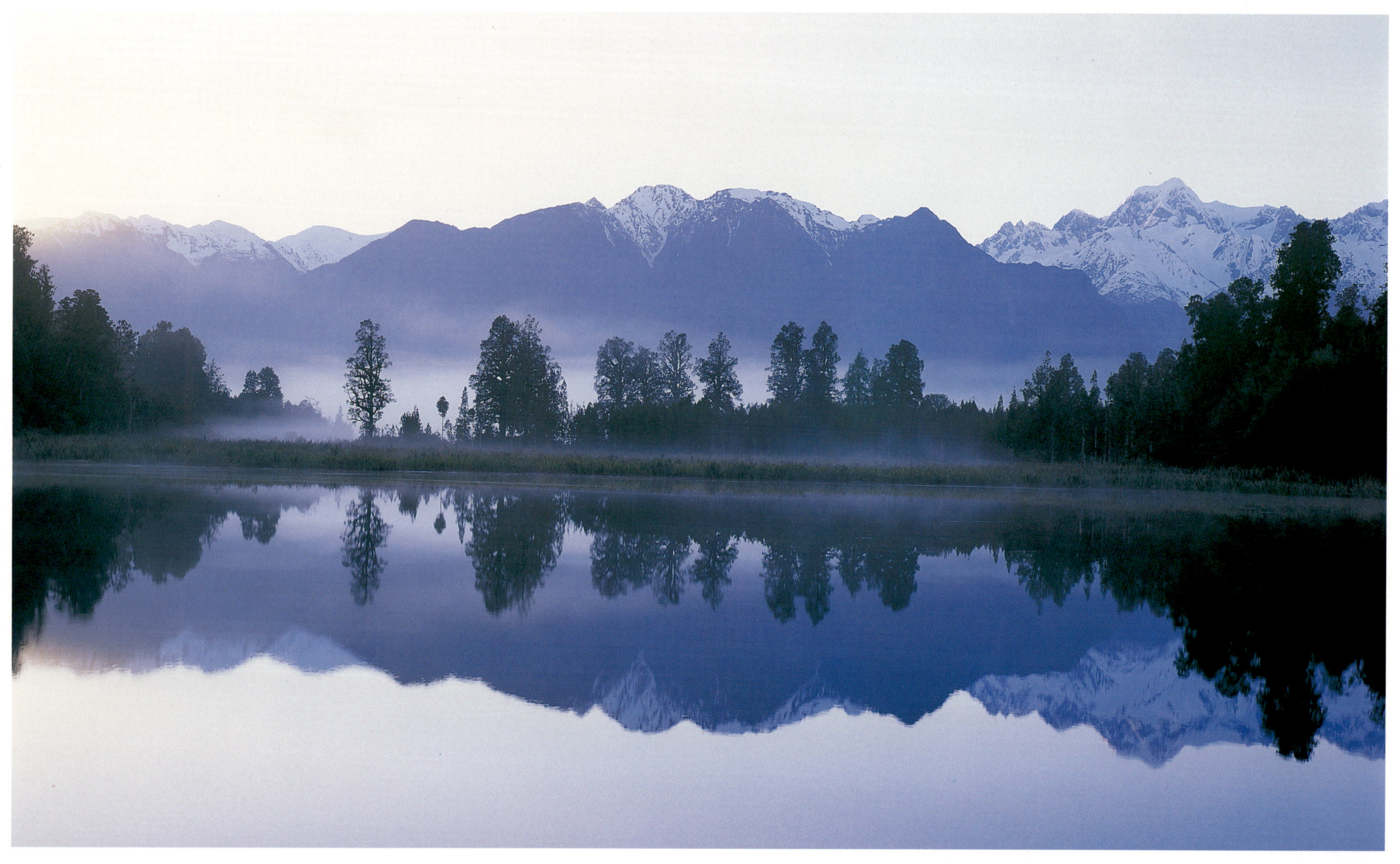

A tranquil dawn at Lake Matheson, with its fringing forest and backdrop of snowy peaks beautifully reflected in its mirror-smooth waters. The prominent mountain at the right is Mt Tasman (3,498 metres).

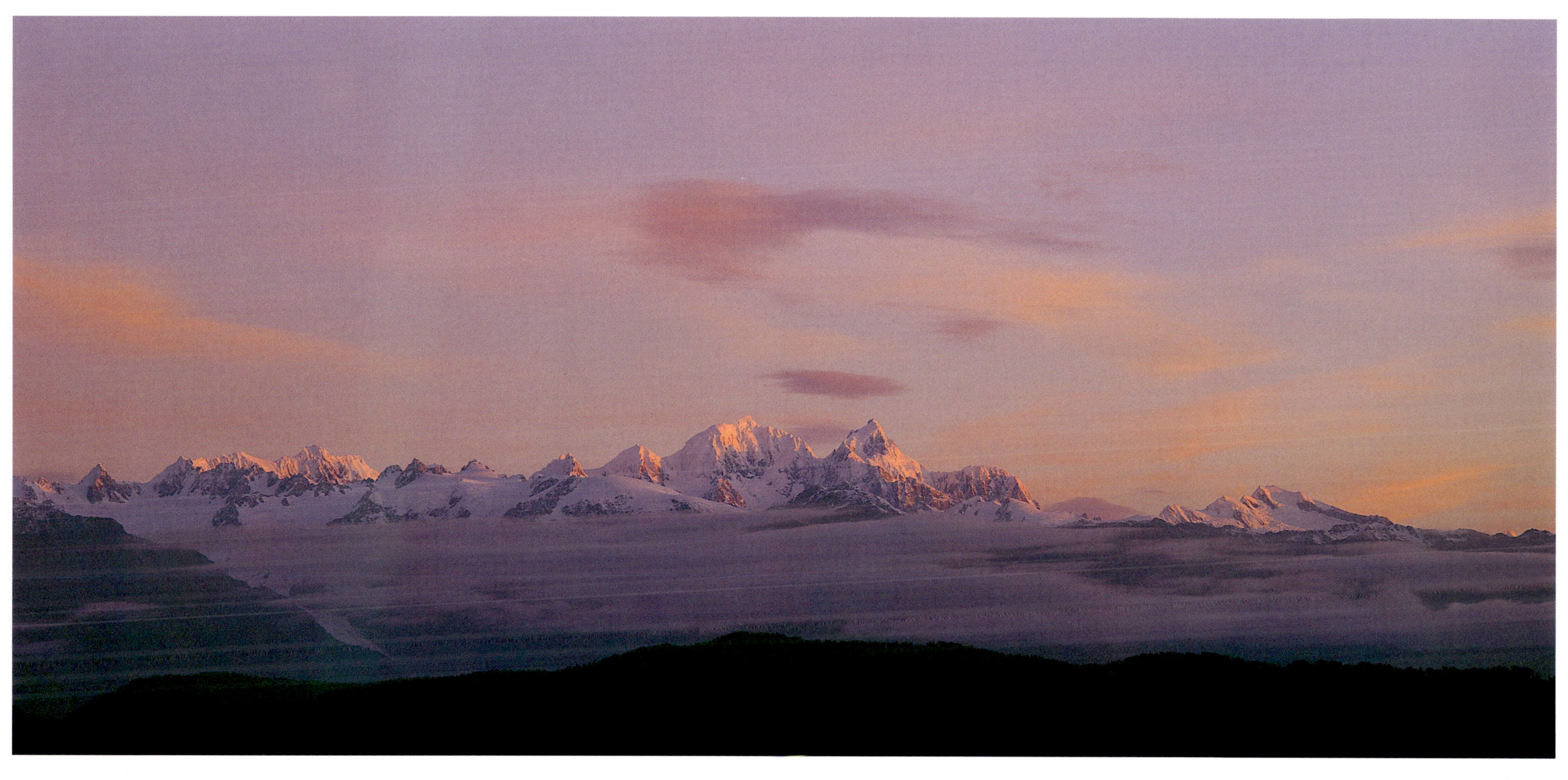

The last rays of the sun redden the summit snowfields of the Southern Alps' highest peaks. This photograph, taken from Okarito Trig, shows Mt Tasman and Mt Cook in the centre, with Mts Douglas and Haidinger (well to the left) and La Perouse (right) also catching this final sublime flourish of the departing day.

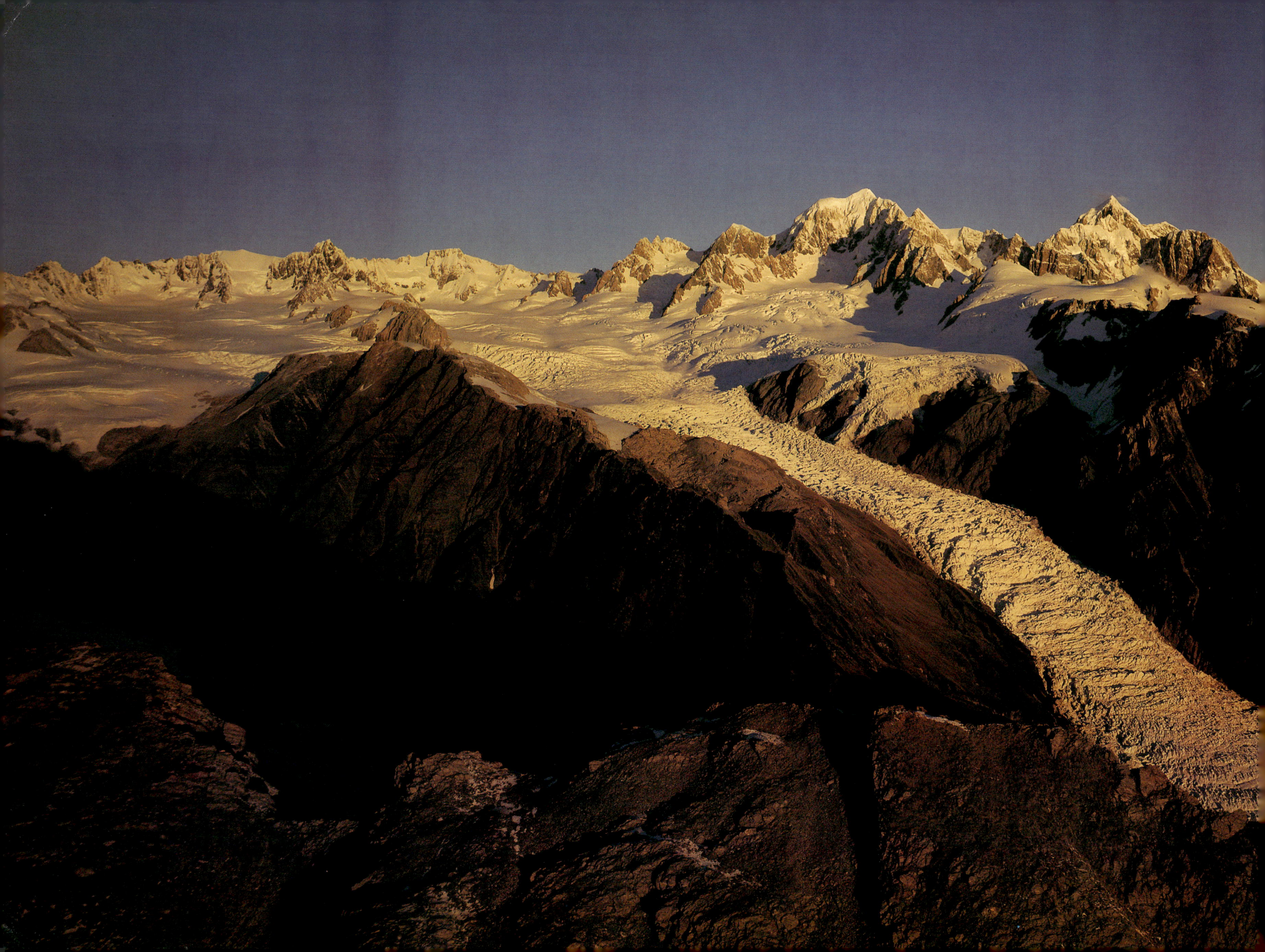

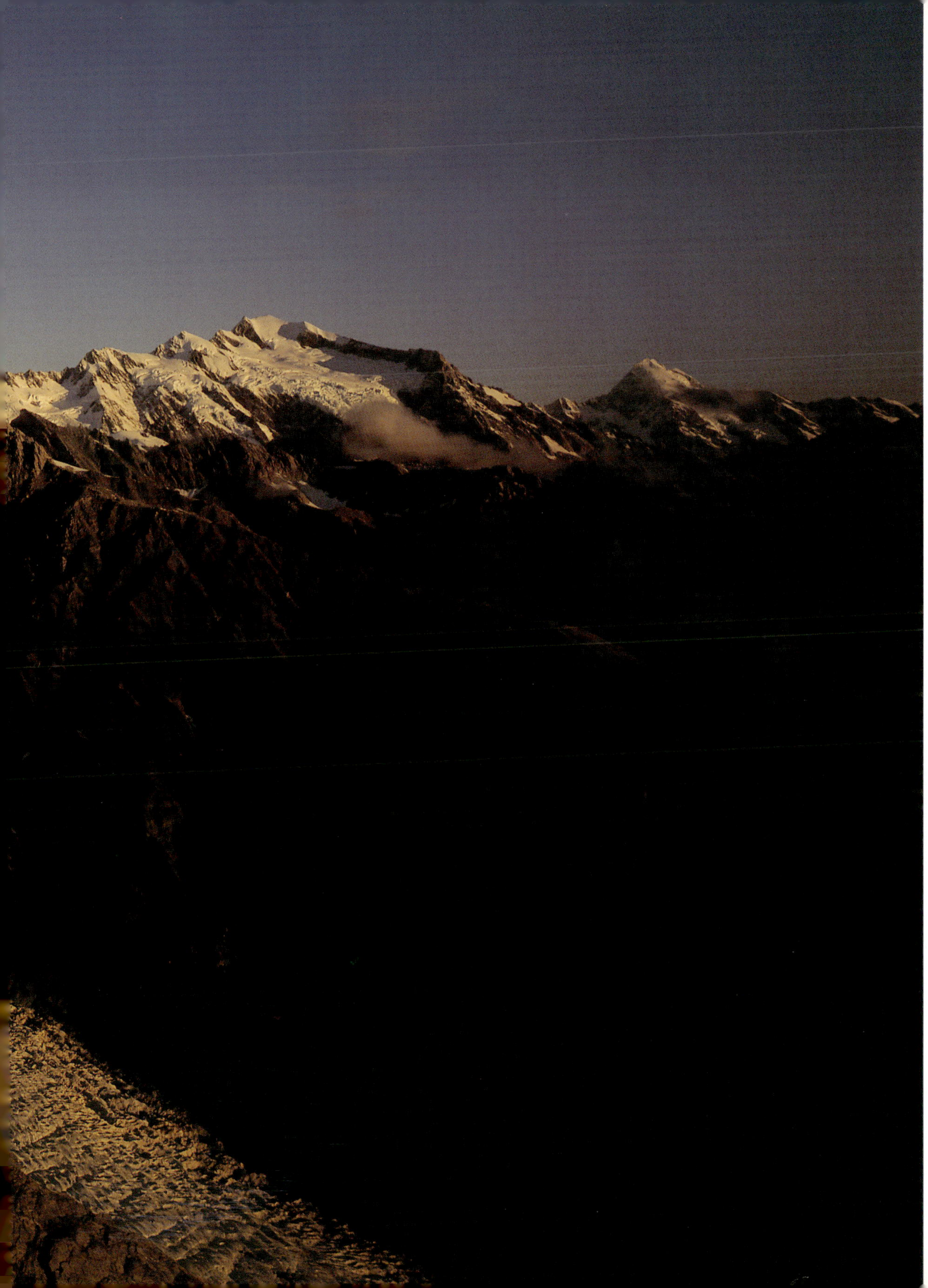

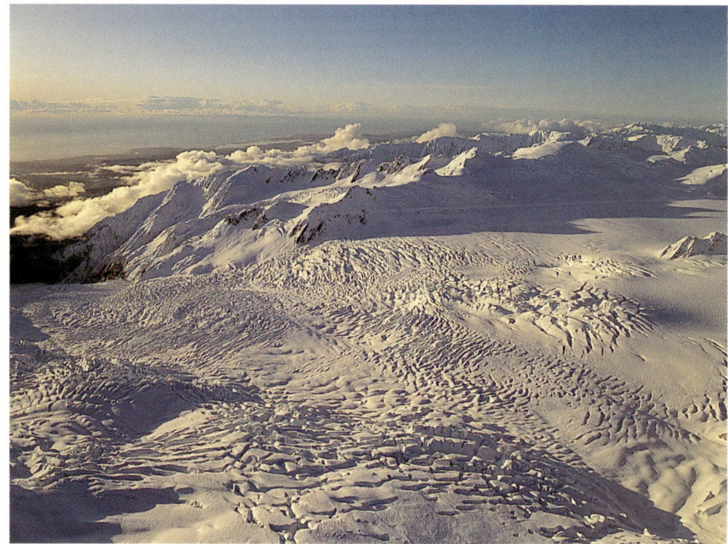

The deep ice reservoir of the Franz Josef névé gradually becomes an imbroglio of seracs and crevasses as this vast mass of accumulated ice seeks to escape to lower altitudes down the tumbling Franz Josef icefall. The inlet on the distant coastline is Okarito Lagoon.

LEFT: Like the Franz Josef, the vast icefields at the head of the Fox Glacier eventually coalesce into the crevasse-ridden tongue of its long icefall. Along with the Franz Josef Glacier to the north, the Fox Glacier is outstanding both for the speed at which its icefall flows down its narrow valley and for the extent to which this rapid rate of descent enables it to trespass into the realms of temperate rainforest, ending at an altitude of only 300 metres above sea level.

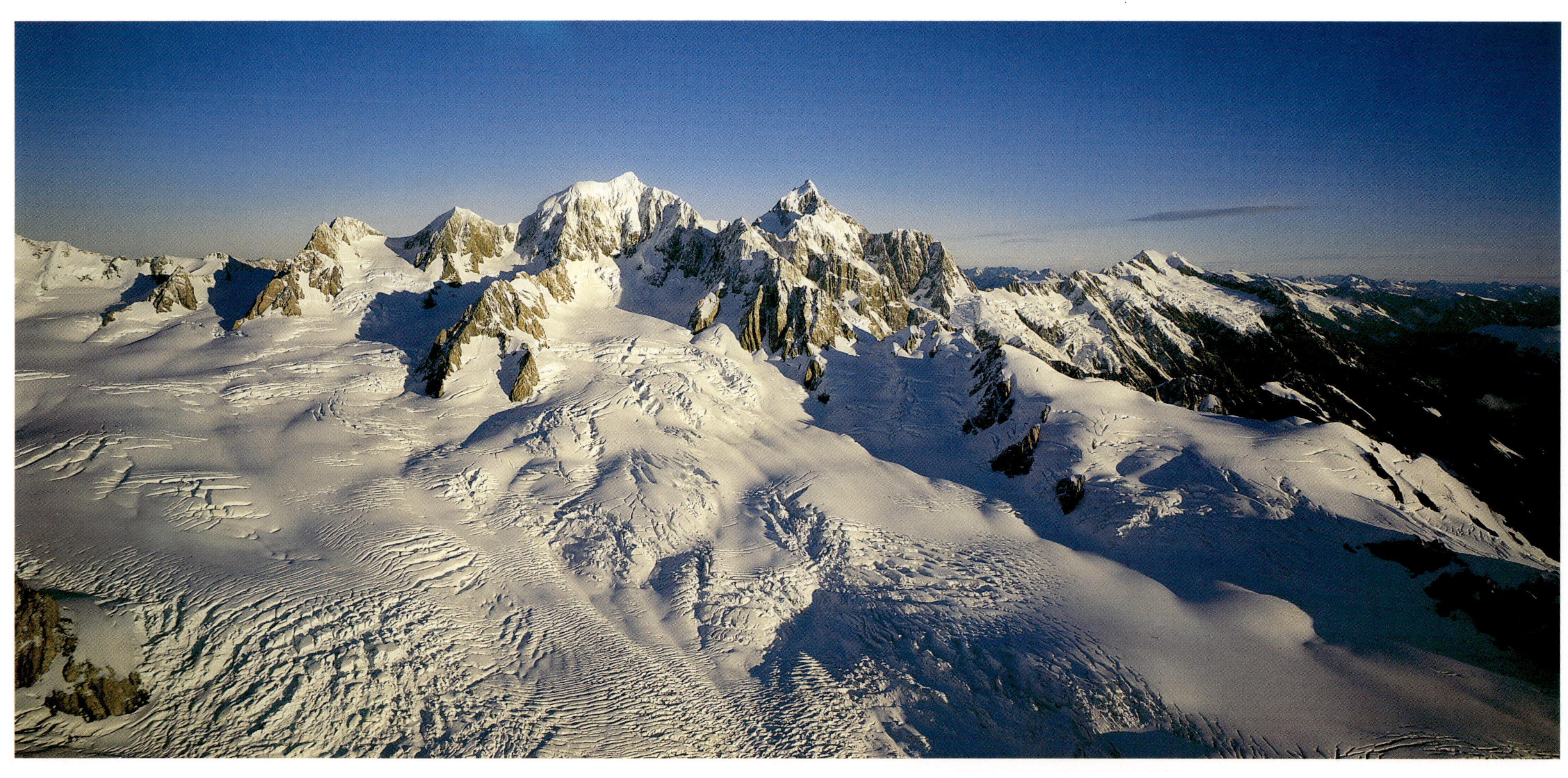

A glorious panorama of peaks and glaciers—evening sunlight on the crevasse-etched snowfields at the head of the Fox Glacier, looking towards the summits of Mt Tasman (3,498 metres) and Mt Cook (3,754 metres).

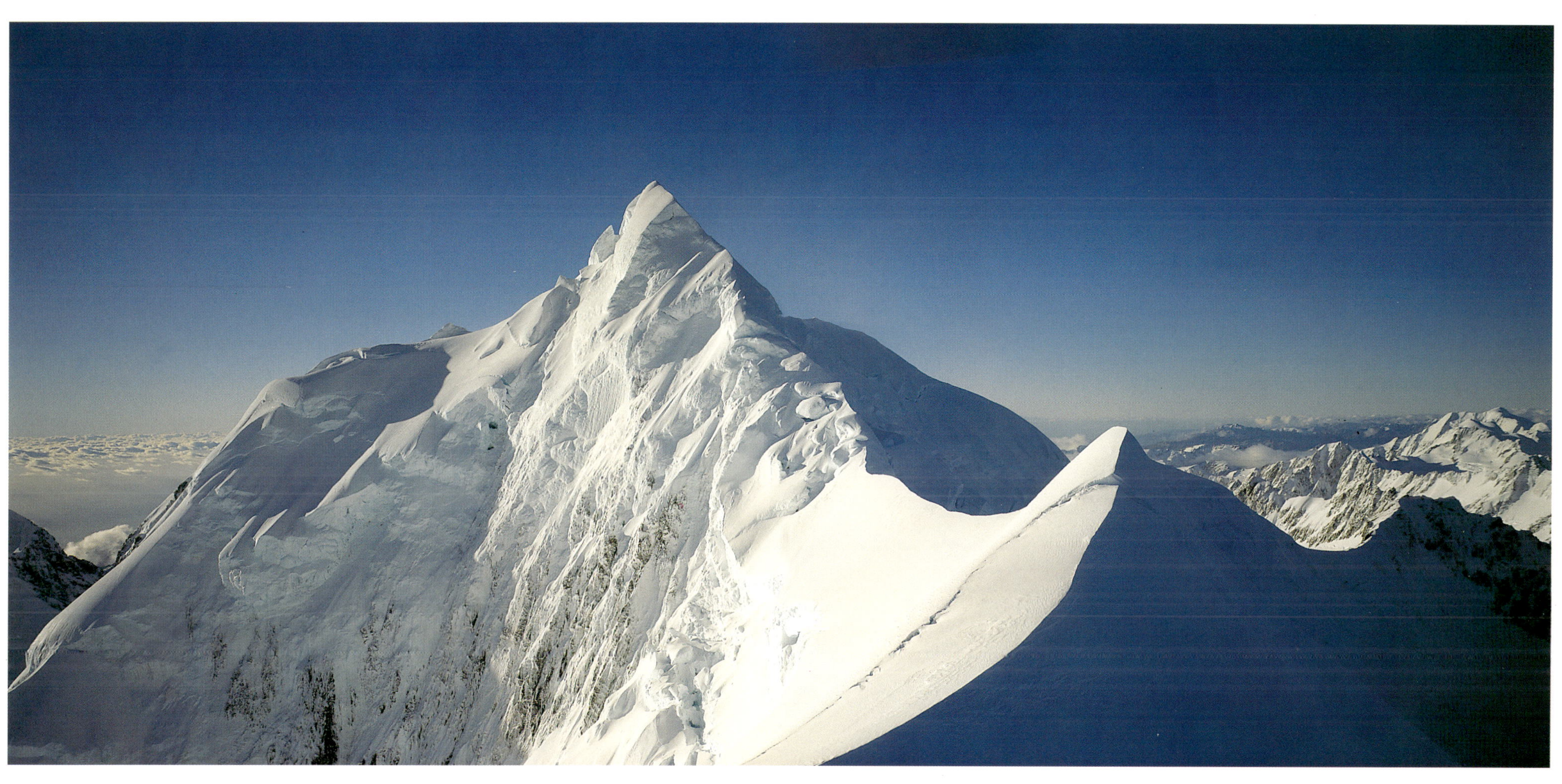

The Silberhorn ridge of Mt Tasman (3,498 metres) with the top of the Balfour Face and summit of Mt Silberhorn (3,279 metres) in the foreground. Mt Tasman is considered by many mountaineers to be the most beautiful mountain in the Southern Alps.

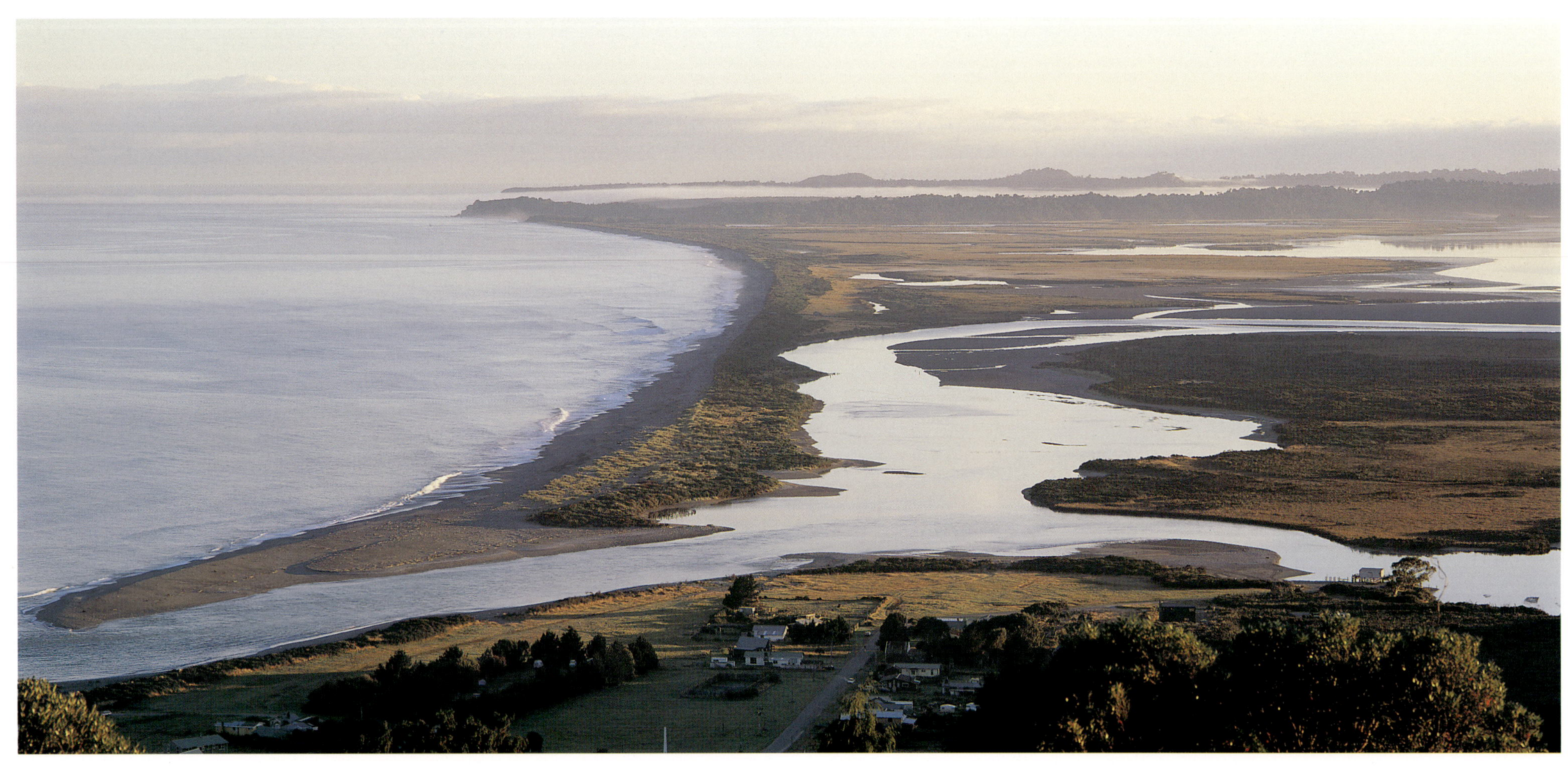

With a tidal area of 2,500 hectares, Okarito Lagoon is the largest estuary in the South Island still in a more or less natural state, and a haven for numerous wading birds—including summer migrants from the northern hemisphere like godwits and knots. During the breeding season the lagoon is the main feeding area for the beautiful kotuku (or white heron) whose only breeding colony is just north of the lagoon.

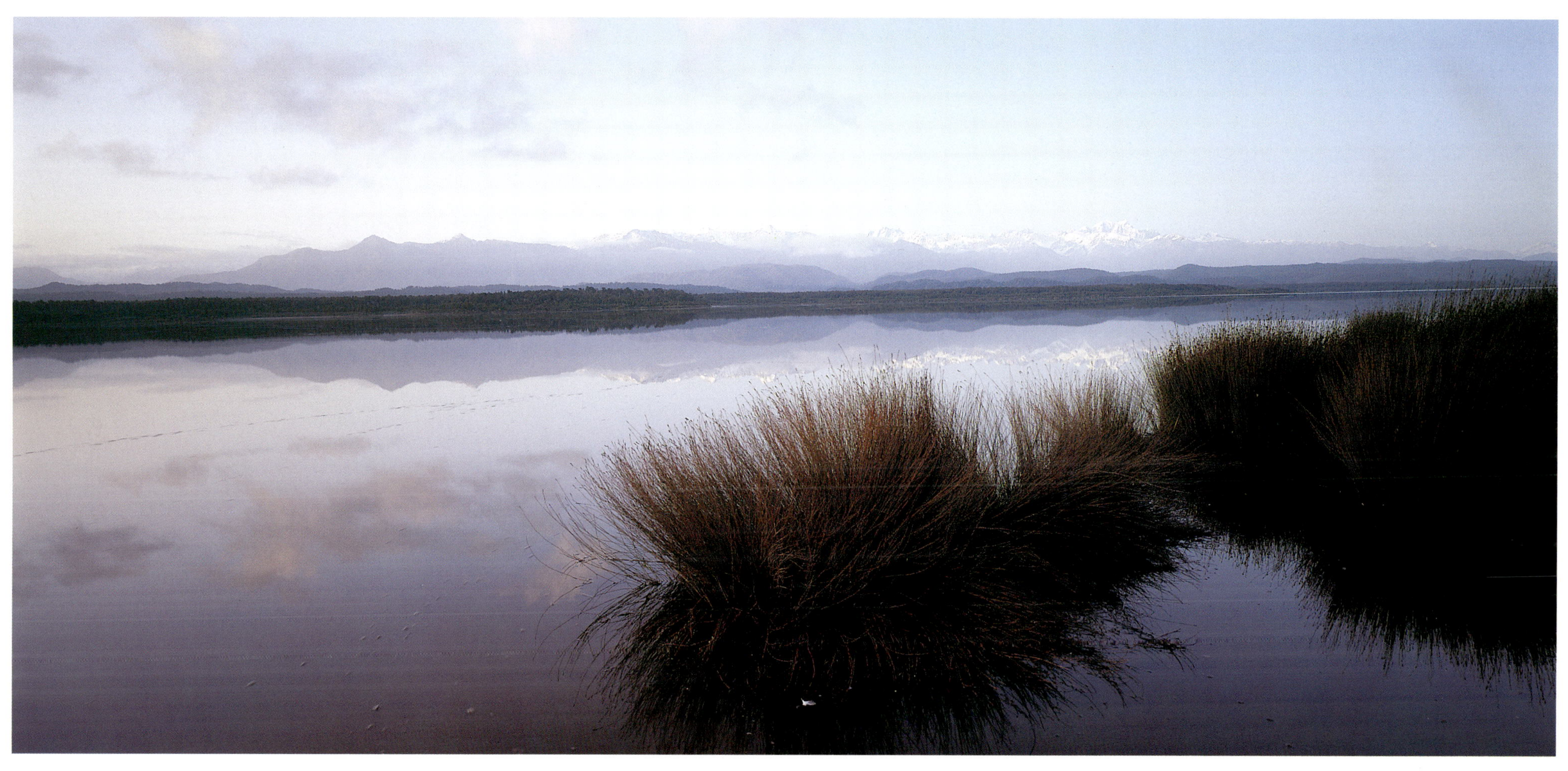

A panorama of the ranges and forested lowlands of Westland National Park spread out beyond the tranquil waters of Okarito Lagoon.

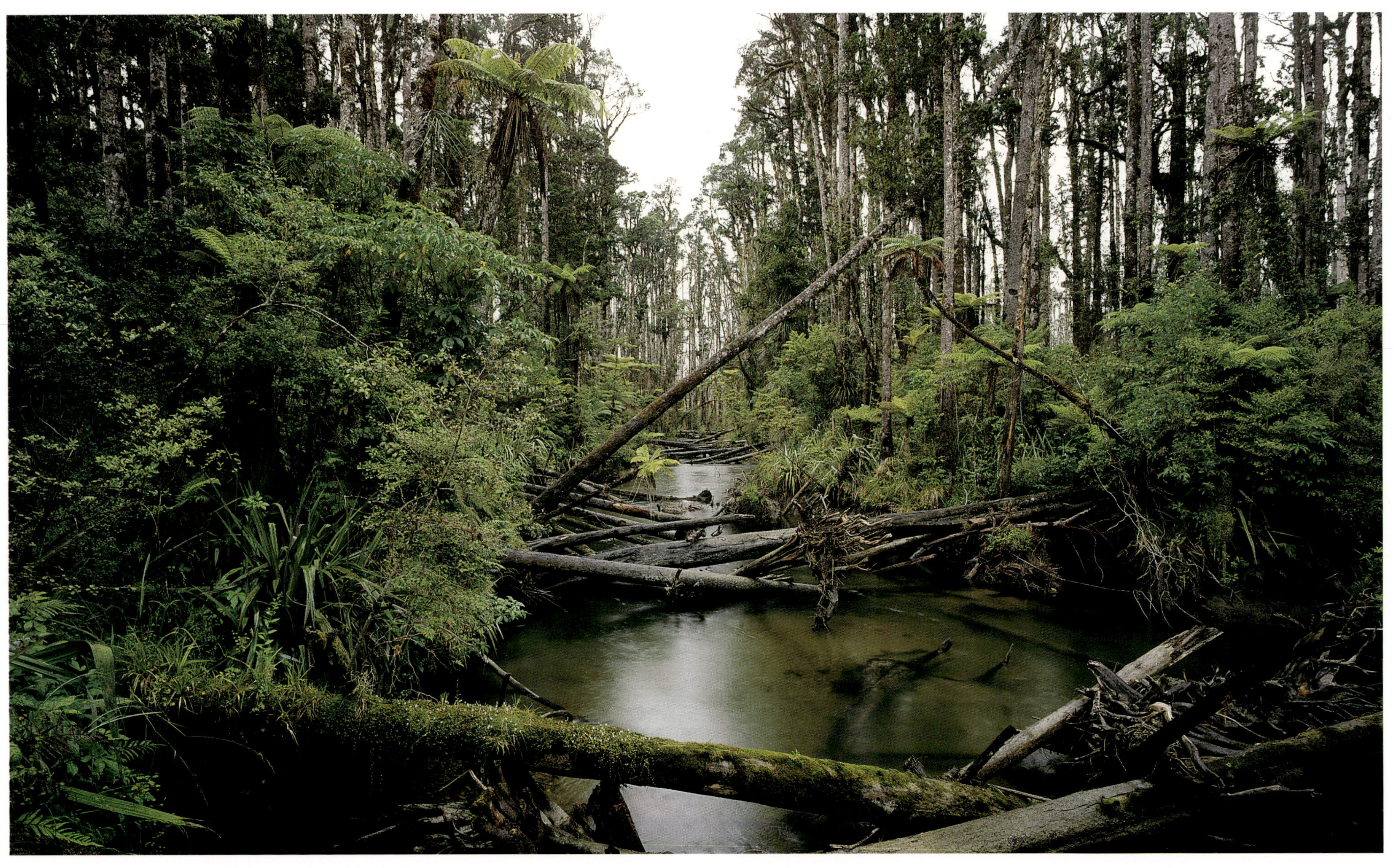

Tall kahikatea forest lines the banks of the Okarito River. A direct descendant from the ancient 'dinosaur' forests of Gondwana, kahikatea forest was once widespread throughout lowland New Zealand until it was comprehensively cleared for farming. Today it remains on only about two per cent of its former range, almost all of which is in South Westland.

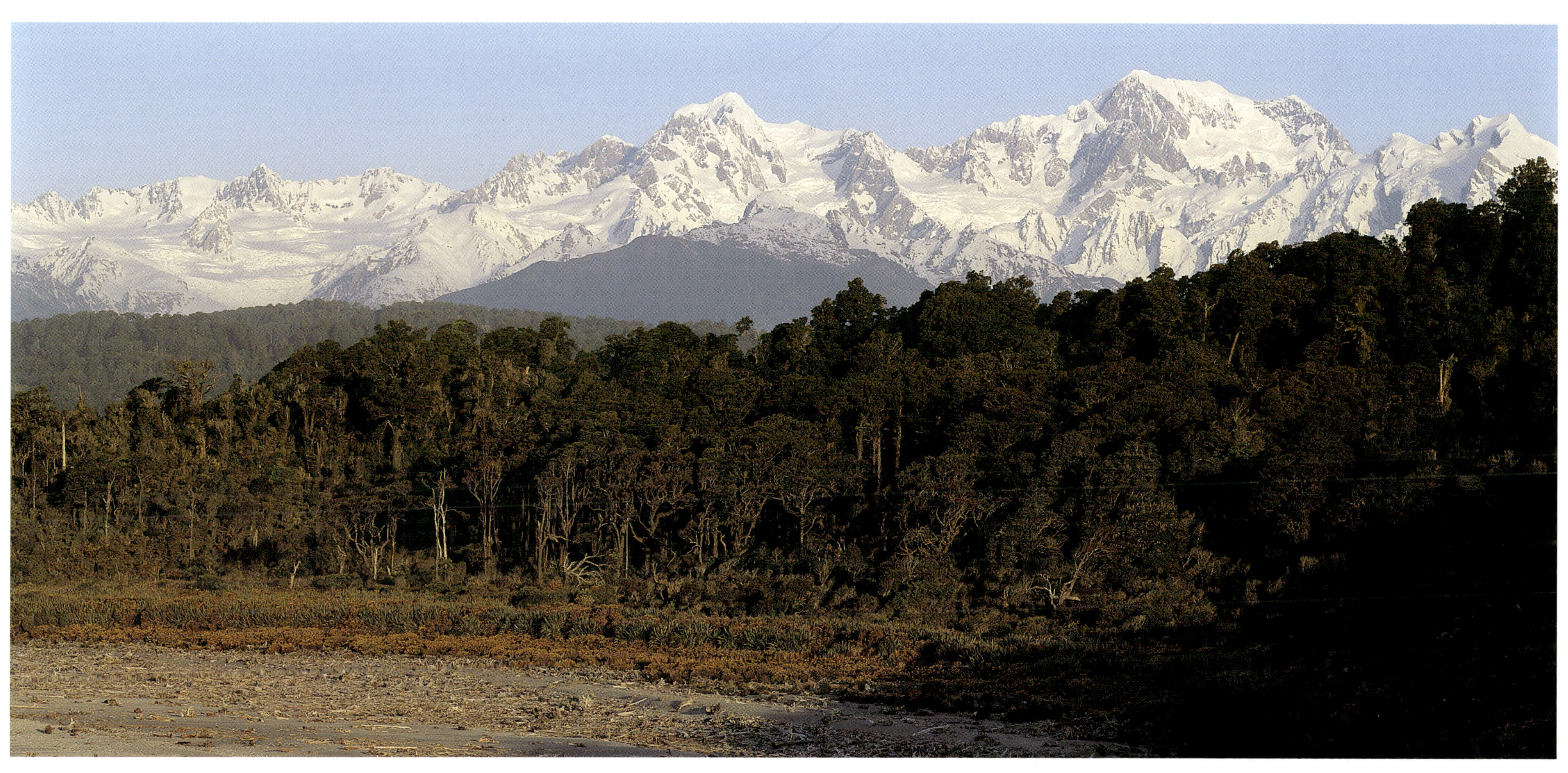

A classic Westland National Park 'mountains-to-sea' vista: Mt Tasman (centre) and Mt Cook (right) form a magnificent backdrop to the dense coastal rimu forest growing behind Gillespies Beach.

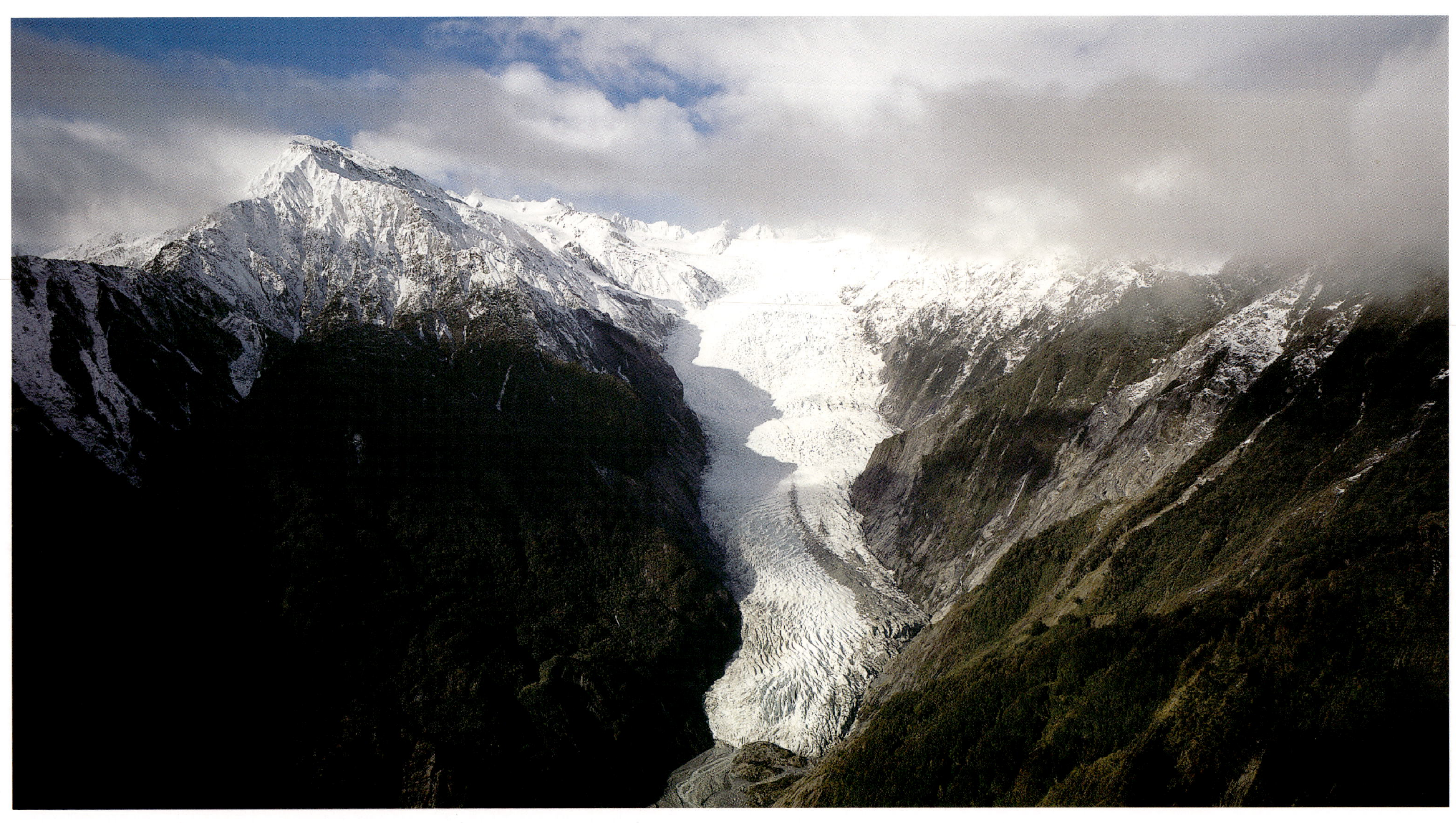

Pioneer geologist Julius Haast, who visited (and named) the Franz Josef Glacier in 1865, noted that "the ploughing and furrowing action of ice" could be better observed here than anywhere else in the world. At that time the glacier presented an even more dramatic spectacle than it does today, with its terminal face located three kilometres further down the valley and its surface up to 300 metres higher.

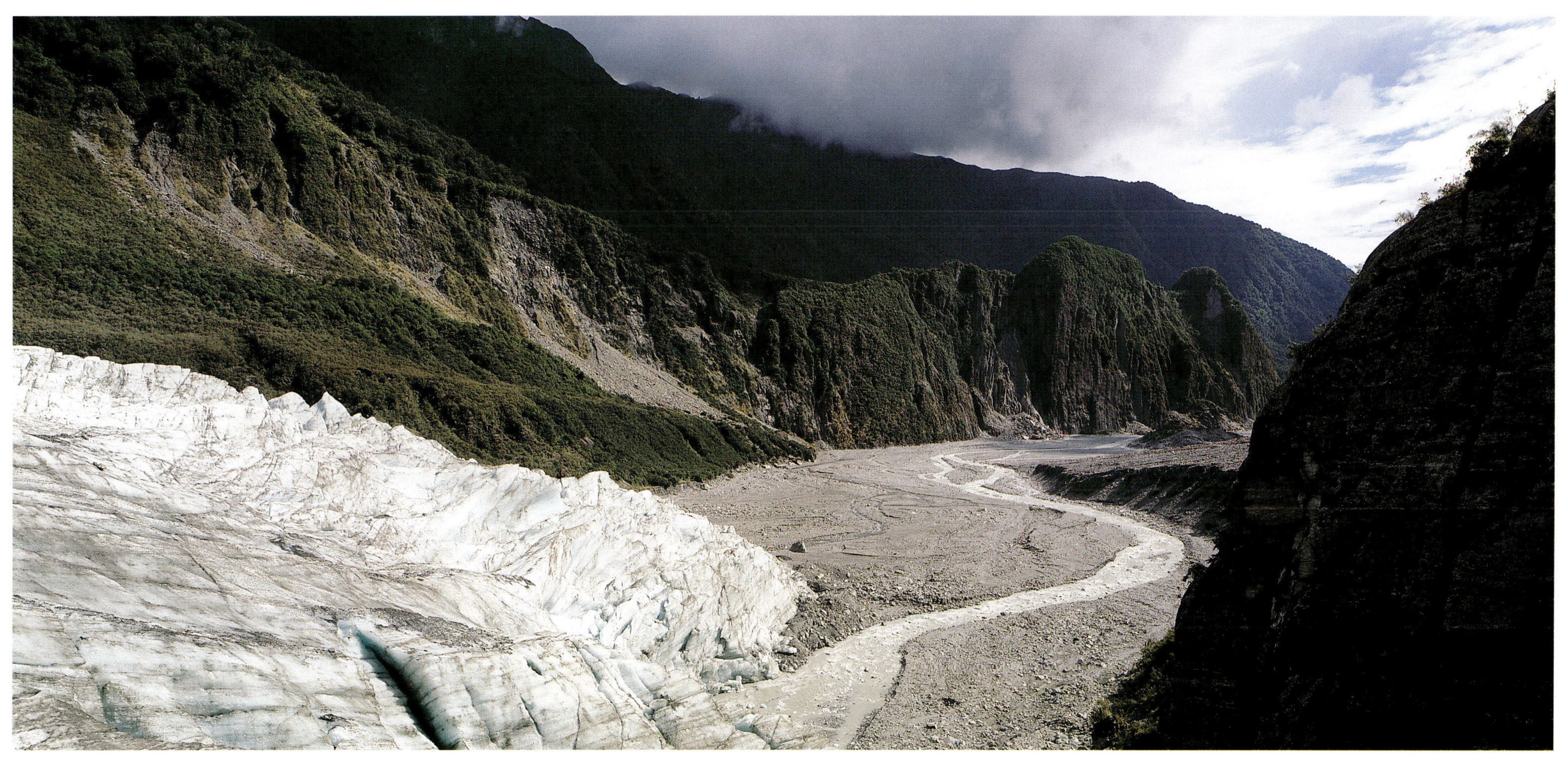

The terminal regions of the Fox Glacier with the murky, grit-laden Fox River draining away meltwater carried within and beneath the ice. When the glacier was first surveyed in 1894 the terminal face was 2.7 kilometres further down the valley, and the depth of ice at the point where the glacier now ends was about 370 metres.

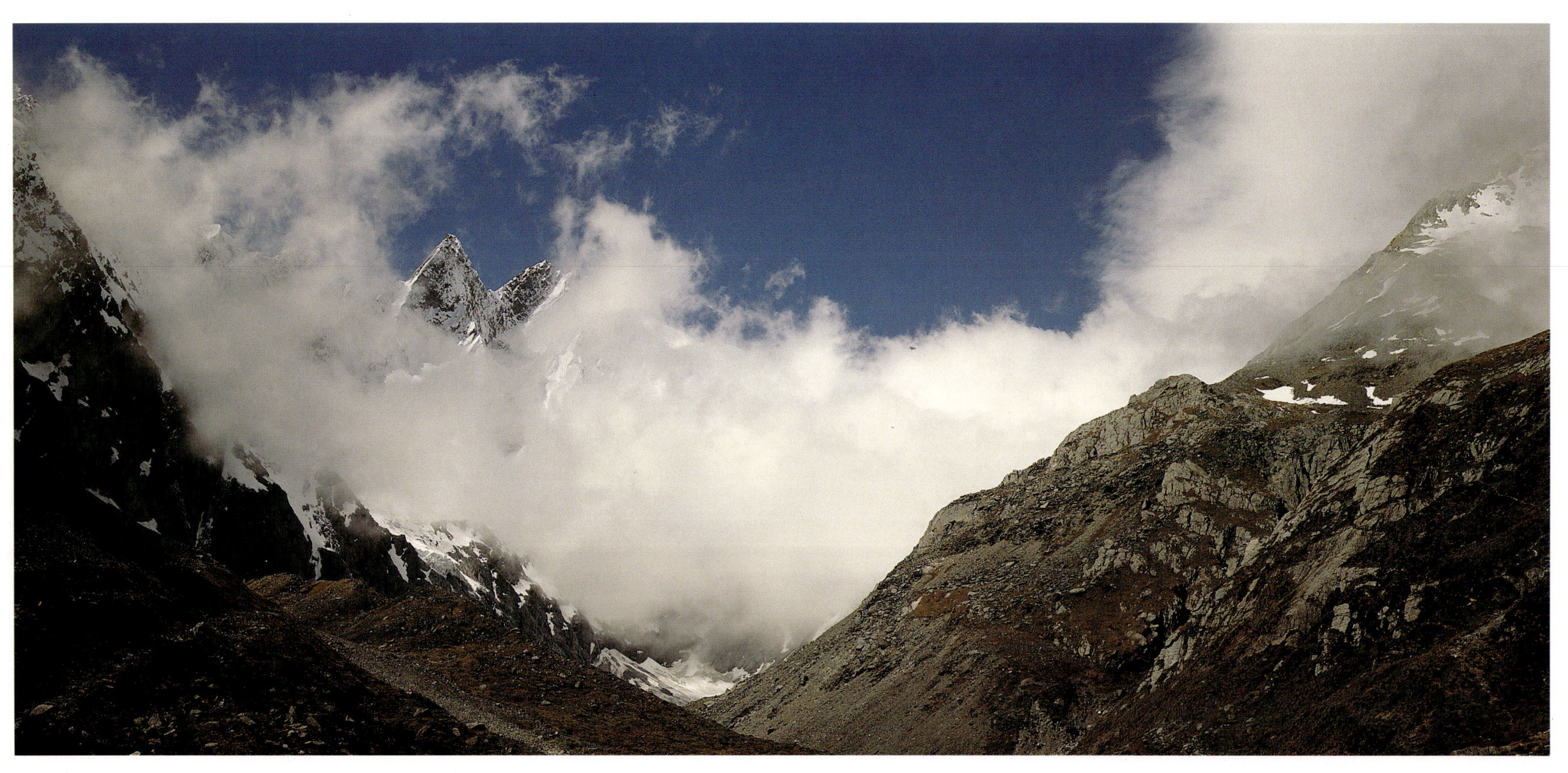

The sharply-pointed summits of Unicorn (2,559 metres) and Dilemma Peak (2,619 metres) at the head of the Copland Valley towards the southern end of Westland National Park.

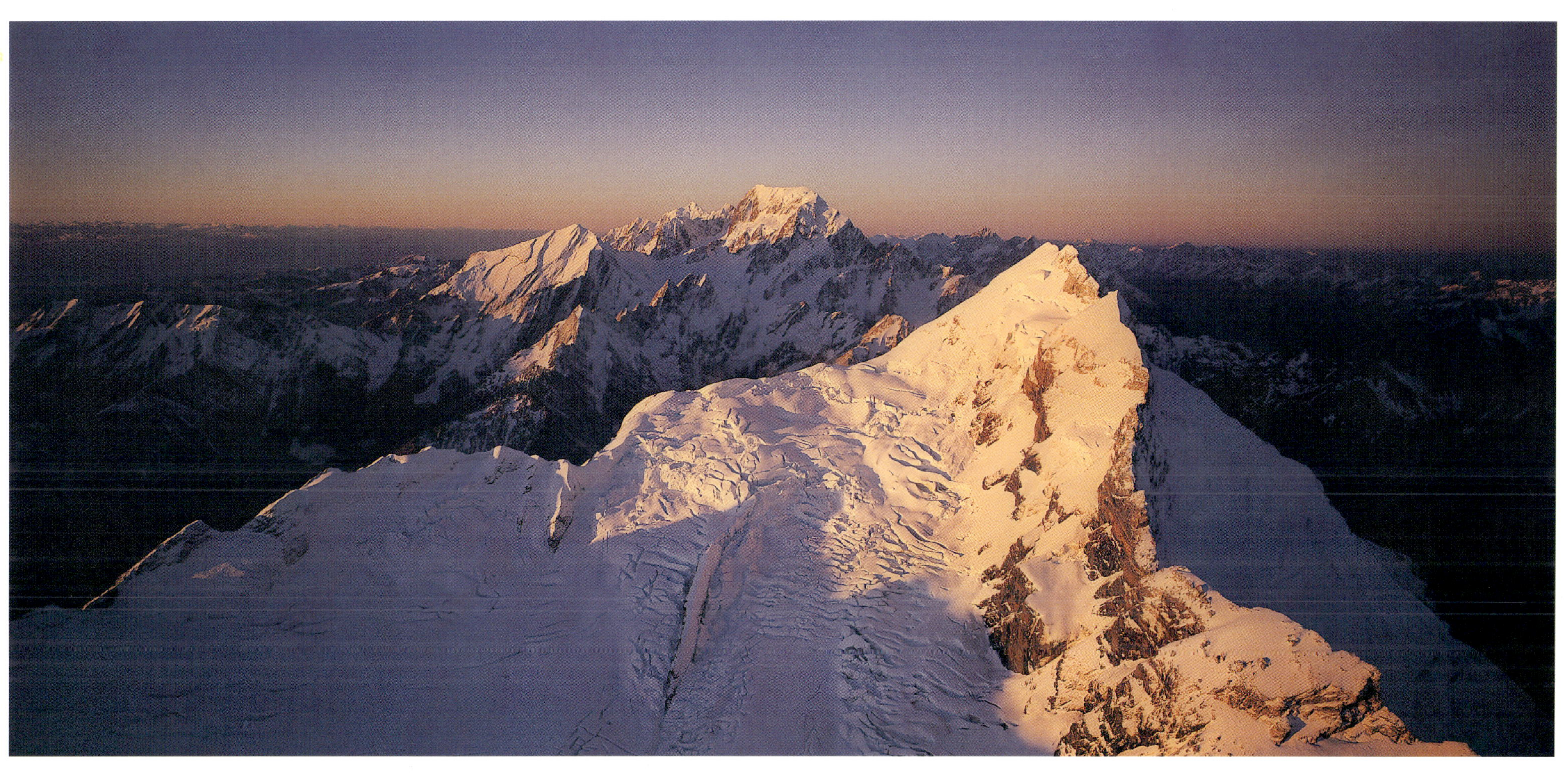

Sunset lights the western faces of the Southern Alps' highest peaks: (from left to right) La Perouse (3,079 metres), Mts Torres (3,163 metres), Tasman (3,498 metres), Dampier (3,440 metres), Cook (3,754 metres) and Sefton (3,157 metres).

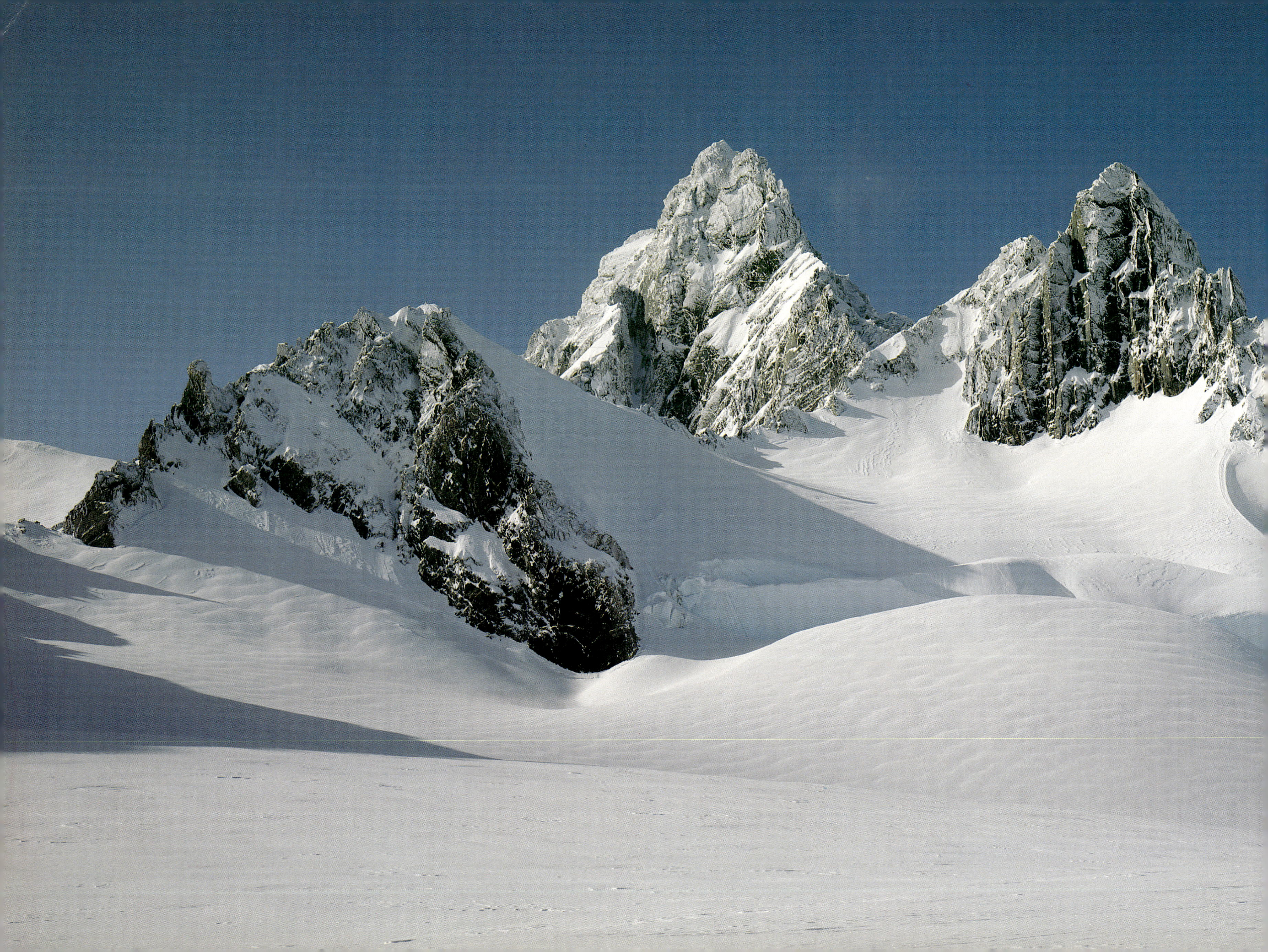

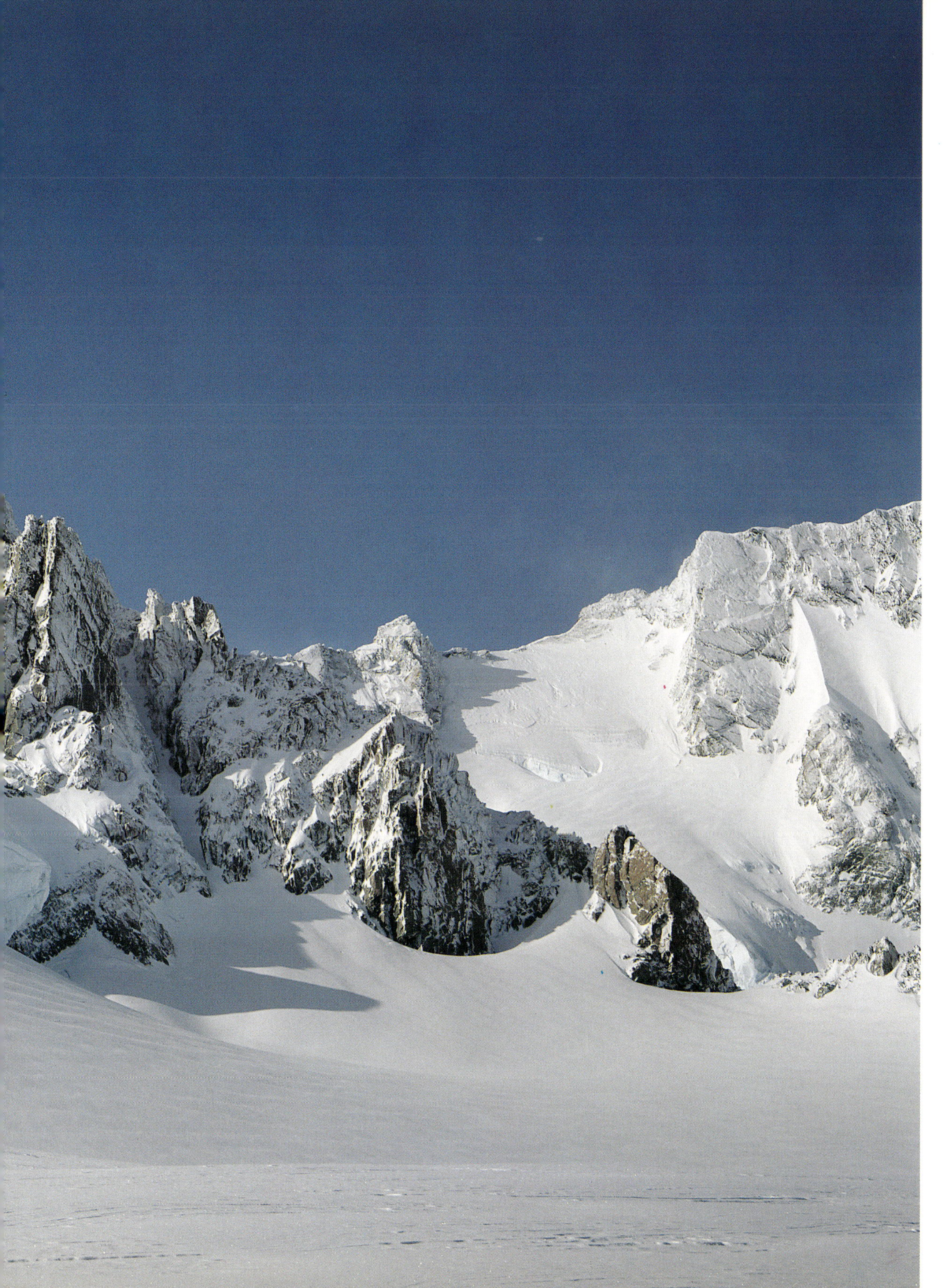

The summits of Douglas Peak (3,085 metres, left) and Mt Alack (2,766 metres) contrast in shape and texture with the gently undulating snowfields above the Fox Glacier.

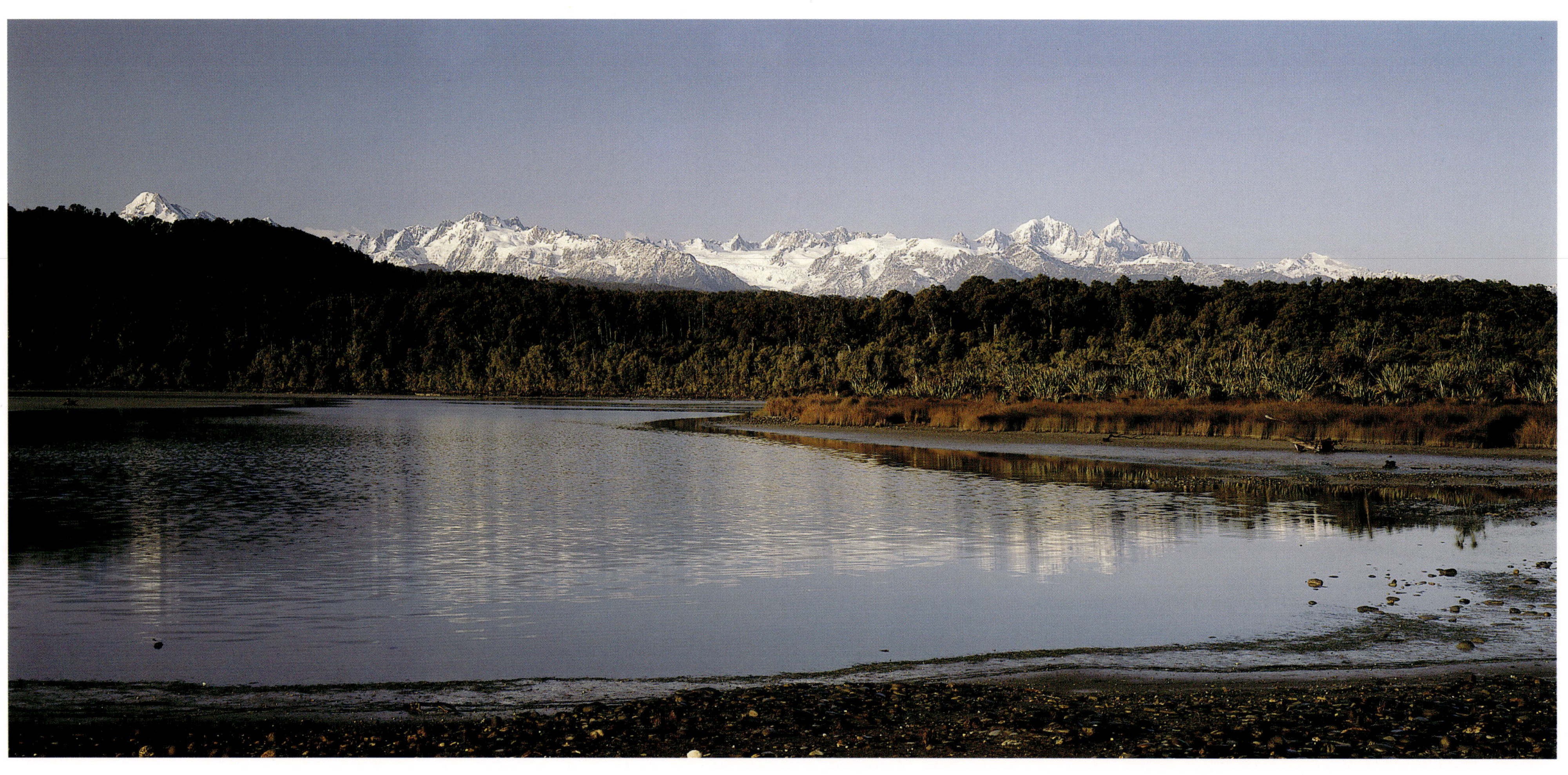

A thirty-five kilometre segment of the Main Divide from Elie de Beaumont (3,117 metres, left) to La Perouse (3,079 metres, right) from Three Mile Lagoon, south of Okarito. The forests here, saved from logging and added to the national park in 1982, have outstanding natural values, including an endangered population of 60 to 100 South Island brown kiwi, which is possibly a unique subspecies.

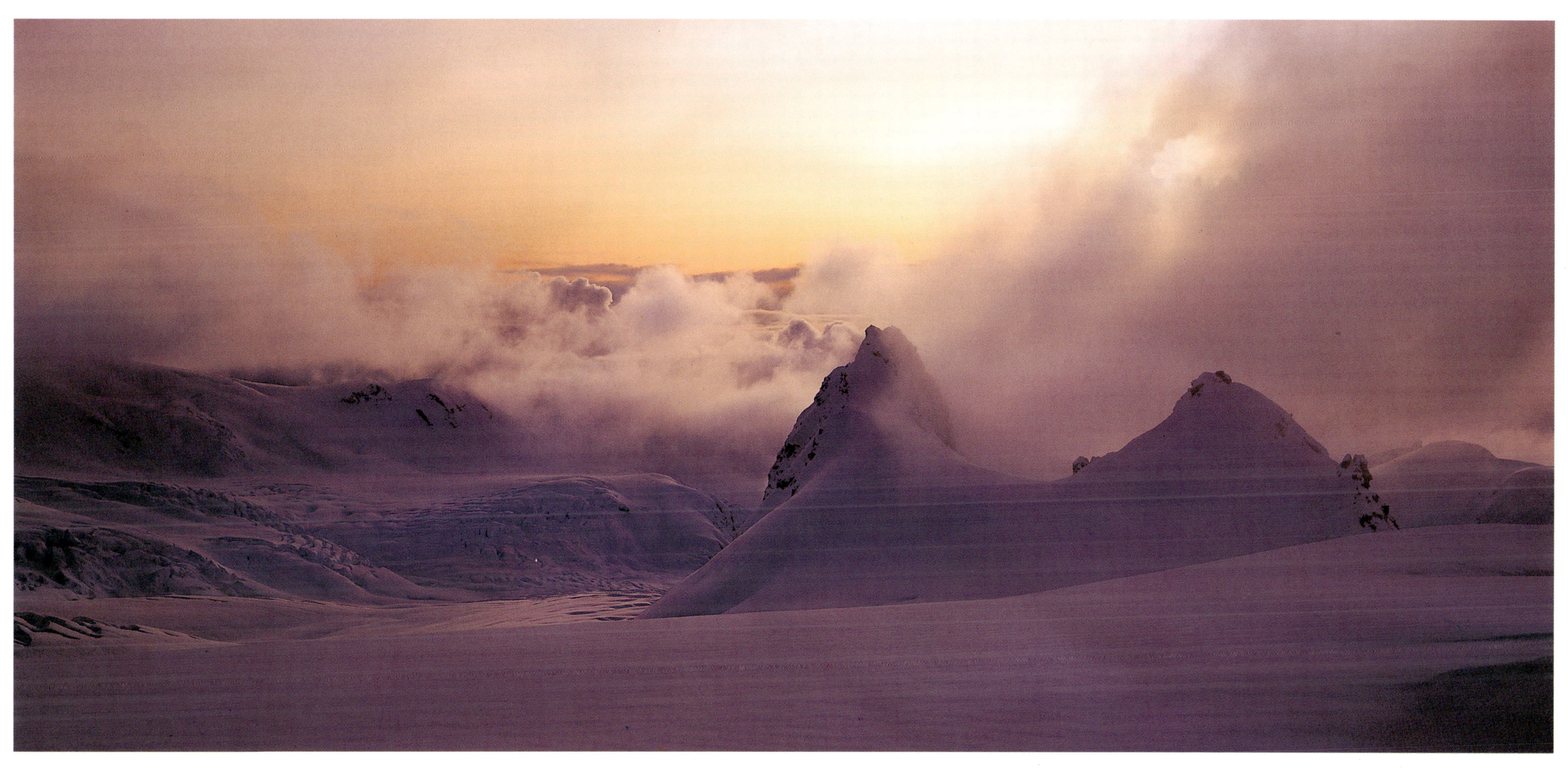

*"The solemn, soundless music/Of the sun's setting reverberates/Along the low red cloud-reefs."*—(Mary Ursula Bethell, '*At the Lighting of the Lamps*'.)
Sunset from the purple snowfields at the head of the Fox Glacier.

# HAAST-LANDSBOROUGH

The Haast-Landsborough component of Te Wahipounamu contains most of the land within the World Heritage Area outside of its four national parks. It includes both the eastern and western flanks of a fifty kilometre segment of the Southern Alps north of Haast Pass, an area of rugged mountains and remote valleys that includes the Hopkins, Huxley and Hunter valleys in the east, and the Hooker Range and Haast-Landsborough river system in the west. The majority of the region, however, is in the South Westland lowlands, where it extends over a distance of 180 kilometres between the Cook River in the north, and Big Bay in the south. In all, this central segment of Te Wahipounamu contains about 800,000 hectares—or half as much again as the combined area of Mount Cook, Westland and Mount Aspiring national parks. It includes many outstanding natural features that are confined to this part of the World Heritage Area, and the drive through South Westland and across the Haast Pass provides probably the best opportunity to discover why the entire south-west corner of the South Island of New Zealand is considered one of the last great tracts of unspoilt temperate wilderness left on earth.

From both a national and international heritage perspective, what particularly distinguishes this part of Te Wahipounamu is its mosaic of lowland forests and wetlands. Prior to human settlement most parts of lowland New Zealand would have been covered in a dense mantle of tall forest (in which kahikatea would have regularly been a major component) with large areas of swampy wetland occupying poorly drained alluvial sites. Today, much of this land has been cleared and drained for farming and settlement, resulting in the loss of over ninety per cent of New Zealand's wetland areas, and all but the last two per cent of once widespread kahikatea forests. Only in South Westland is there today something resembling the older natural order over extensive areas of lowland landscape, which gives these areas immense ecological significance. They are also museum pieces of great cultural value, preserving the kind of landscape that would have greeted both Maori and European settlers when they first waded ashore in this strange new country, and in which many of these early settlers would have established their first homes.

Further enhancing the heritage value of these lowland areas is the fact that ice age glaciers didn't totally overwhelm the coastal country between the Karangarua and Haast rivers and between the Cascade River and Big Bay (as they did in most other parts of South Westland and Fiordland) and consequently these areas provided important refuges for plants and animals. Moreover, major plant and animal pests today occupy a restricted range, or are present in lower numbers, in the Haast region than is the case elsewhere in the West Coast lowlands, enabling a number of rare or threatened species to survive better here than they have elsewhere. Prominent examples include: tokoeka (Haast brown kiwi) which is confined to the Haast area; tawaki (Fiordland crested penguin) whose main population is near Jacksons Bay; kaka (whose highest mainland densities occur in lowland forests south of the Cascade River; and mohua (yellowhead), which has one of its last strongholds in the Landsborough valley.

*'Far South Westland is as remote from the settled centres of New Zealand as one can reach and its extent is vast enough to test all the powers of the body and the imagination. Set between sky-propping peaks of the alps and the vast emptiness of the western seas are forests and lakes, rivers and seashores, as beautiful, as mysterious, as rich in elemental spirit as any left on earth.'*

Peter Hooper

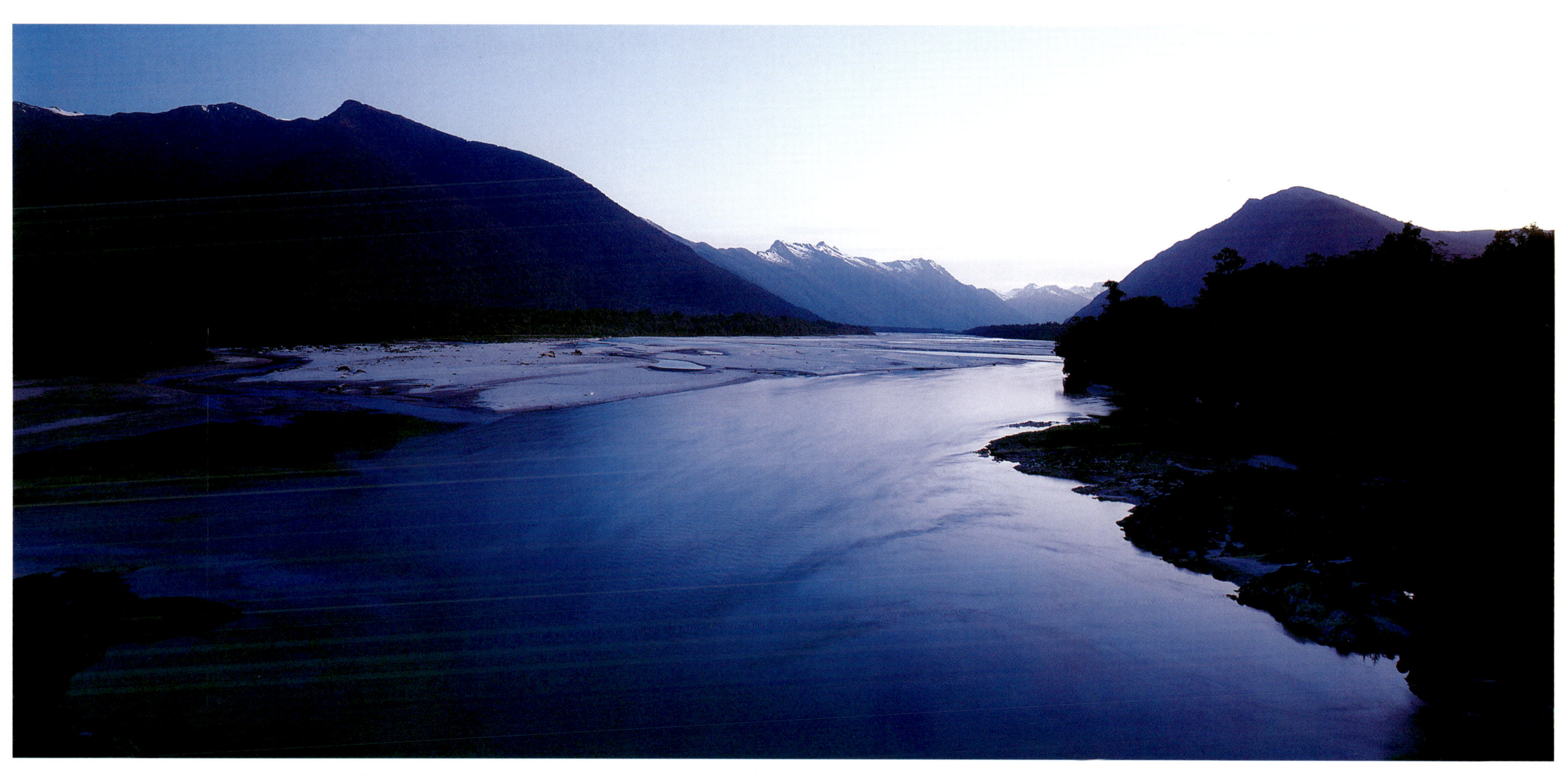

Last light on the Arawhata River near Jacksons Bay.

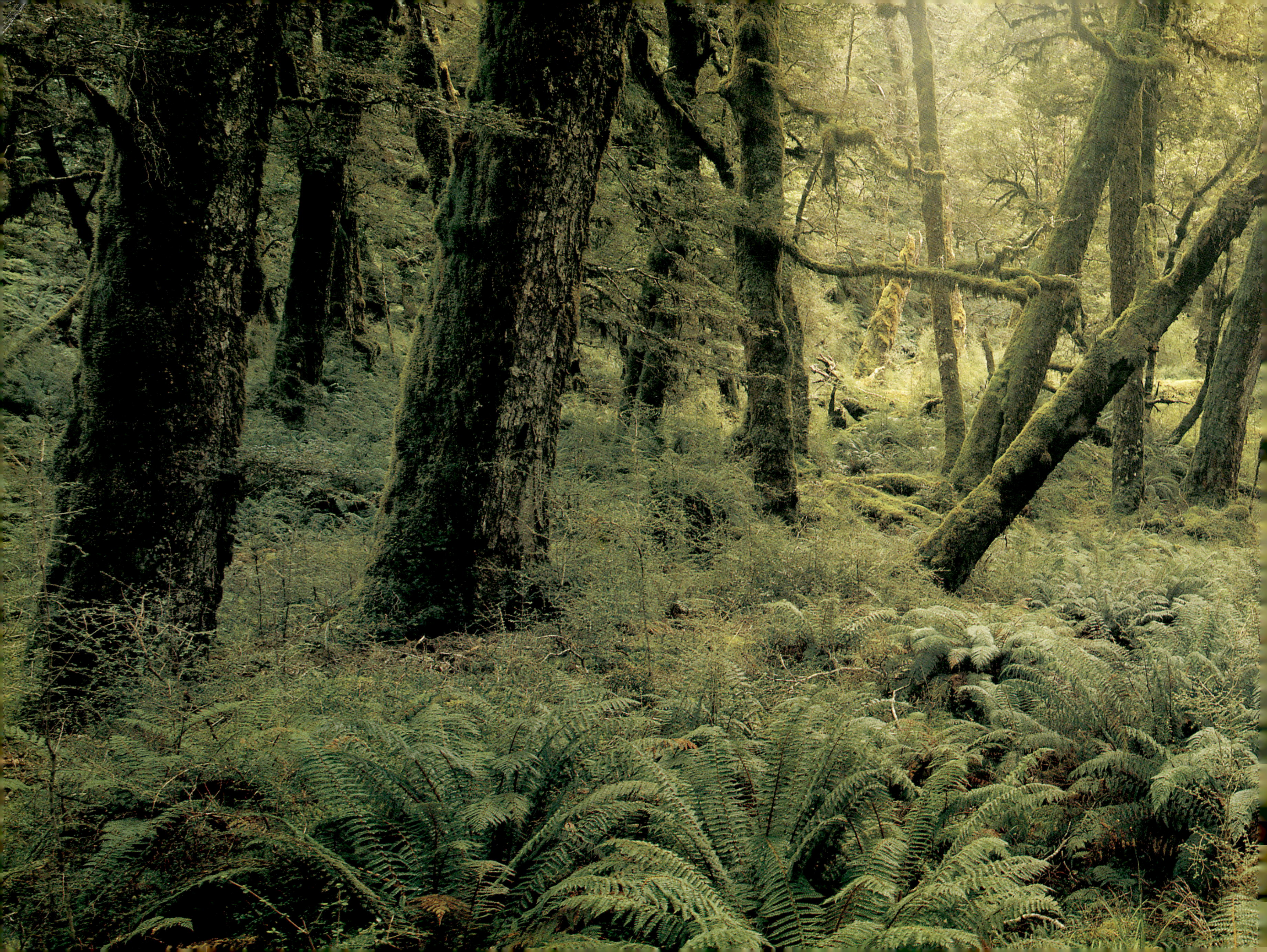

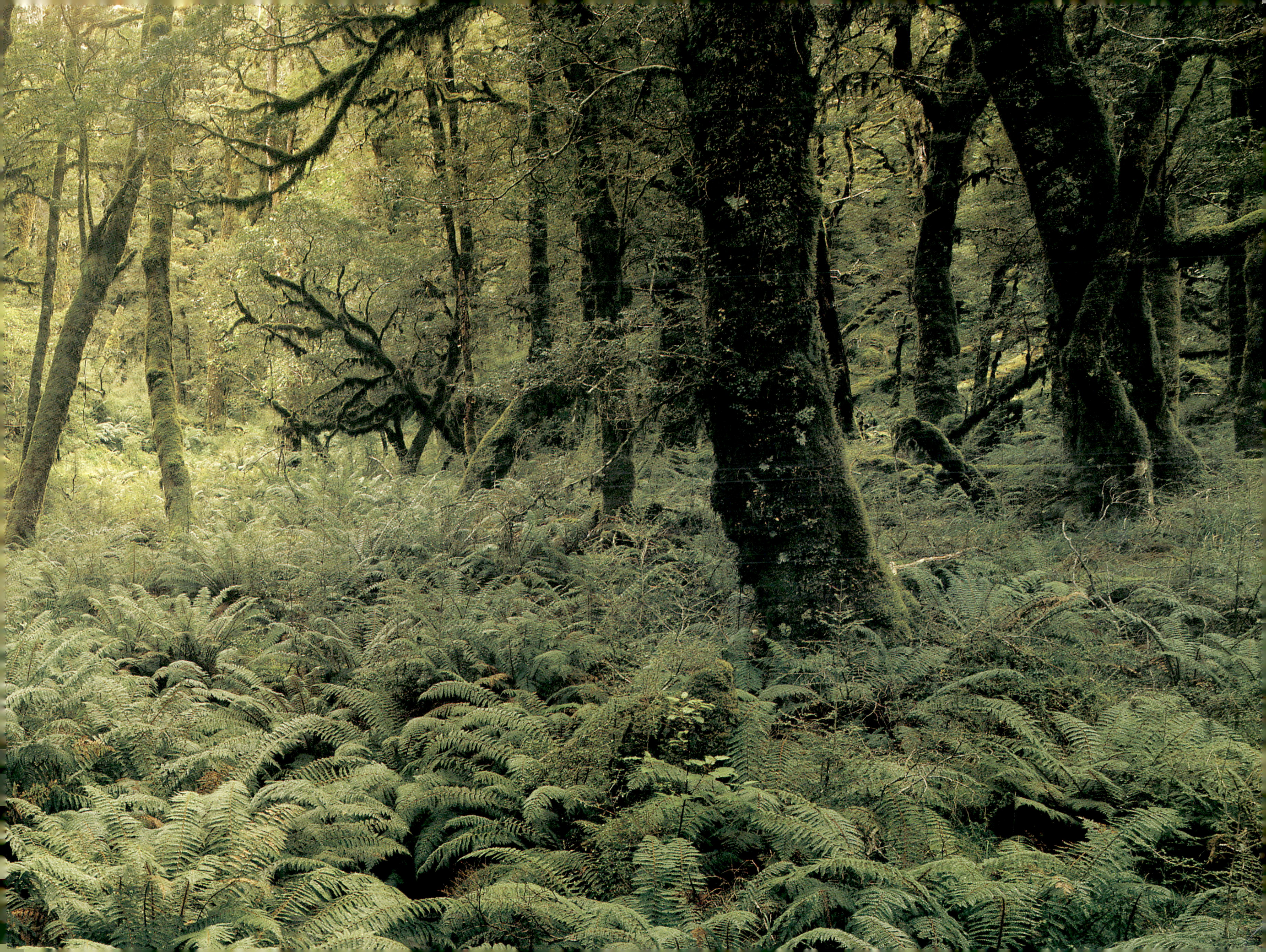

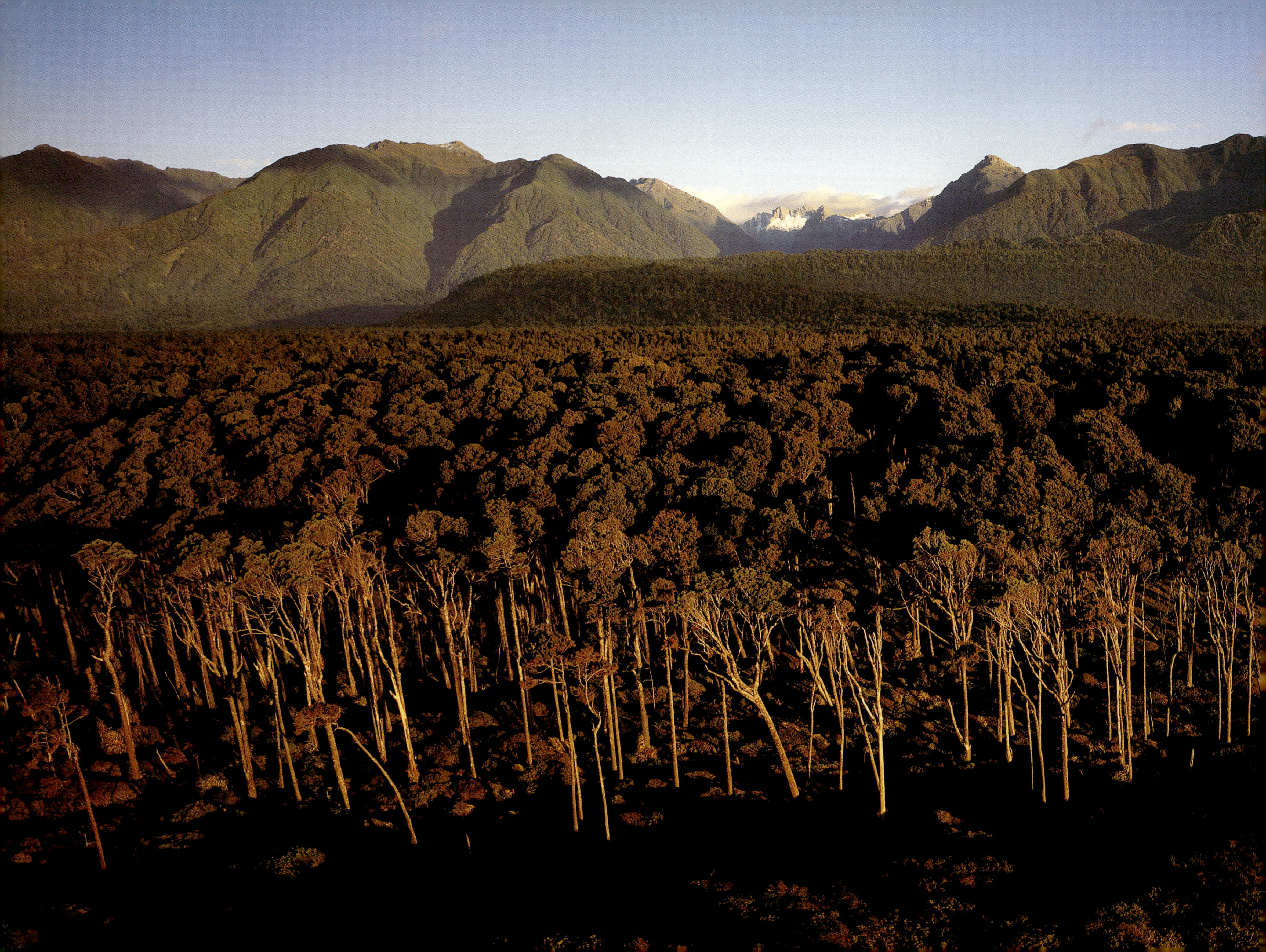

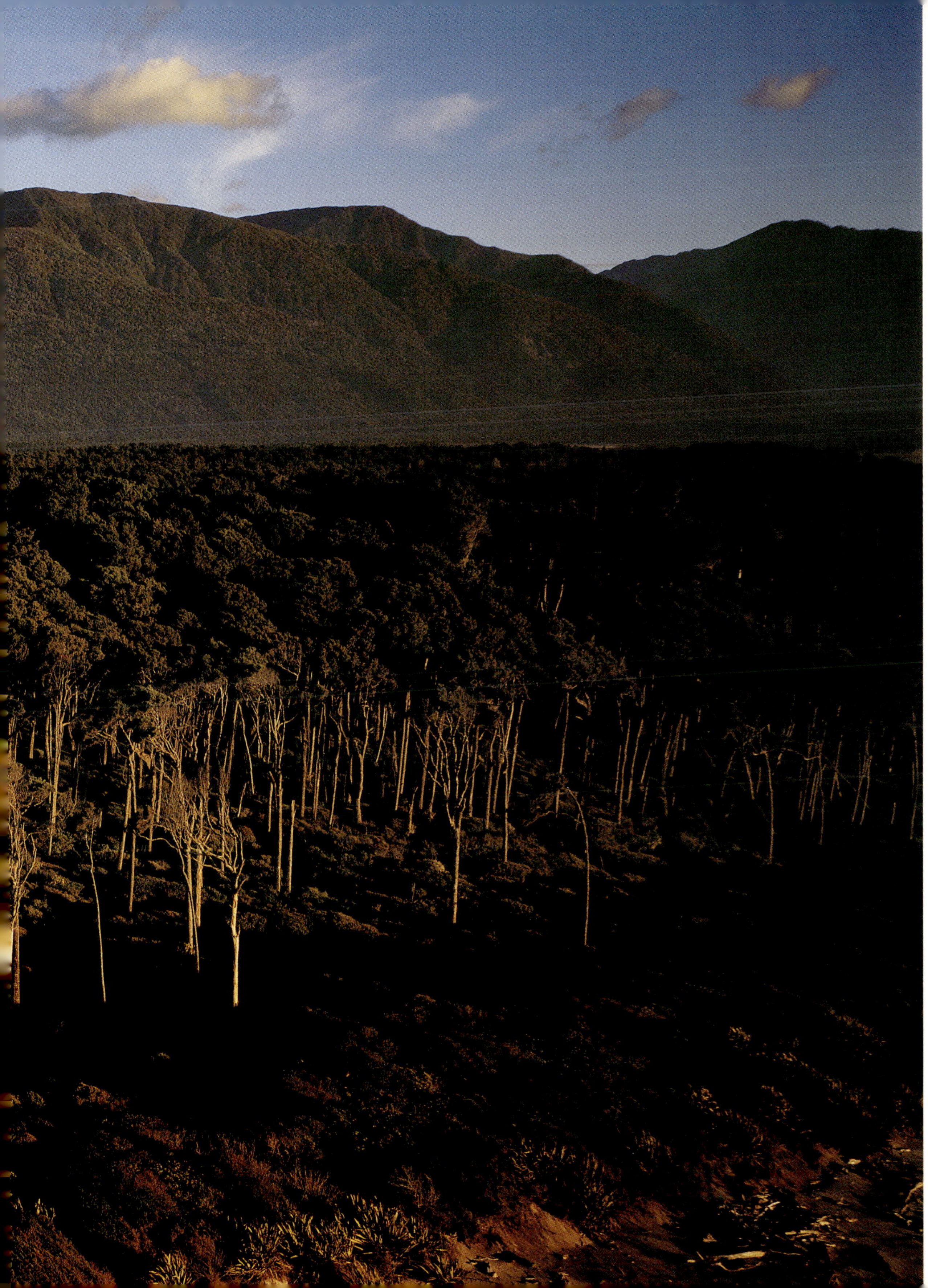

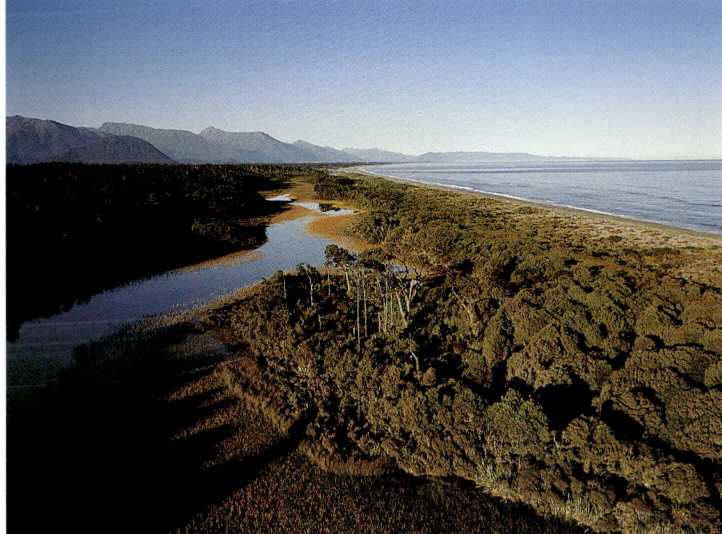

Above: Impounded dune lakes near Ship Creek at the northern end of the Haast coastal plain separate shrubland-covered younger dunes from taller podocarp forest growing on older dune ridges inland of the lakes. Beyond the last of the lakes visible here is a unique series of five to six parallel dune ridges built up over the past 6,000 years as a result of uplift of the coastal plain, climatic oscillations causing sea-level changes and possibly also fluctuations in the volumes of sediment being delivered to the coast by the Haast/Landsborough river system.

Left: Evening light illuminates rimu forest behind the beach at Bruce Bay.

Previous Pages: Beech forest on the floor of the Landsborough valley, north of the Haast Pass highway. Along with beech forests in Fiordland's Eglinton valley, the Landsborough is one of the last strongholds for the rare mohua (or yellowhead) and has also good numbers of other increasingly rare indigenous forest birds, notably kaka and kakariki.

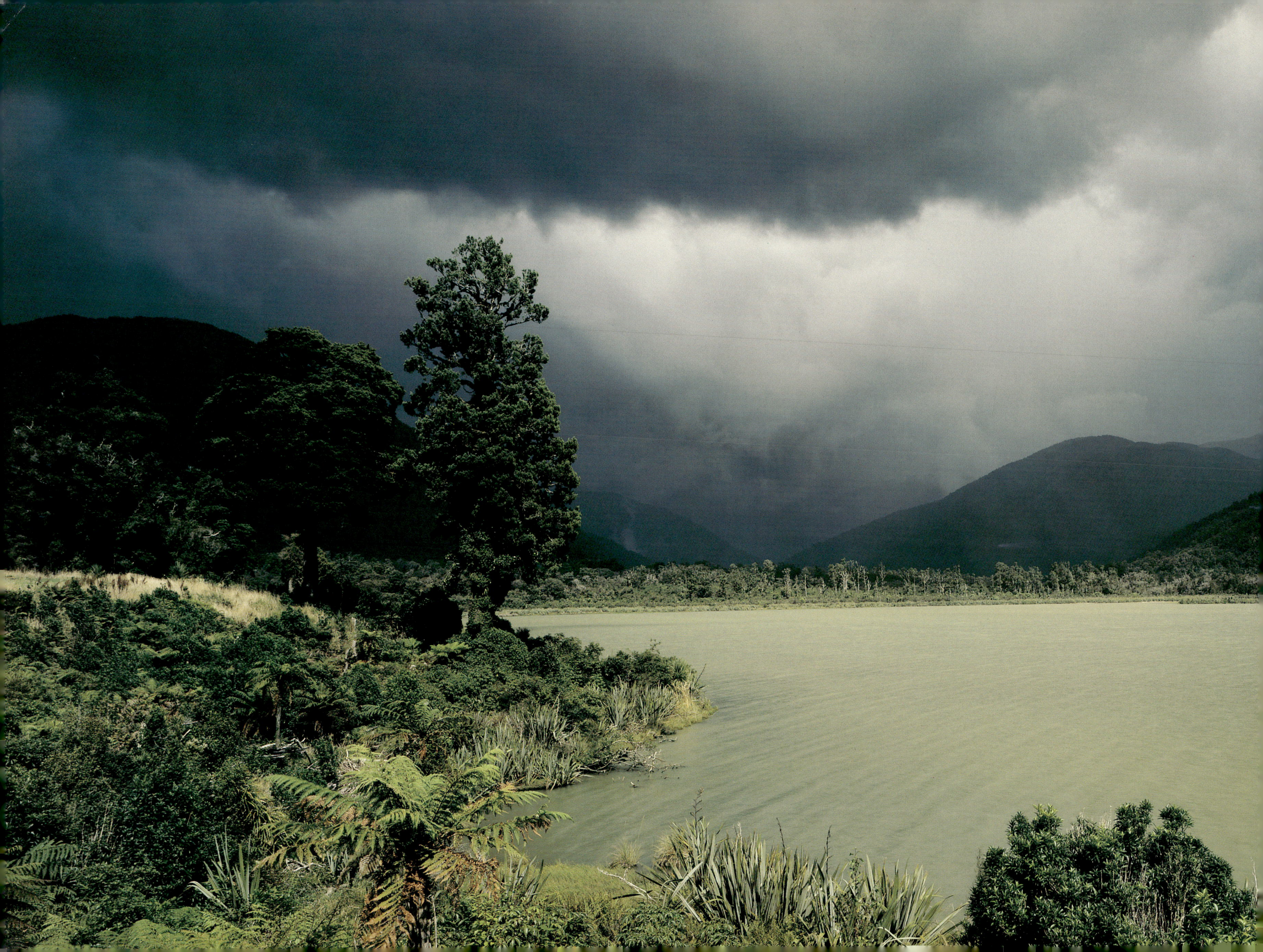

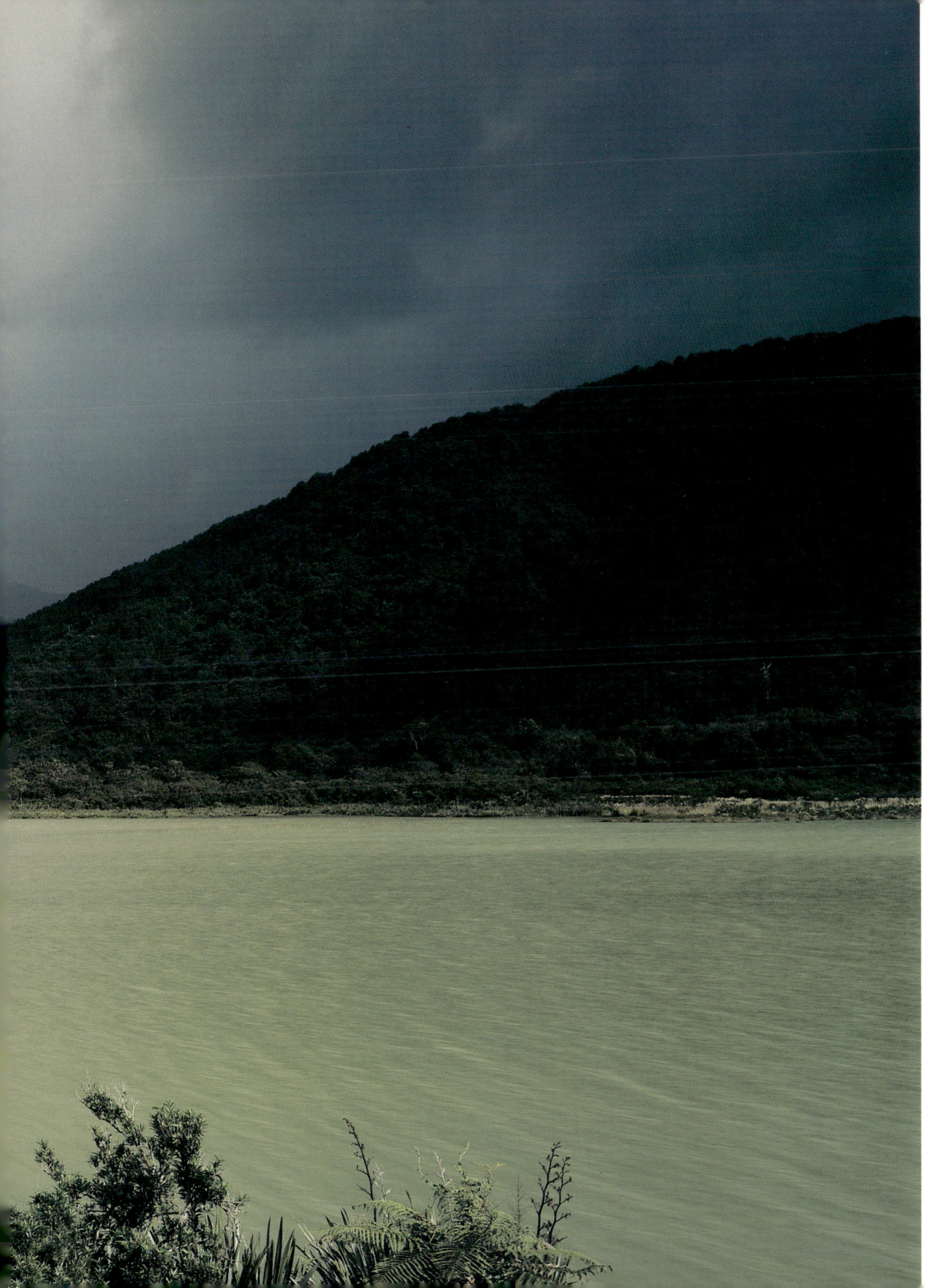

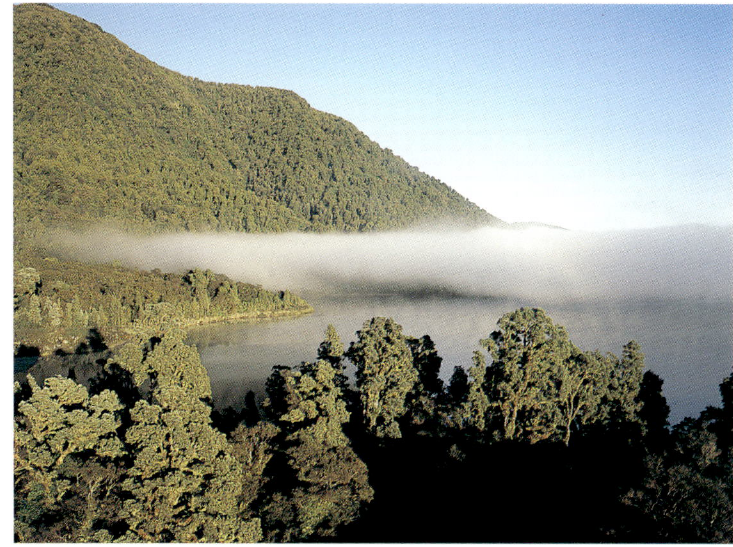

Morning sunlight rolls back a blanket of mist from the tranquil waters of Lake Paringa.

LEFT: A break in storm clouds illuminates the waters of Lake Moeraki, the southernmost and shallowest of a sequence of large lakes (Wahapo, Mapourika, Paringa, and Moeraki) that have filled old, moraine-dammed glacial depressions in the South Westland lowlands. At Lake Moeraki the gradual process of infilling with sediments has resulted in outstanding wetland-to-forest sequences (flax swamp to swamp shrubland to 'floating' kahikatea forest), especially along the alluvial parts of its shoreline. These kahikatea forests are thought to be the best representation anywhere of the Mesozoic swamp forests that existed on the ancient southern super-continent of Gondwana over 100 million years ago.

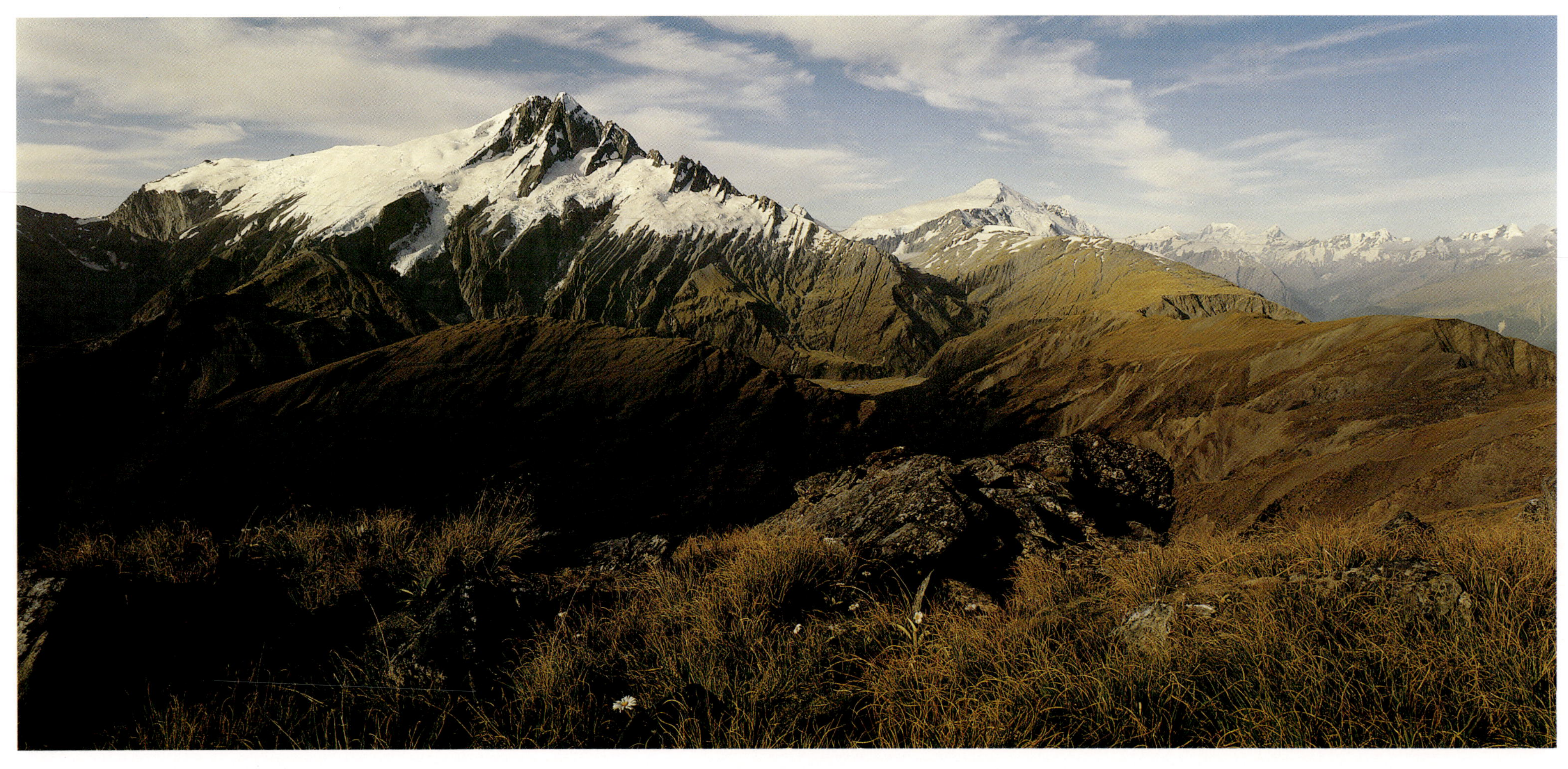

Mt Hooker (2,652 metres) and Mt Dechen (2,630 metres) from the crest of the Solution Range, with Mt Cook visible to the right between the pointed summits of Fettes Peak (left) and Mt Sefton.

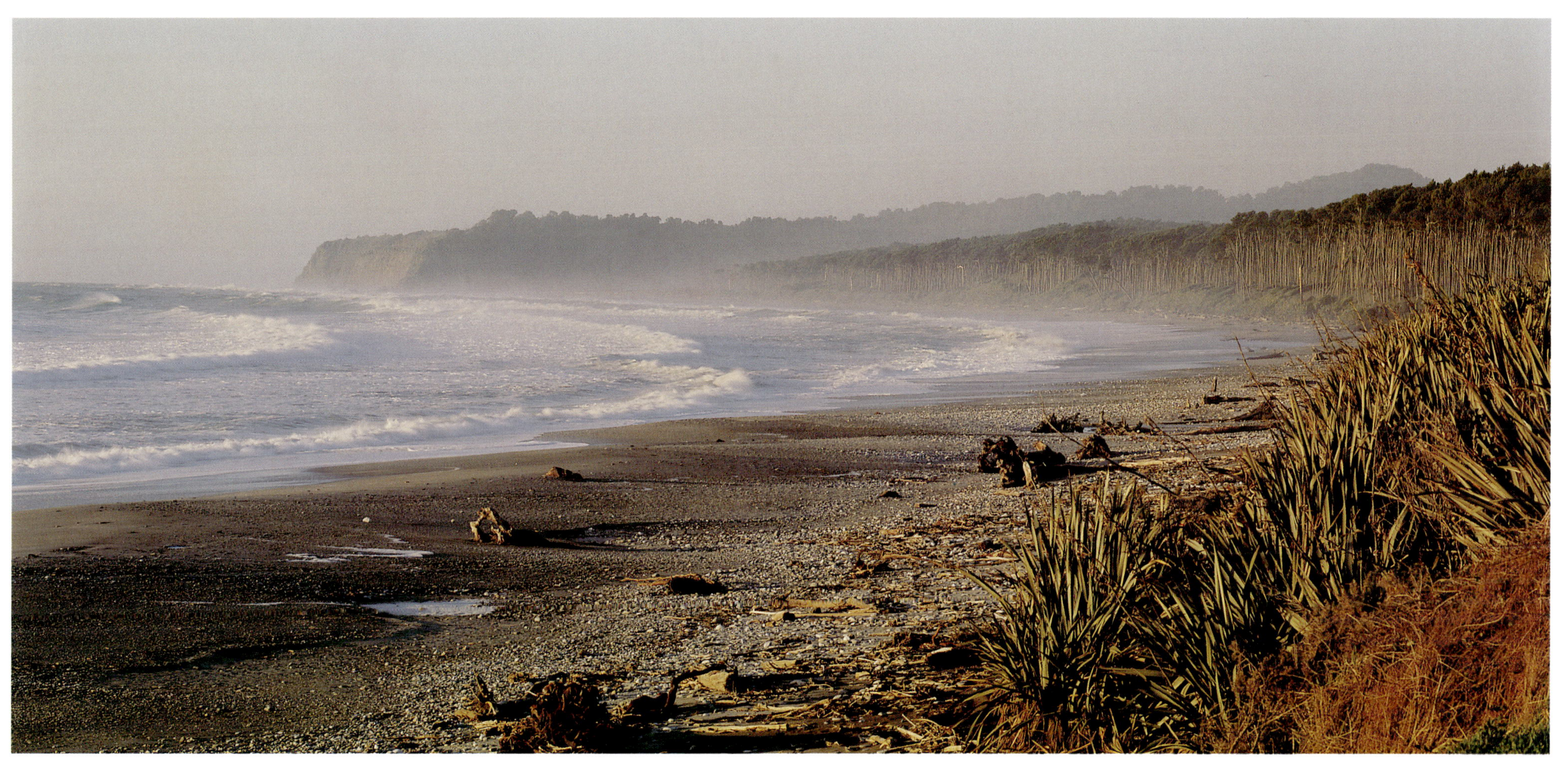

The beach at Mahitahi (Bruce Bay) looking northwards towards Makawhio Point.

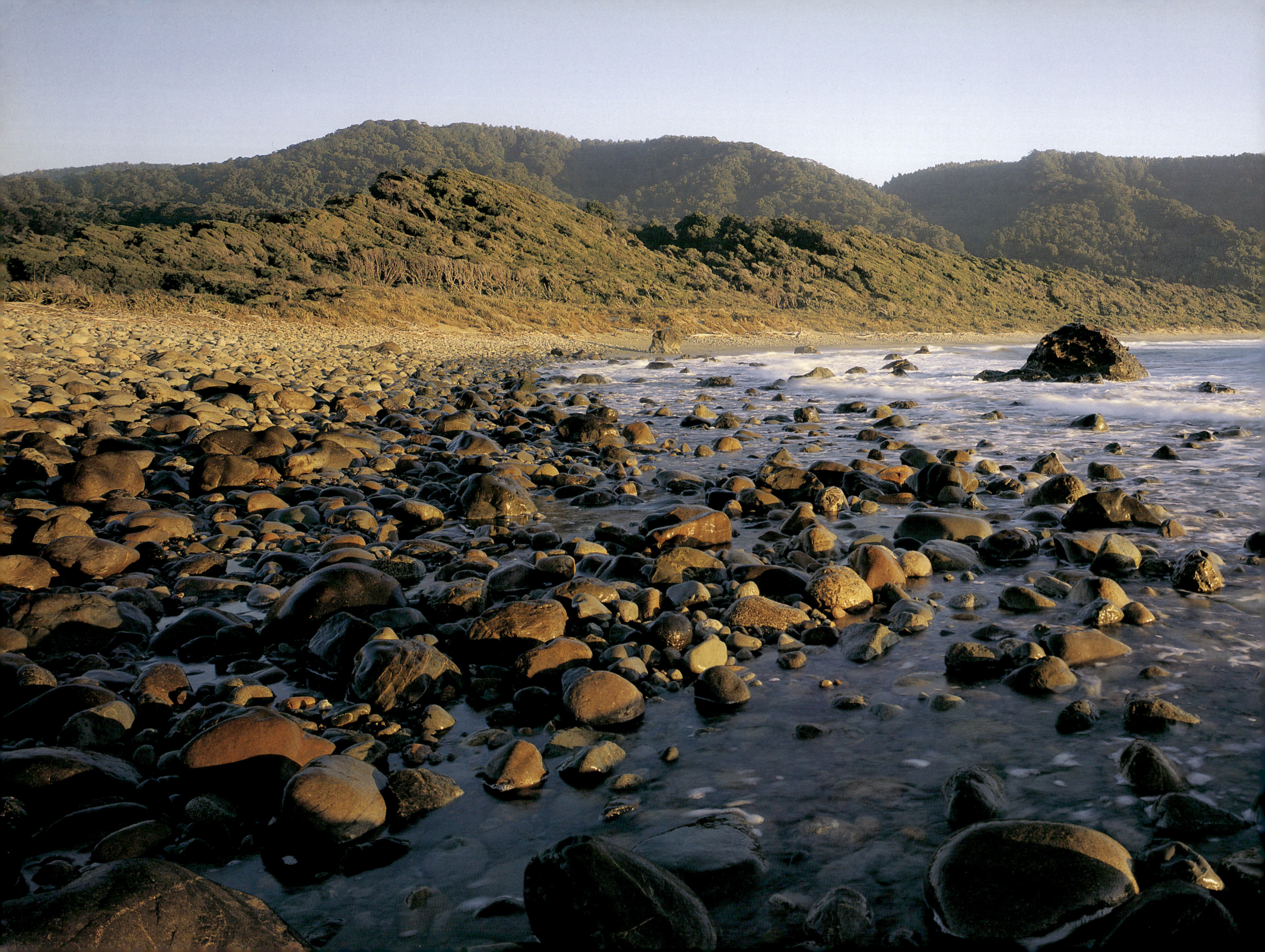

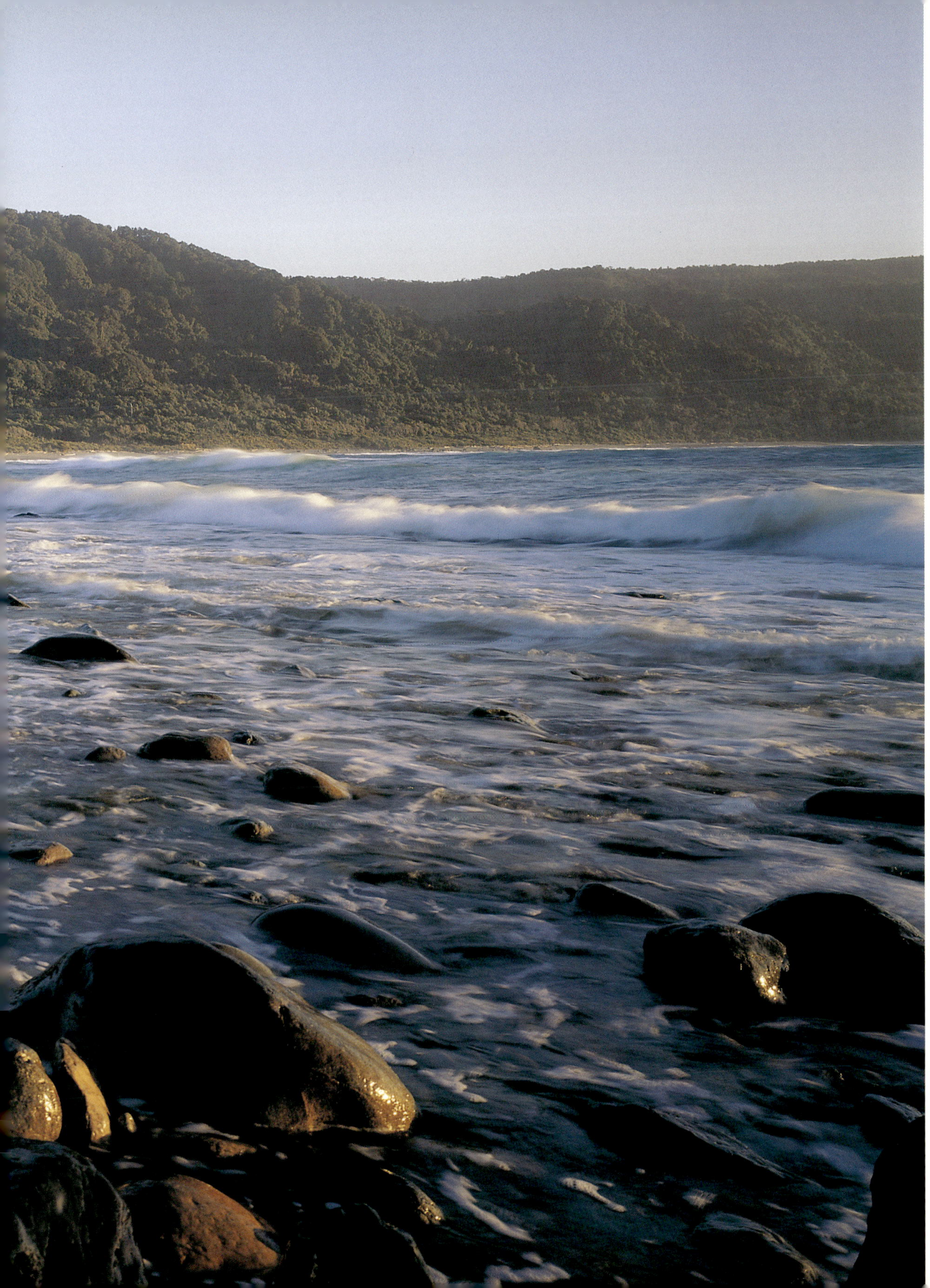

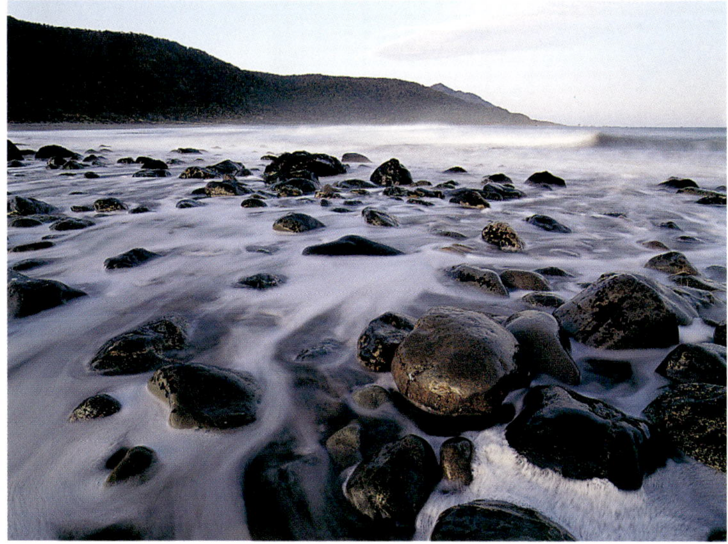

Sunset on the forested coastal hills near the mouth of Spoon River between the Cascade River and Big Bay. Evidence of ancient Maori camps or work-stations associated with the pounamu trade exist at the mouths of most of the main rivers along this section of the South Westland coast, the oldest of which date from the thirteenth century.

LEFT: Dawn on a bouldery beach near the mouth of Spoon River. The peak in the distance is Mt Malcolm (721 metres) at the western end of the Malcolm Range, south of Gorge River.

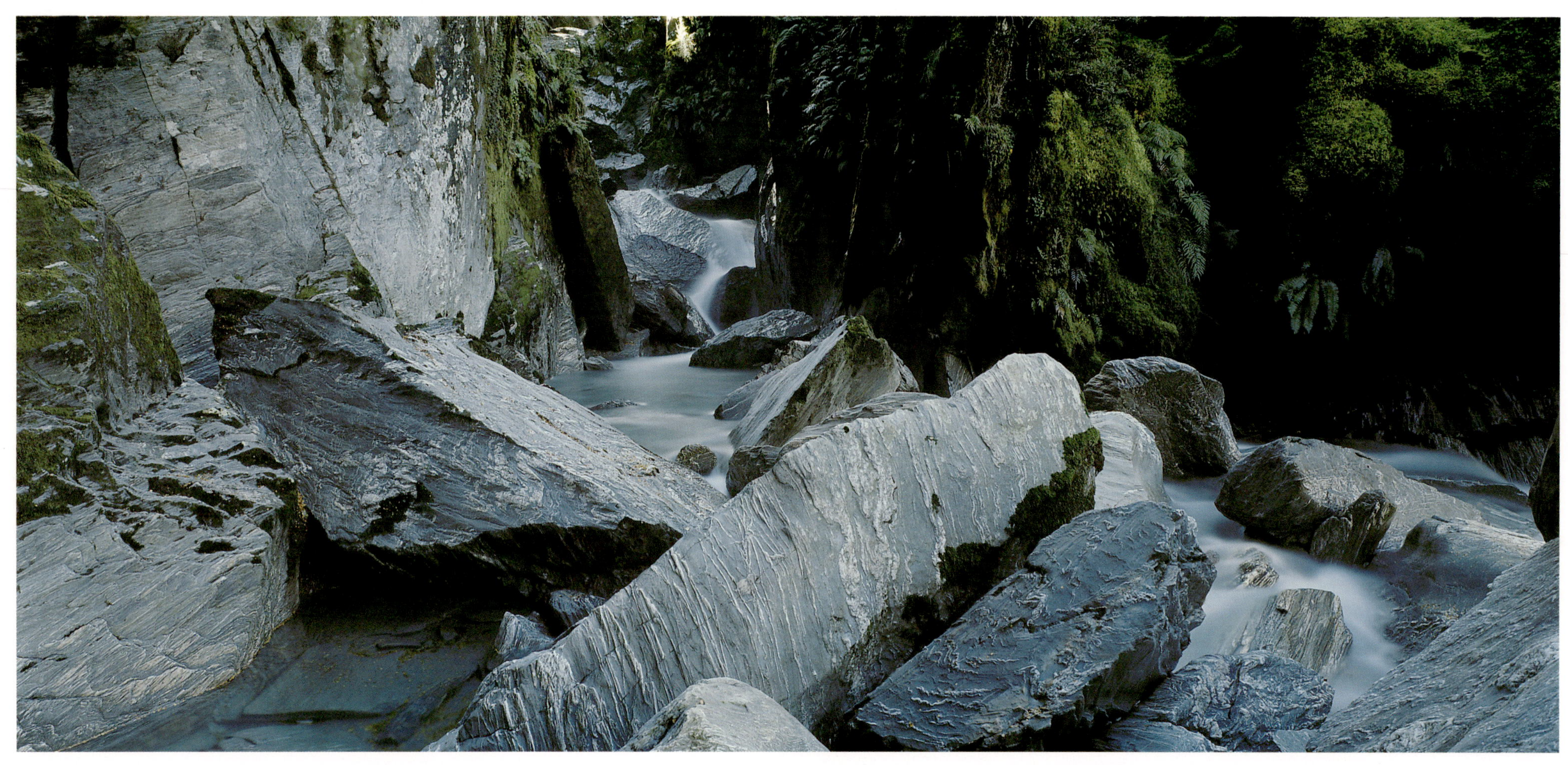

A small stream flowing through a schist gorge in the upper Clarke River, which drains southwards from Mt Hooker, north of the Haast Pass highway.

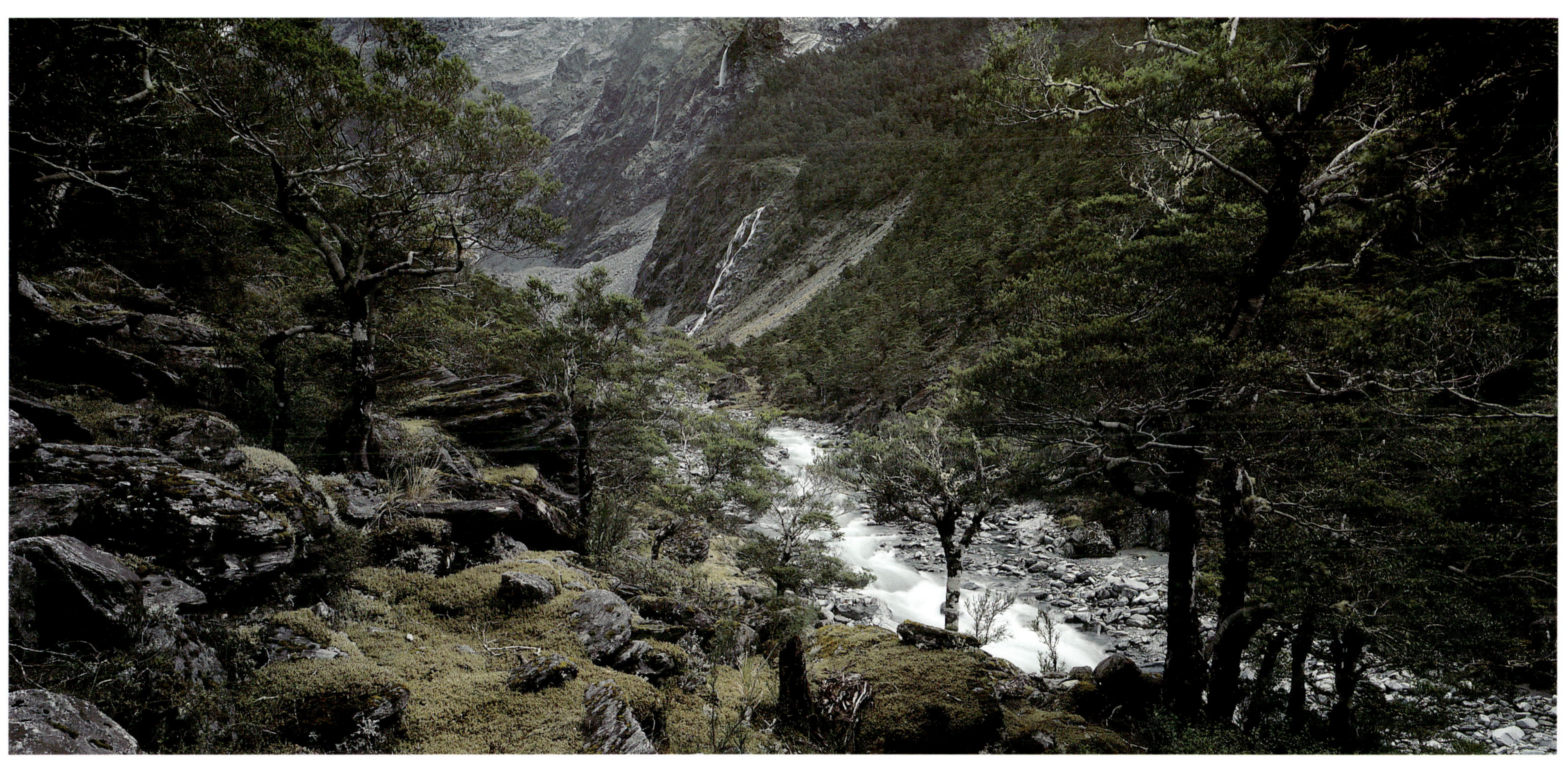

Beech forest, bluffs and waterfalls near the head of the Landsborough River. During the ice ages easily one of the the longest glaciers in the Southern Alps (which at its maximum was probably 125 kilometres in length) occupied the Haast-Landsborough valley system. Since it was first explored in 1887, the Landsborough has become legendary among trampers, hunters and mountaineers for its remote and challenging wilderness valleys.

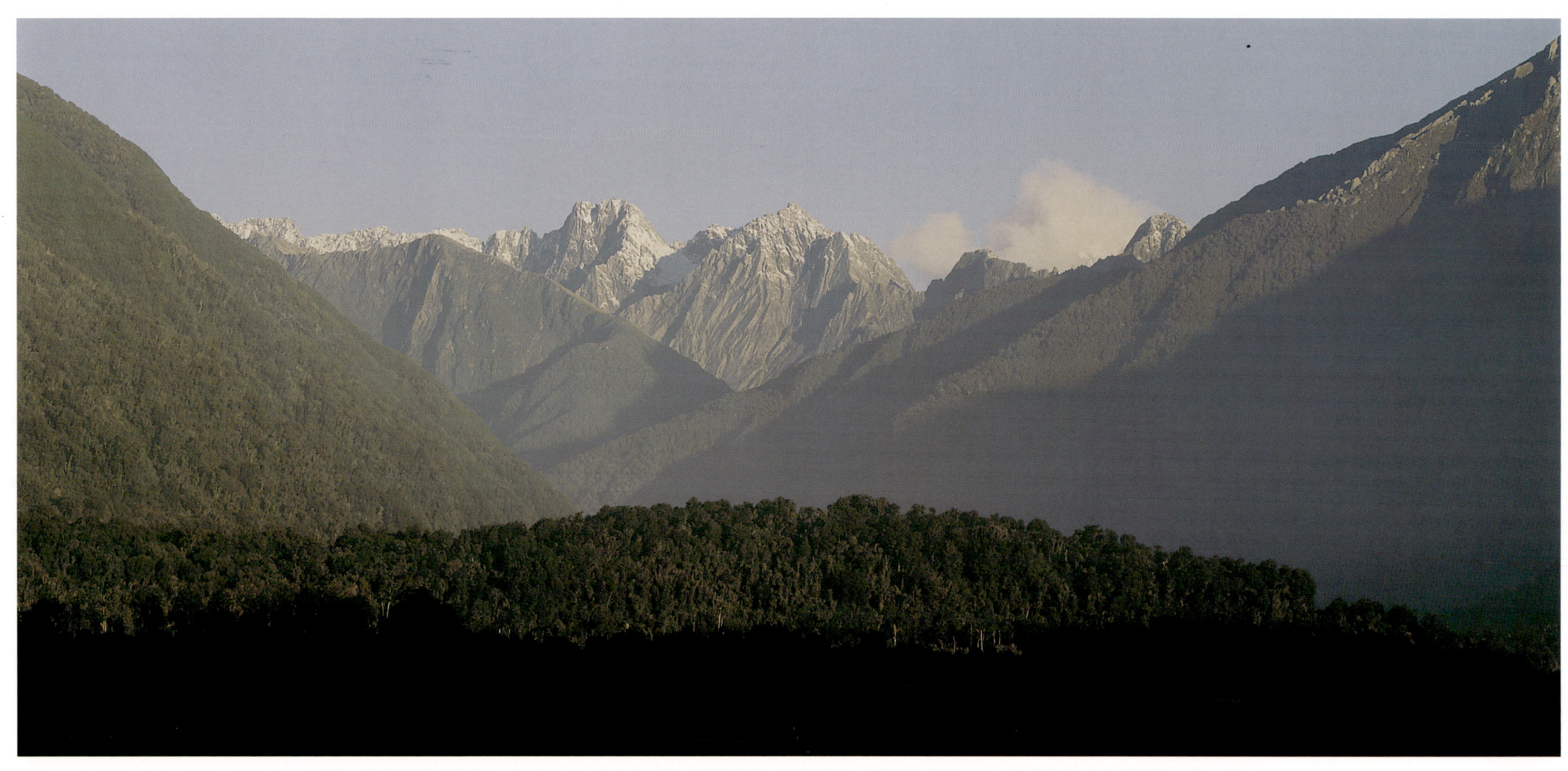

The sheer schist summits of the Strachan Range separate the Mahitahi and Paringa river catchments south of Bruce Bay.

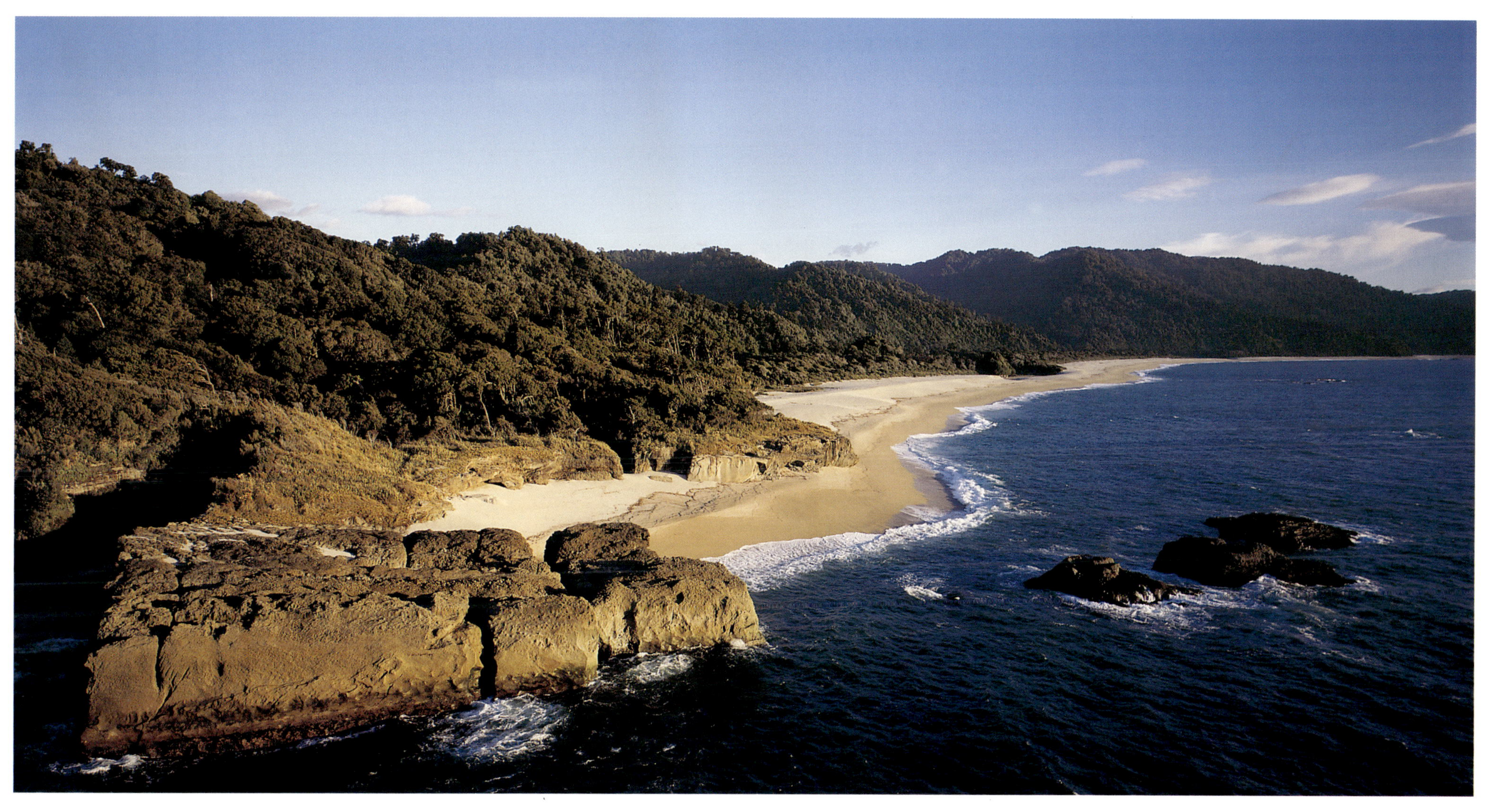

Coastal hills formed from sandstones, limestones and basalt have resulted in a series of intimate golden beaches between the Paringa River and Knights Point—a striking contrast to the gritty grey/black glacial sands that characterise beaches further north.

# MOUNT ASPIRING NATIONAL PARK

Mount Aspiring National Park straddles the southern end of the Southern Alps from the Haast Pass region in the north to the Humboldt Mountains near the head of Lake Wakatipu 140 kilometres to the south (where it shares a common boundary with the huge Fiordland National Park). In the west the park takes in the mountain country inland from the Haast coastal plain, including most of the catchments of the Waiatoto, Arawhata, and Cascade rivers and the highly distinctive Red Hills Range inland from Big Bay. In the east it encompasses the spectacular mountain terrain between the headwaters of lakes Wanaka and Wakatipu, including most of the forested parts of the Dart, Rees, Matukituki, Wilkin and Makarora catchments. Among the park's principal values are the pristine condition of both its alpine environments and deep forested valleys (especially on the eastern side of the Main Divide), its stunning panoramas of mountains and glaciers rising beyond idyllic grassy river flats and forested valley walls, and the magnificent terrain it provides for tramping, mountaineering and wilderness exploration. Symbolising these values is the park's principal scenic icon, the elegant 3,027 metre ice pyramid of Mt Aspiring and its encircling skirt of large glaciers, the highest mountain in the country outside the Mount Cook region, and the centrepiece of the park both geographically and in terms of public perception.

The park contains numerous soaring angular schist mountains and upwards of 100 separate glaciers, remnants of the massive ice sheets that issued from this region of the Southern Alps during the ice ages and carved out the deep troughs now occupied by lakes Wanaka and Wakatipu in the east, and, in the west, deposited the huge lateral moraine that today forms the coastal hill country between Jacksons Bay and the lower Cascade River. Great tilted slabs, huge vertical rock faces, cirques and hanging valleys are all a legacy of this past glaciation, as is the shape of the now densely forested valleys that make up most of the lower altitude landscapes of the park. East of the Main Divide these forests are a botanically significant mosaic of red, silver and mountain beech that, prior to the 1960s, was ravaged by large herds of red deer, but which are now in a much healthier condition as a result of the introduction of helicopter hunting and the subsequent dramatic reductions of deer populations. In the west, where rainfall can be four to five times higher than in the east, forests are usually much denser tangles of beech, podocarp and broadleaf species. An outstanding feature of the western parts of the park are the stark landscapes of the Red Hills region, where reddish ultramafic rocks and screes, sparse vegetation, and a much lower treeline contrast strikingly with the dense forests and grey schist mountains of the surrounding areas.

A proposal to create a national park in this part of the Southern Alps was first mooted by the Otago section of the New Zealand Alpine Club in 1936, but access to the area was difficult, and it was not until 1964 when the road link across the Haast Pass and through South Westland was close to completion, that this vision finally became a reality. Initially the park covered 199,227 hectares, but a series of major additions both sides of the Main Divide have seen it increase to its present 335,543 hectares—making it the third largest of New Zealand's 13 national parks after Fiordland (1.25 million hectares) and Kahurangi (450,000 hectares).

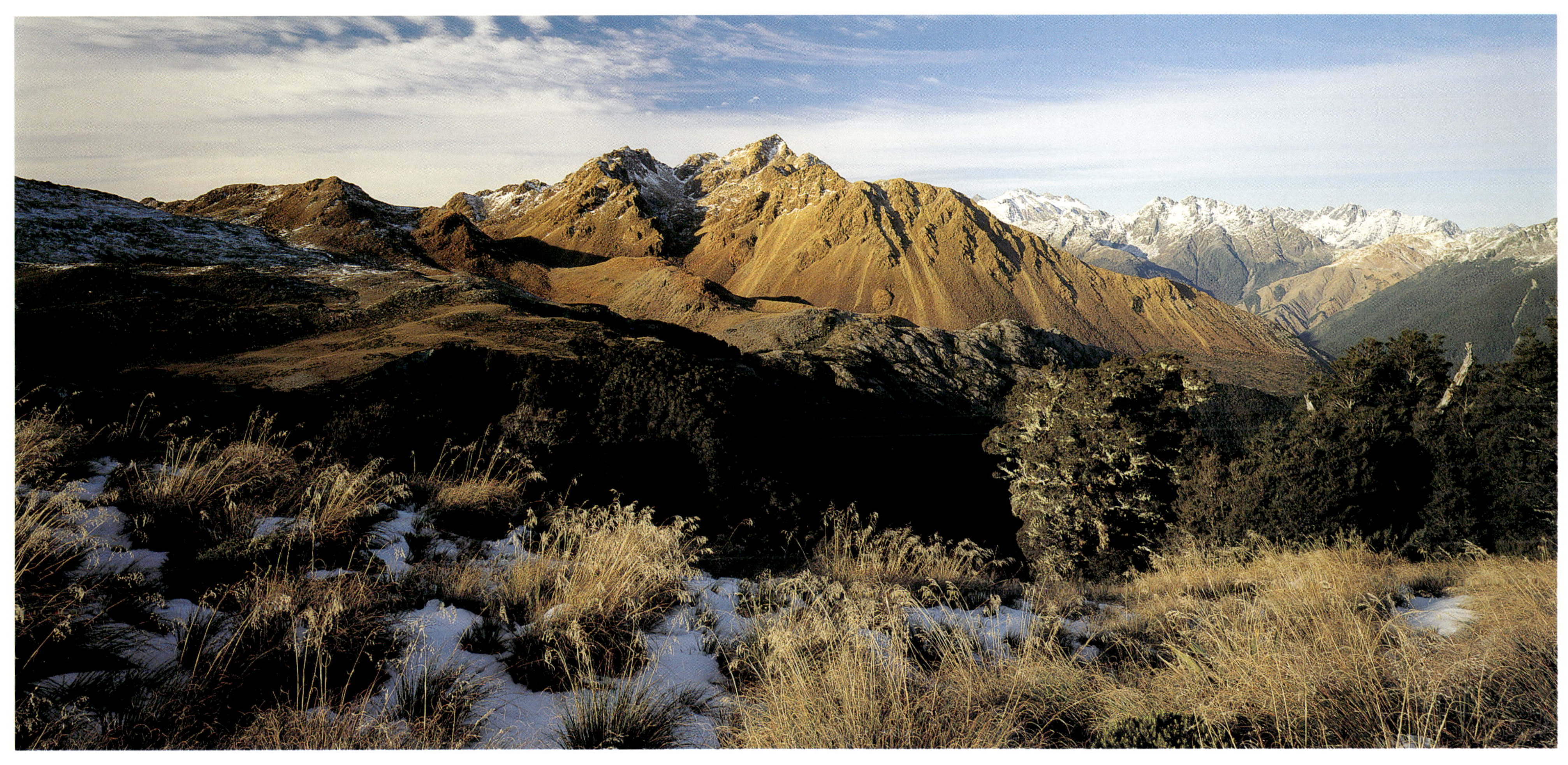

Dominated by Red Mountain (1,704 metres), the Red Hills Range provides the most graphic exposure of a highly distinctive belt of reddish ultramafic rock that extends for about 150 kilometres from the Cascade valley to Lake Ronald (page 86) south of Milford Sound. The characteristically barren topography of ultramafic areas is because the rock contains high levels of magnesium and other minerals which are toxic to all but the most hardy of plants.

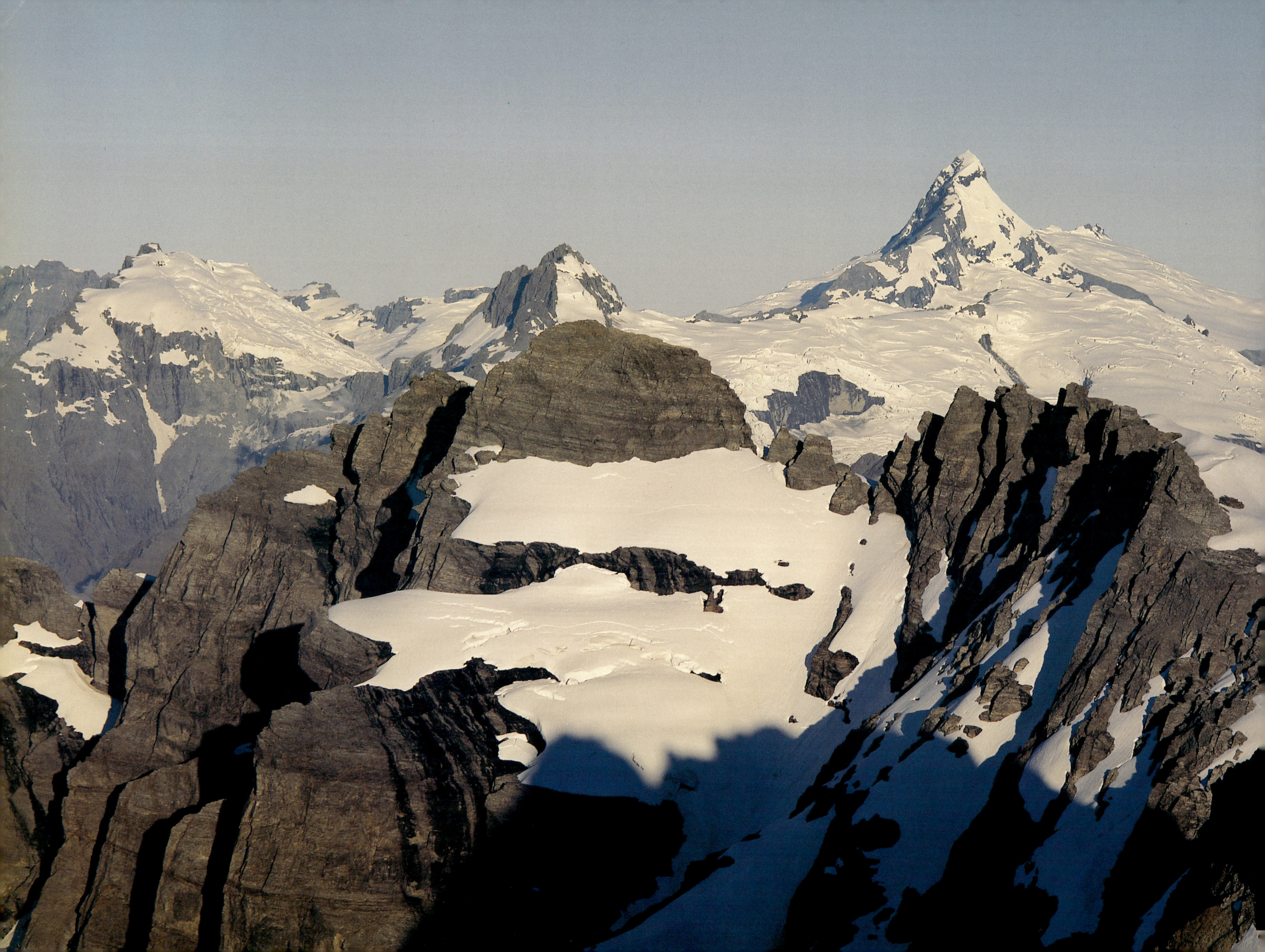

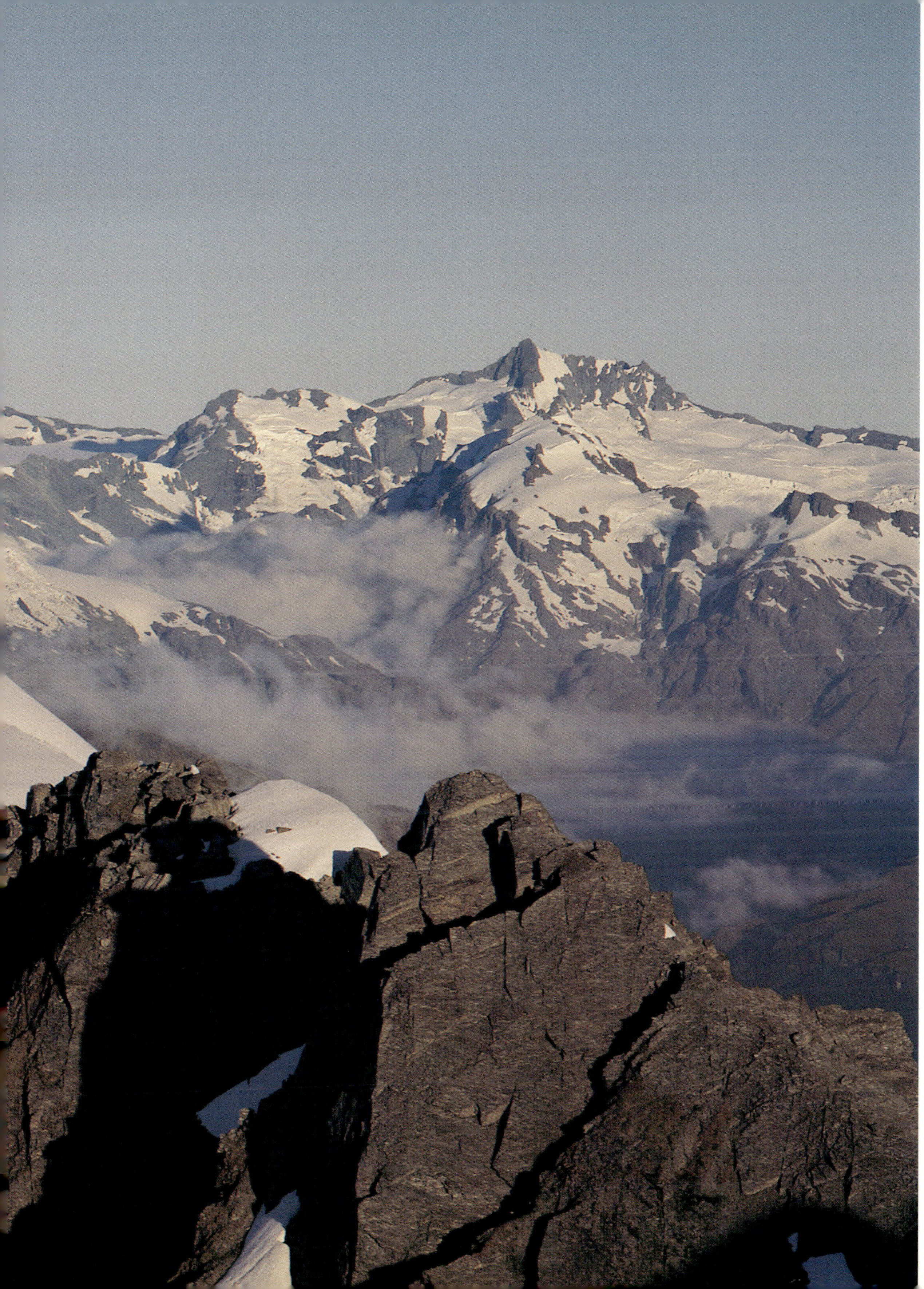

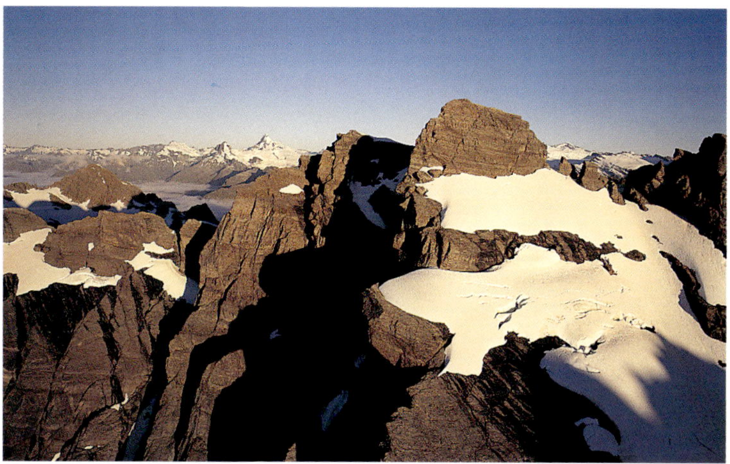

A jagged schist ridgecrest and vanishing remnant glacier on the Olivine Range west of Mt Aspiring (left centre) between the headwaters of the Arawhata and Cascade rivers.

Left: Mt Aspiring (3,027 metres) rises elegantly from the icefields of the Bonar Glacier and surrounding glaciated mountains. The photograph is from the west above the Olivine Range looking across the headwaters of the Arawhata valley. The mountain to the right of Mt Aspiring is Mt Avalanche, and to the left, Mt Ionia.

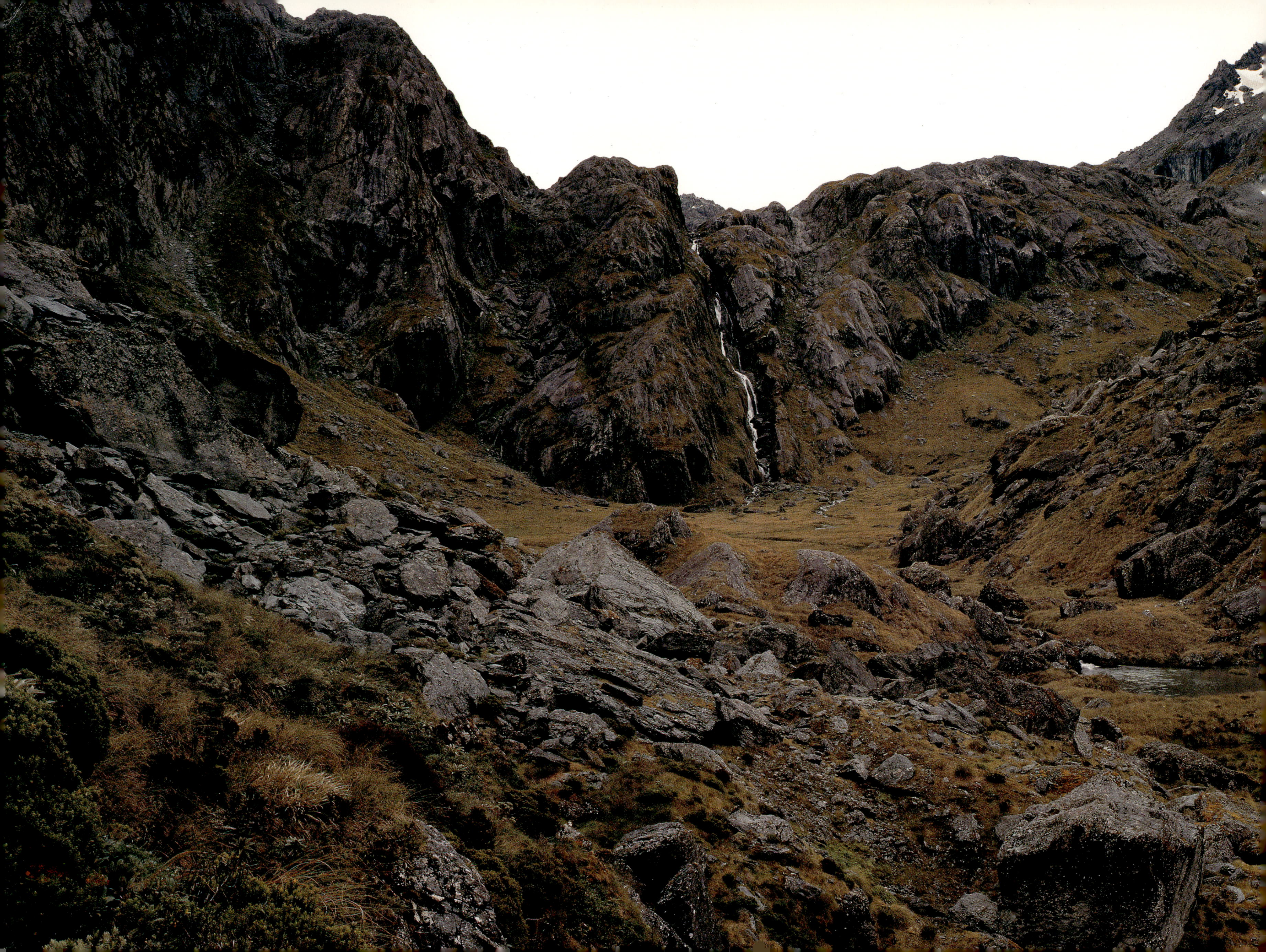

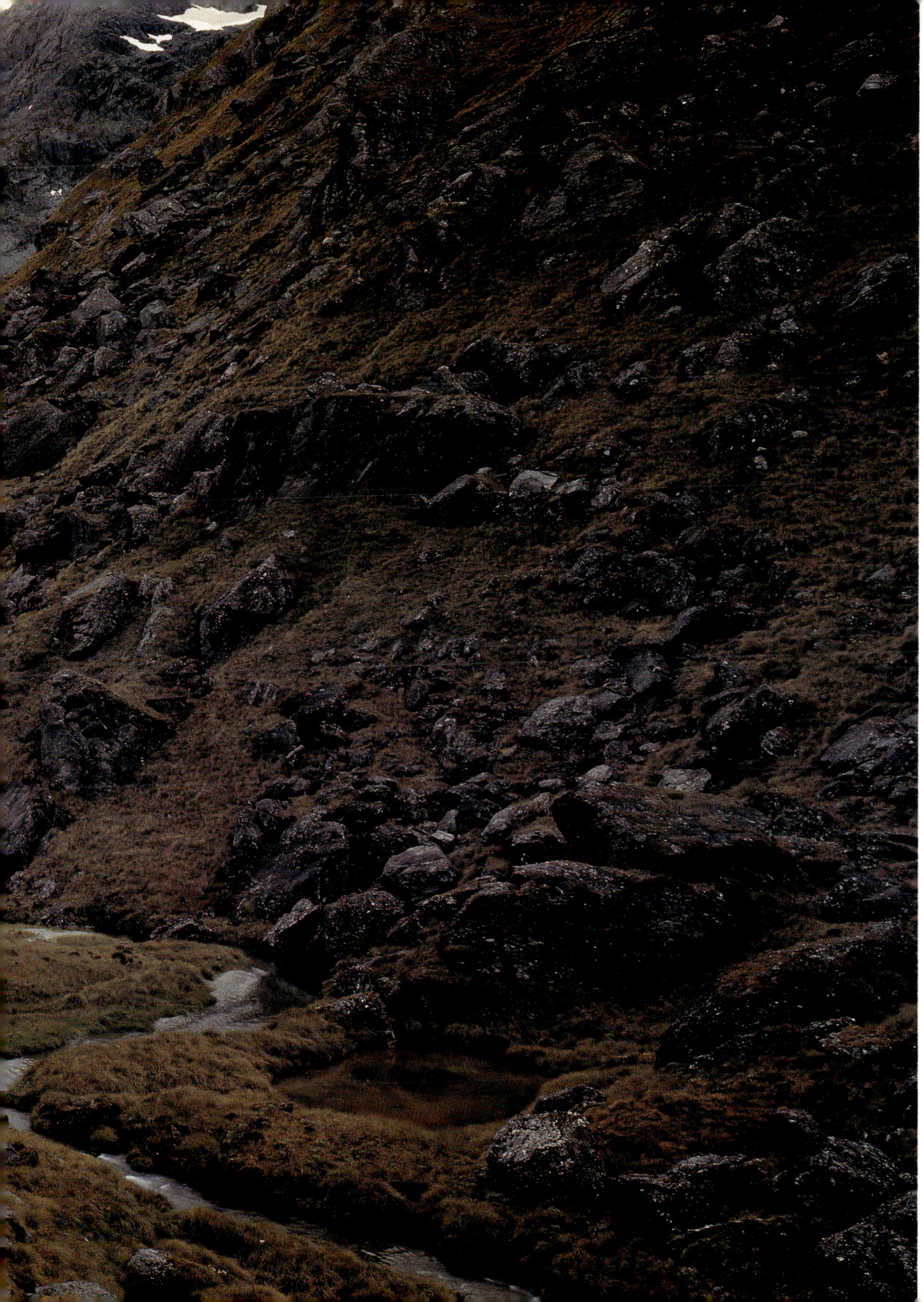

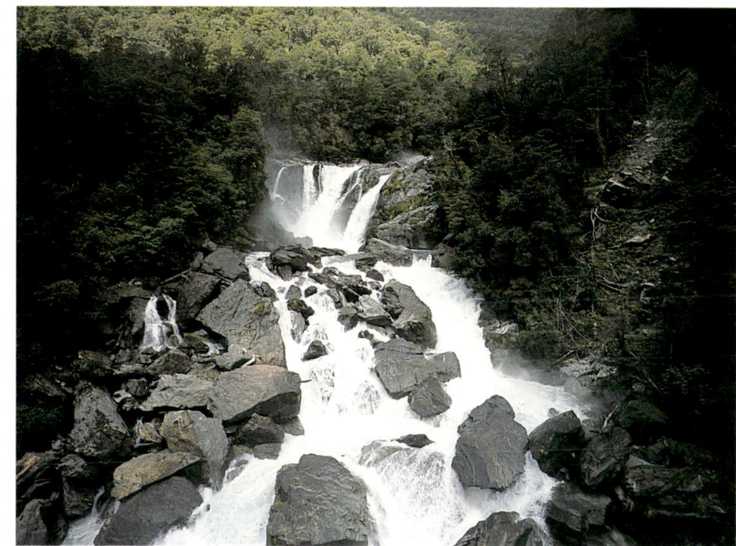

In contrast to the broad unhurried meanders of its lower reaches the upper sections of the Cascade River live up to its name, tumbling over a series of waterfalls and spillways as it drains the forested valley between the Olivine and Red Hills ranges.

LEFT: Fed by Lake Wilson high in the Serpentine Range, the left branch of the Route Burn plunges over grey schist bluffs into the alpine valley popularly known as the 'Valley of the Trolls' at the head of Lake Harris.

OVERLEAF: Climbers on the 3,027 metre summit of Mt Aspiring. The photograph looks southwards towards the Harris and Richardson mountains between lakes Wanaka and Wakatipu, and, further to the right, the twin summits of Mt Earnslaw (2,819 metres) and heavily glaciated Barrier Range. The cloud filling the eastern valleys gives some idea of the kind of landscapes that would have been found in this part of New Zealand during the ice ages, when huge glaciers would have filled the valleys to much the same altitude as this blanket of cloud, leaving only the tops of the ranges protruding.

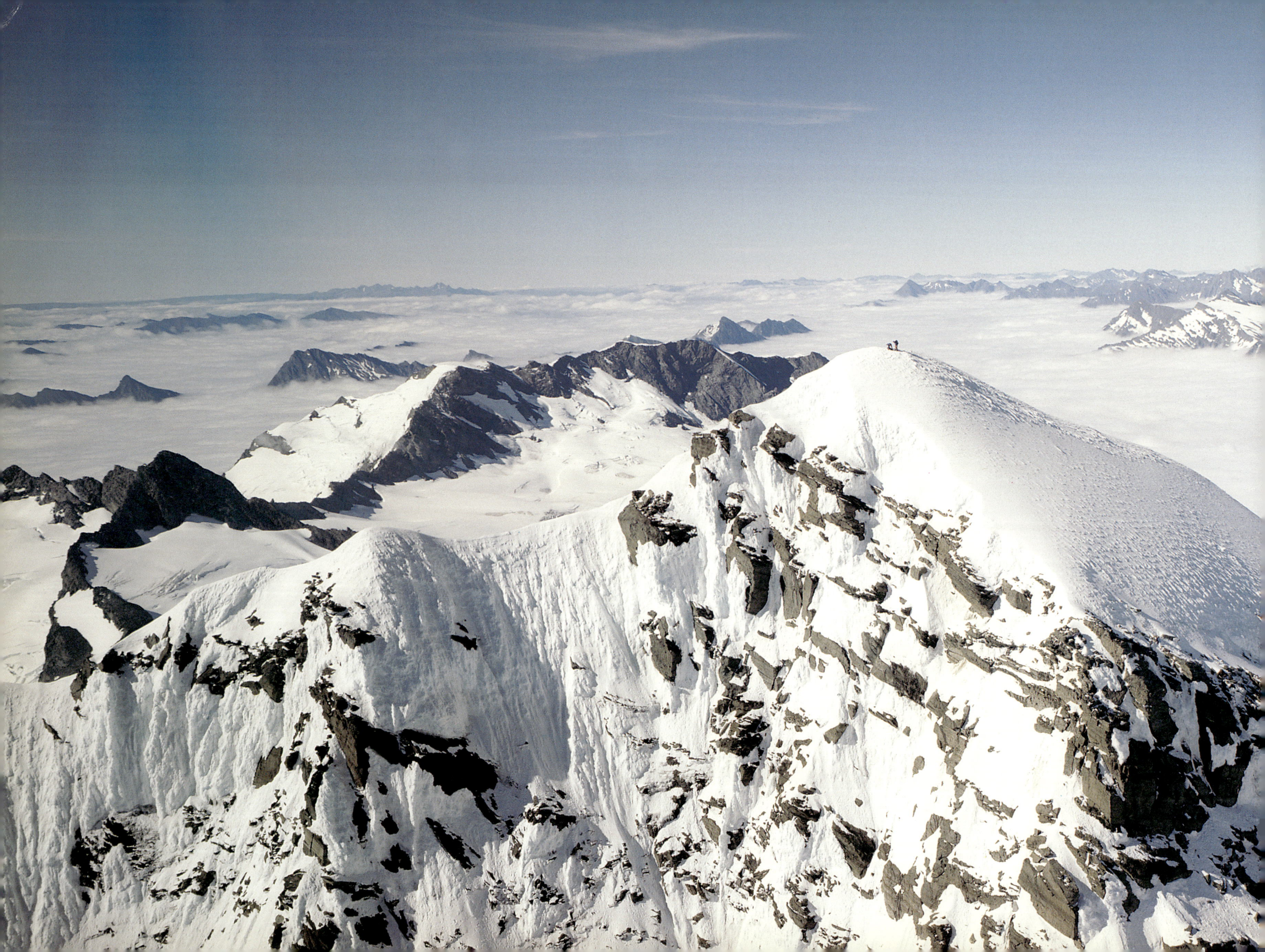

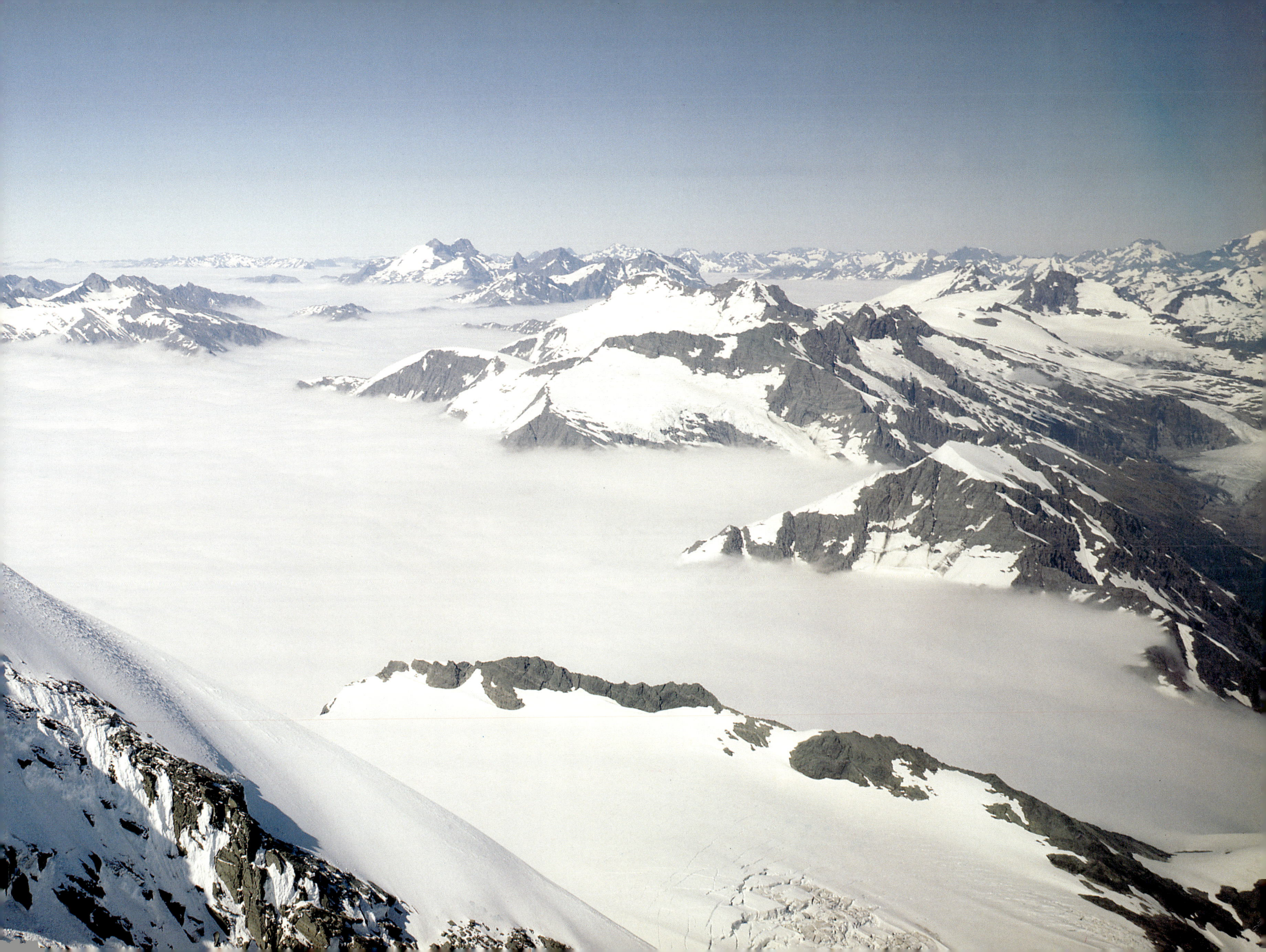

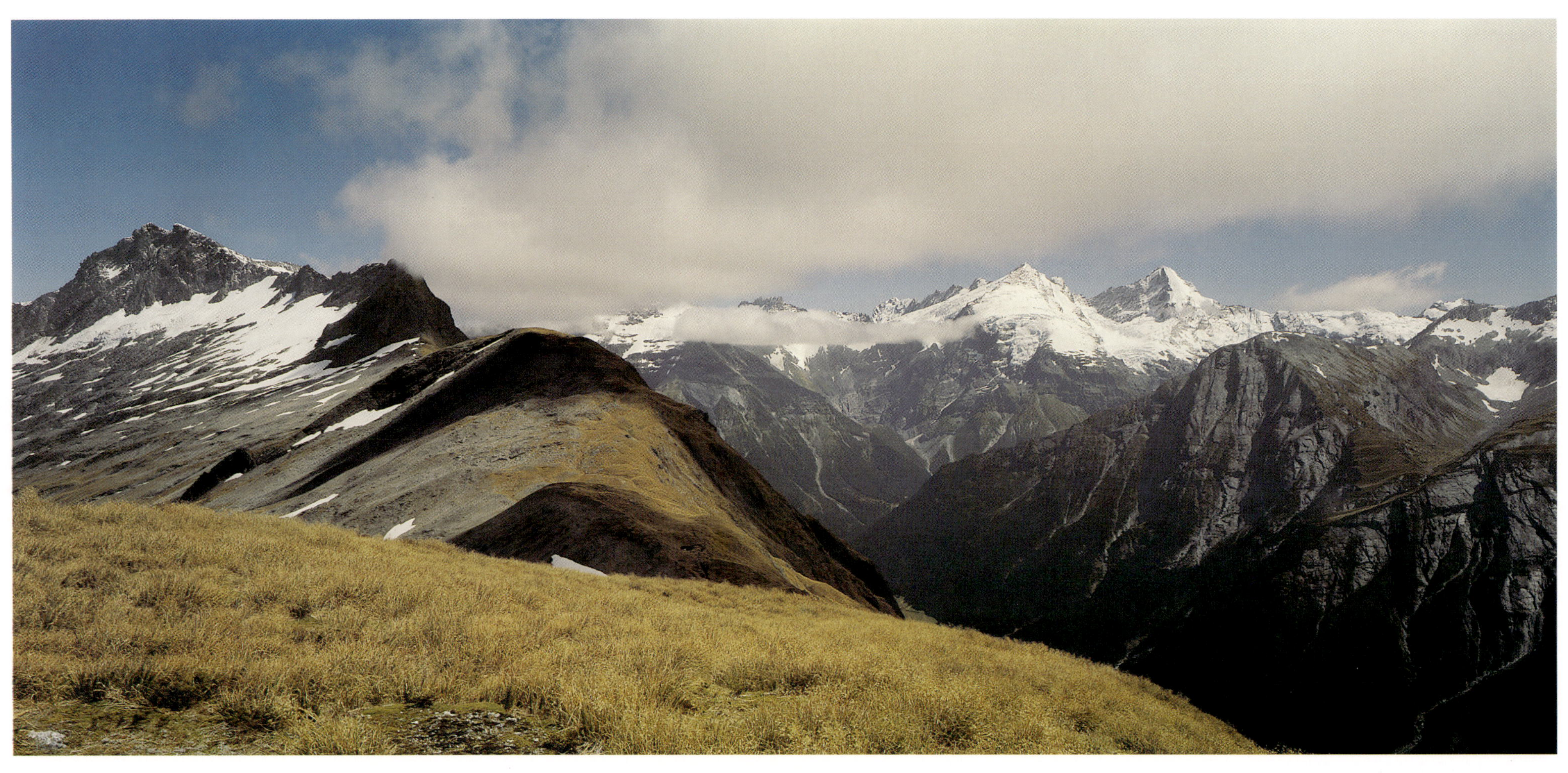

Pollux (2,542 metres) and Castor (2,524 metres) separate the headwaters of the Wilkin River on the eastern side of the Main Divide from the head of the Waiatoto River in the west.

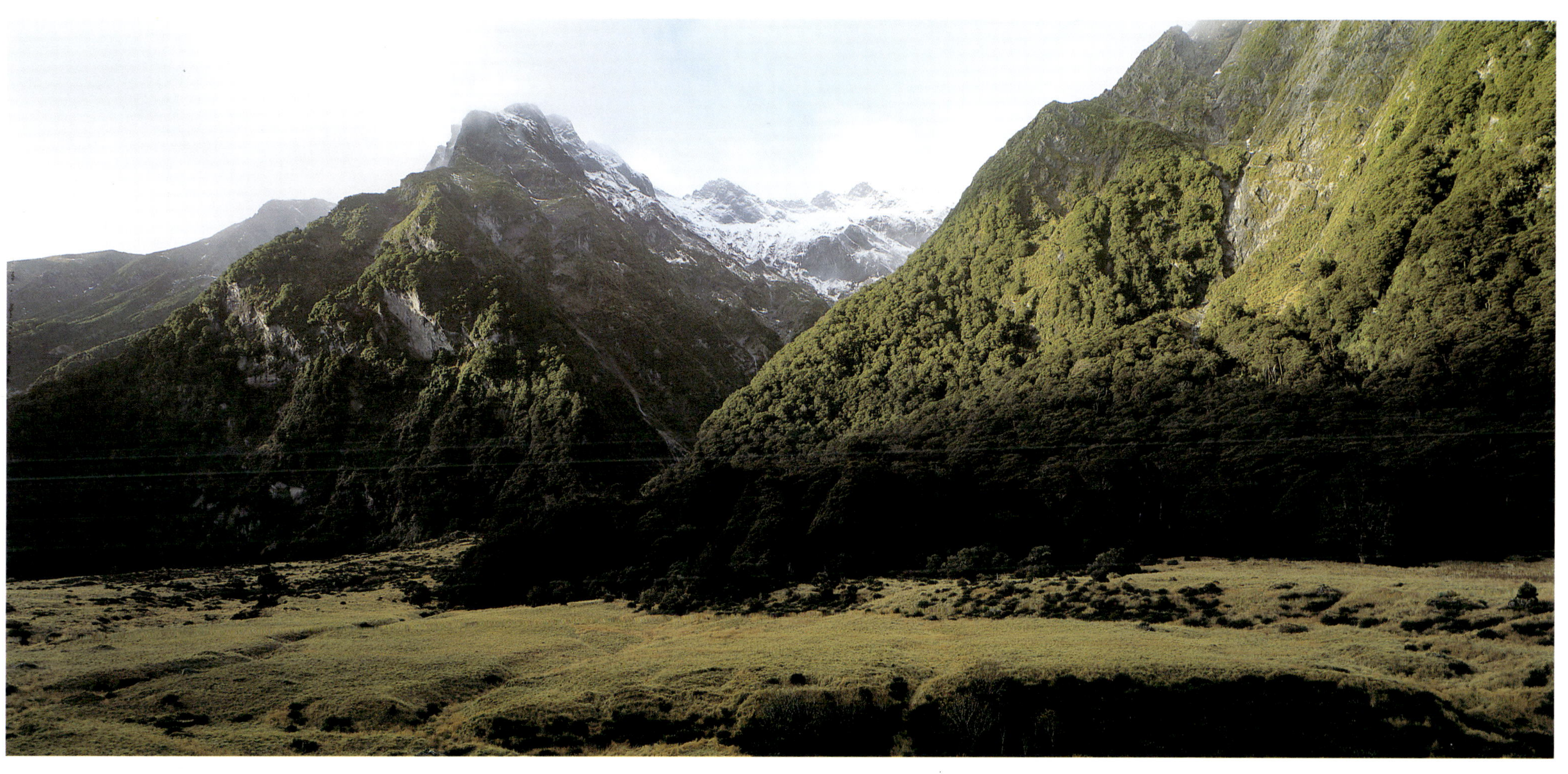

Large areas of the floors of the main eastern valleys of Mount Aspiring National Park are climatically unsuitable for beech forest and instead carry open grasslands like the one shown here in Siberia Stream, the main northern tributary of the Wilkin River.

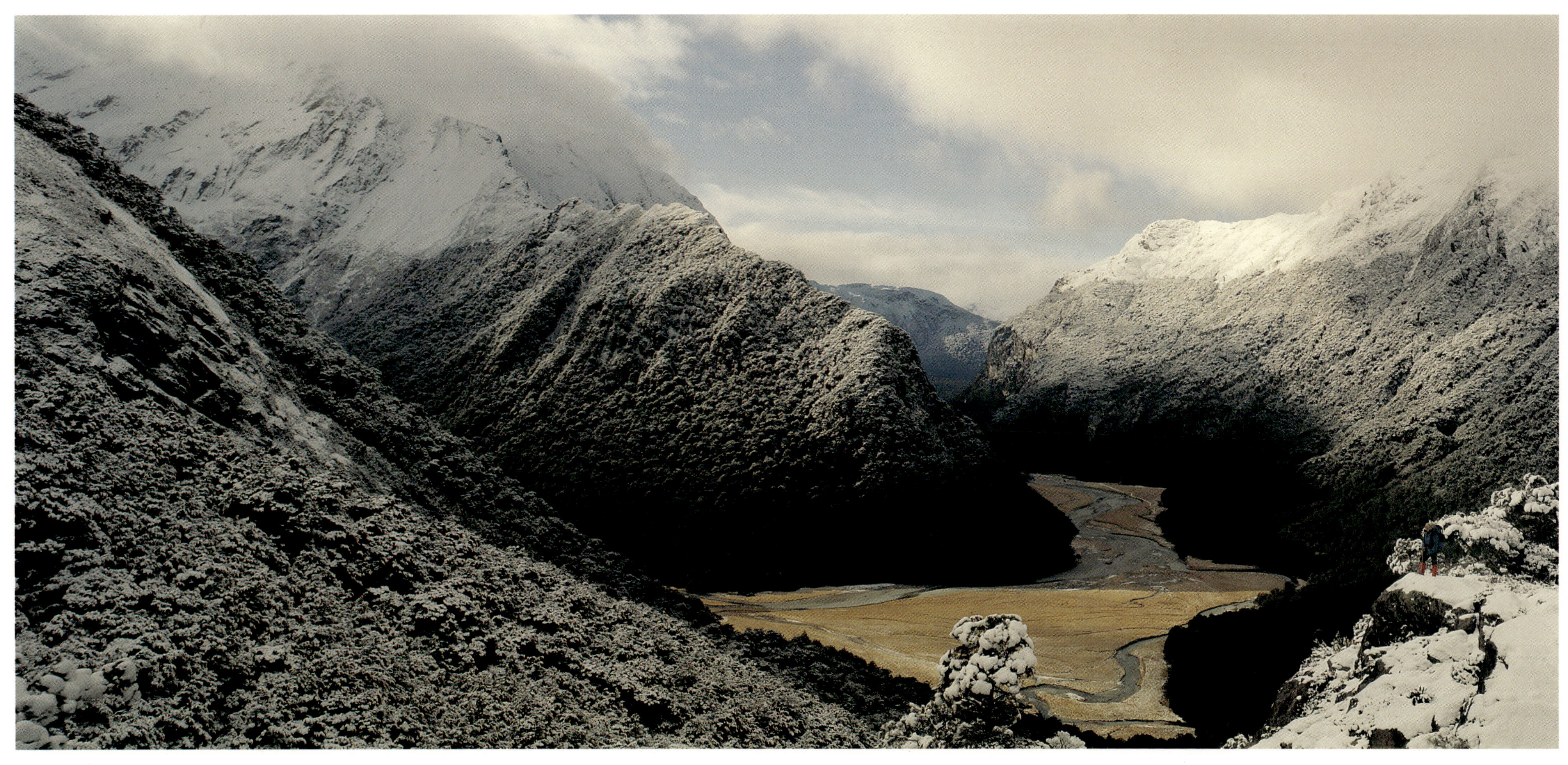

A winter tramper surveys the lower Route Burn from a rock outcrop near Routeburn Falls hut.

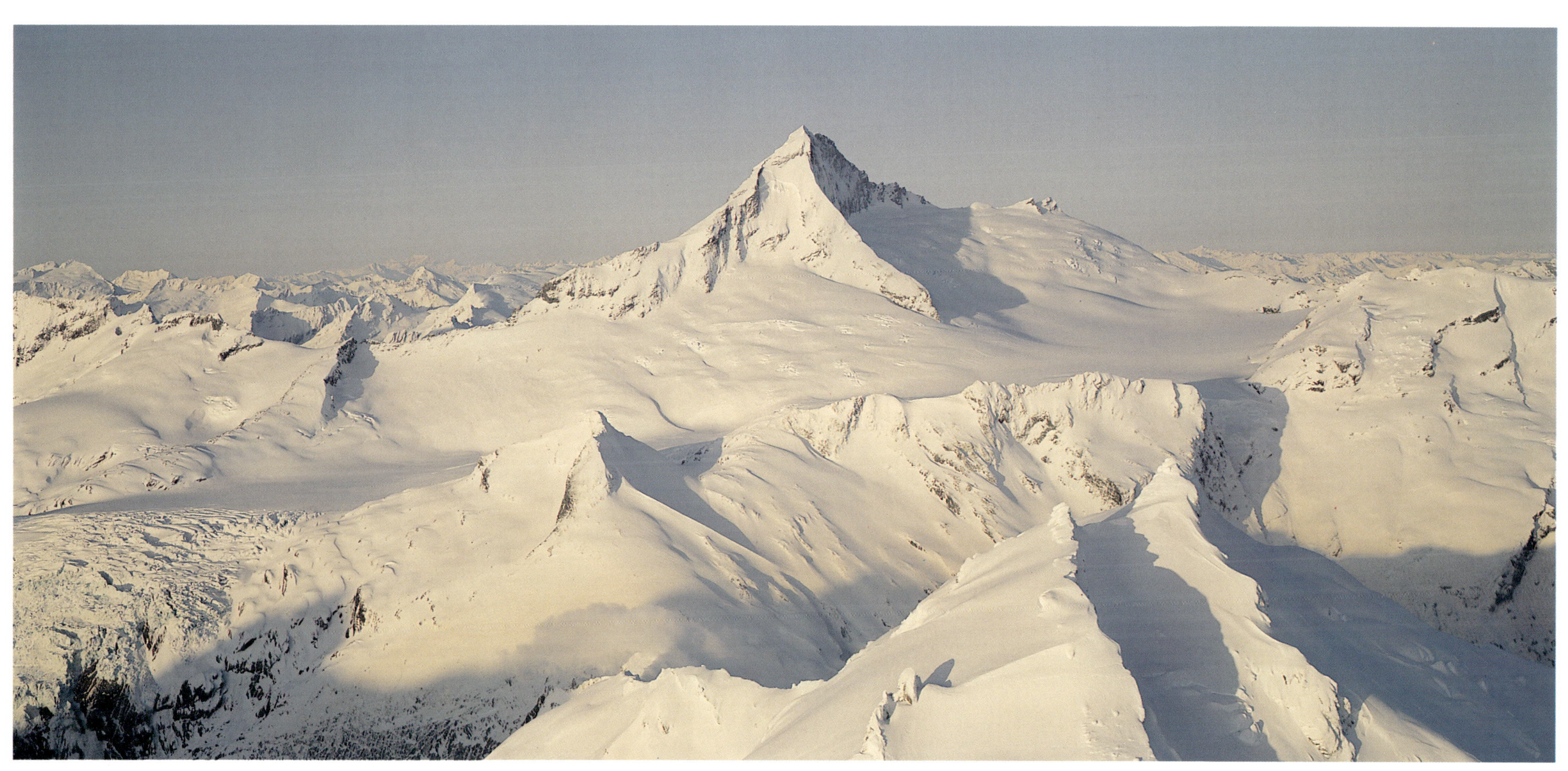

Mt Aspiring, known for centuries to Maori as Tititea 'Glistening Peak', photographed in winter from the south-west.

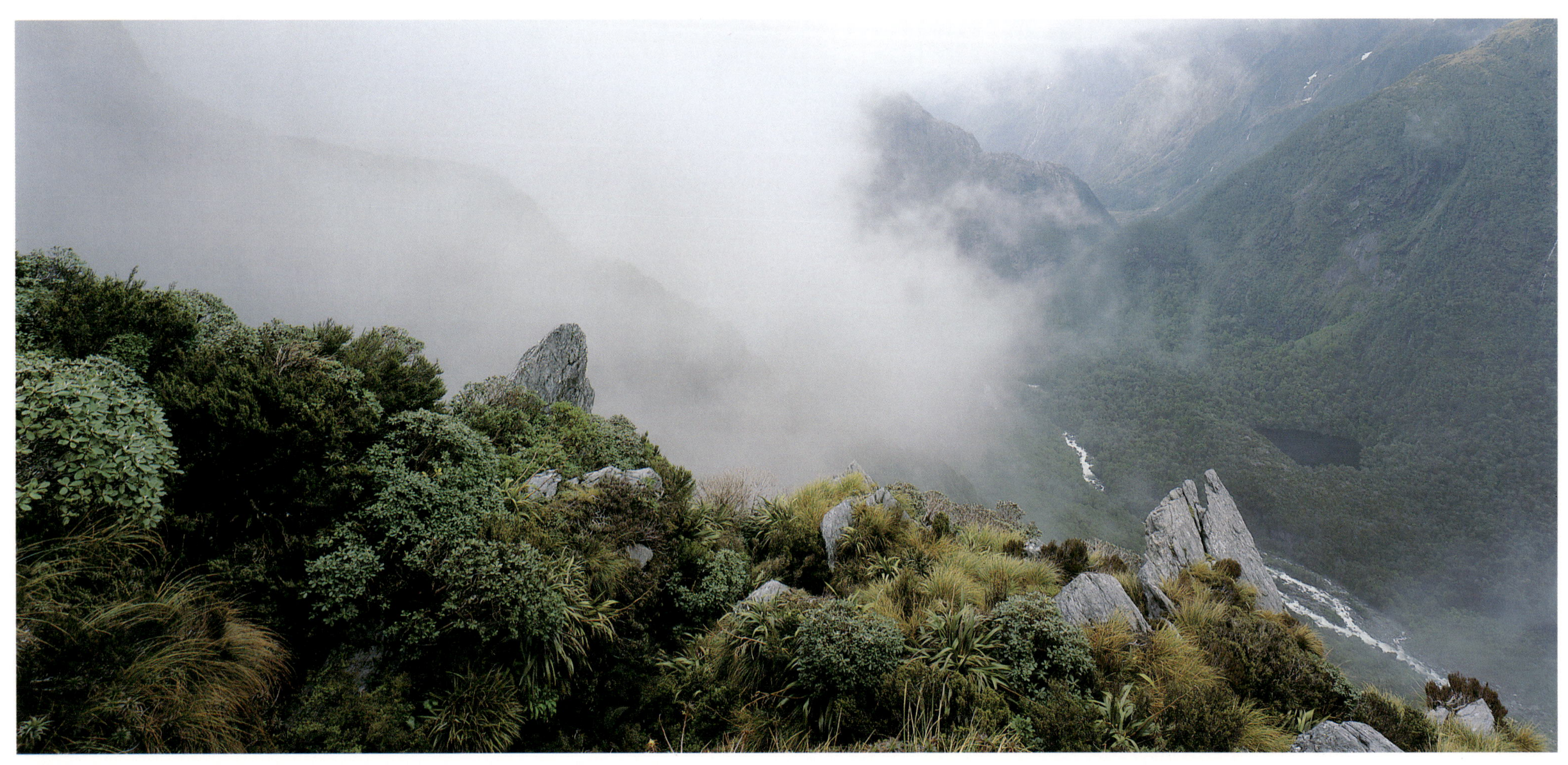

Snow tussocks, flax and subalpine shrubs on a spur above the Mueller River, which drains westwards from a complex jumble of ranges and valleys south of Haast.

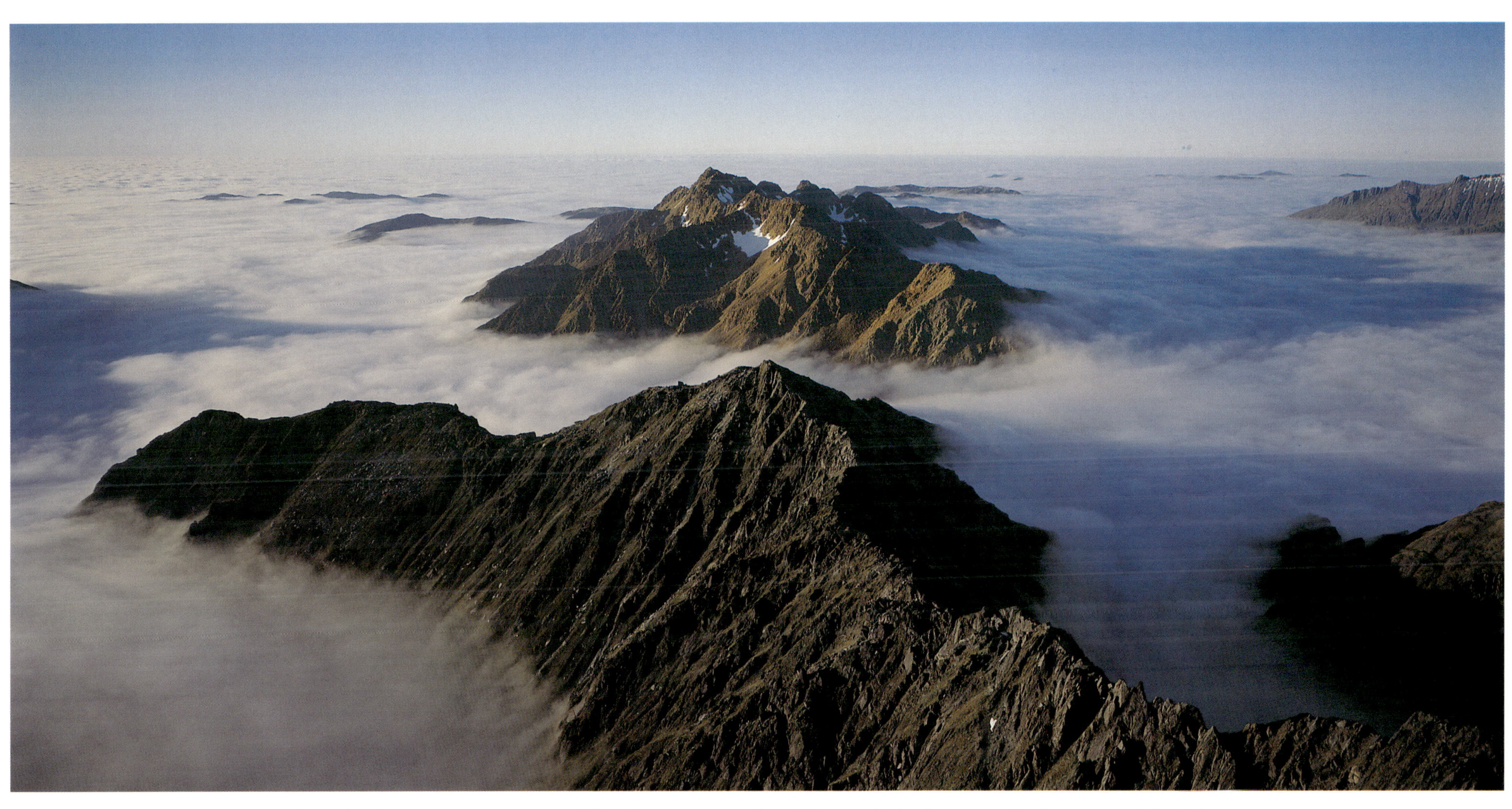

The Red Hills Range, western spurs of the Olivine Range and neighbouring hills, above an unbroken ocean of cloud from the Tasman Sea that blankets western parts of Mount Aspiring National Park.

# FIORDLAND NATIONAL PARK

Fiordland is New Zealand's great wilderness national park—a 1.25 million hectare maze of precipitous granite mountains, long narrow fiords, sheer-walled valleys, deep lakes, dense forests, wild rivers, high waterfalls and the most remote and pristine coastline in the country. Created in 1952 from reserves set aside half a century earlier, it is the world's fifth largest national park and is far and away the largest in New Zealand. Indeed it is so big that prior to the creation of Kahurangi National Park in 1996, Fiordland contained more land than the other eleven national parks added together. It is most frequently described as the wildest, wettest, most remote and most natural part of New Zealand, and as well as its unique fiord topography, its mountains, valleys and lakes are also strikingly different from those elsewhere in Te Wahipounamu. While much of the vast Fiordland wilderness is only accessible by helicopter, boat or by long and arduous journeys on foot, the two main tourist routes through the park—the road from Te Anau to Milford Sound, and the boat and bus journey from Manapouri to Doubtful Sound—incorporate outstanding examples of all major Fiordland landforms except for the outer coast.

As in other parts of Te Wahipounamu, the basic shape of Fiordland today is a legacy of huge ice age glaciers that ground their relentless way to lower altitudes over hundreds of thousands of years, patiently steepening valley walls and deepening the troughs now inundated by the fiords and larger lakes. However, because the rocks of Fiordland are very much harder than the generally rotten sandstones and schists of the Southern Alps, post-glacial weathering and erosion has been much less extensive, with the result that the imprint of major glaciation remains much more emphatic in Fiordland today than it does elsewhere. It is this resistance to the ravages of the elements that gives much of Fiordland its distinctive character, most strikingly illustrated on the road through the Darran Mountains to Milford Sound where a stunning sequence of ice-carved landforms is on display: towering rock walls, jagged knife-edged ridges, pointed peaks, cirque basins, side valleys that 'hang' high above the main valley floor, and classic glacial U-shaped valleys.

While the scenic attractions of Fiordland are amply conveyed in the photographs that follow, what makes this park important as a conservation area is the sanctuary it has provided (and hopefully will continue to provide) for plants and animals whose tenure elsewhere in New Zealand has become increasingly precarious. Parts of southern Fiordland were clearly important refuges for plants and animals during the ice ages, and in more recent times the remoteness and fortress-like topography of Fiordland generally has resulted in a continuation of this critical sanctuary role. Birds that were once widespread in New Zealand like kakapo and takahe (and possibly also moa) survived in Fiordland long after they had disappeared from other parts of the country, and today a lengthening catalogue of threatened animals have some of their last strongholds in the vast uninhabited wilds of Fiordland National Park. The park is also a major area of invertebrate endemism, with over 350 of the 5,000 species of invertebrates so far recorded not known to occur anywhere else.

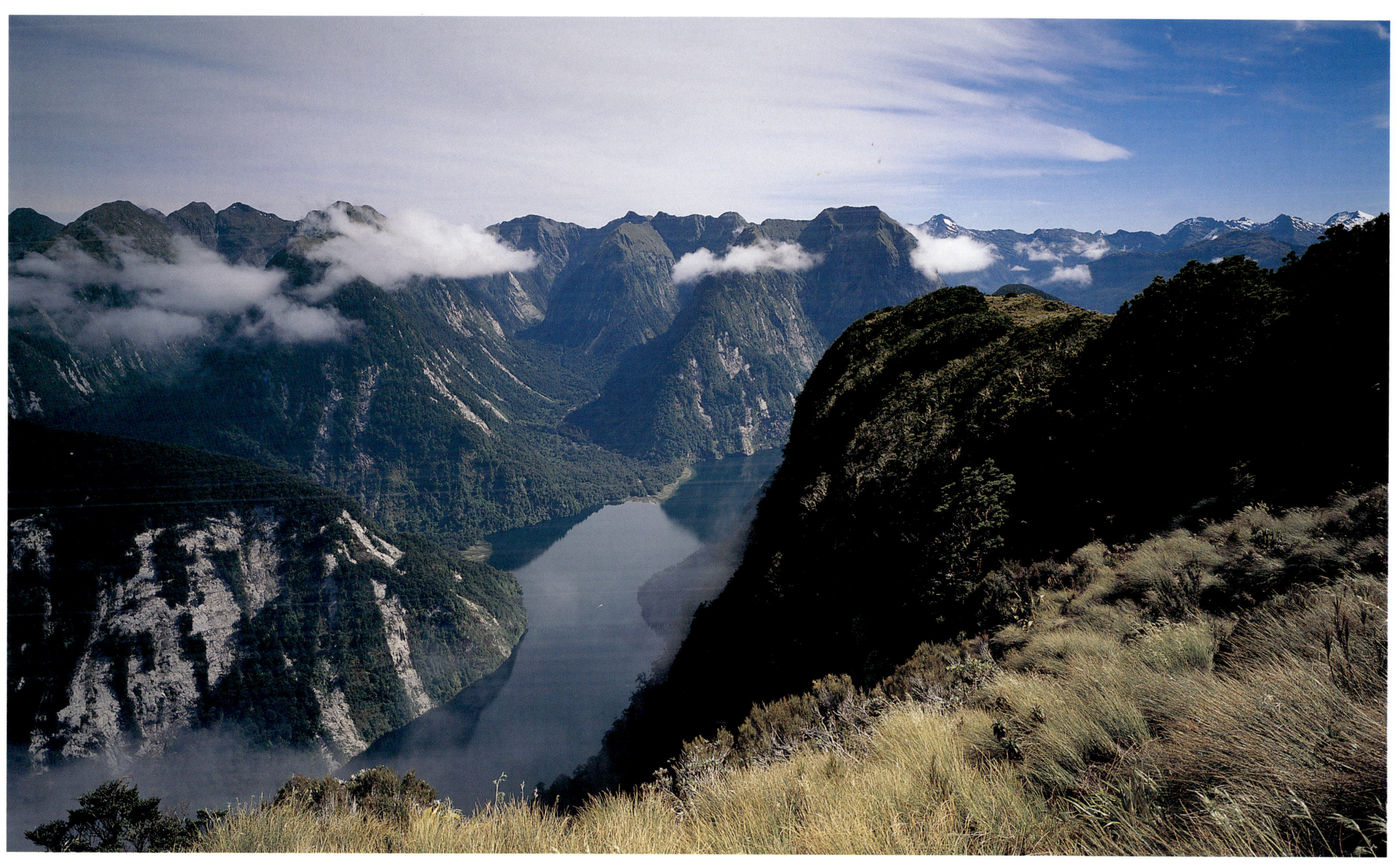

With its soaring cliffs and narrow waterway, Hall Arm at the head of Doubtful Sound provides one of the most dramatic settings in the southern fiords.

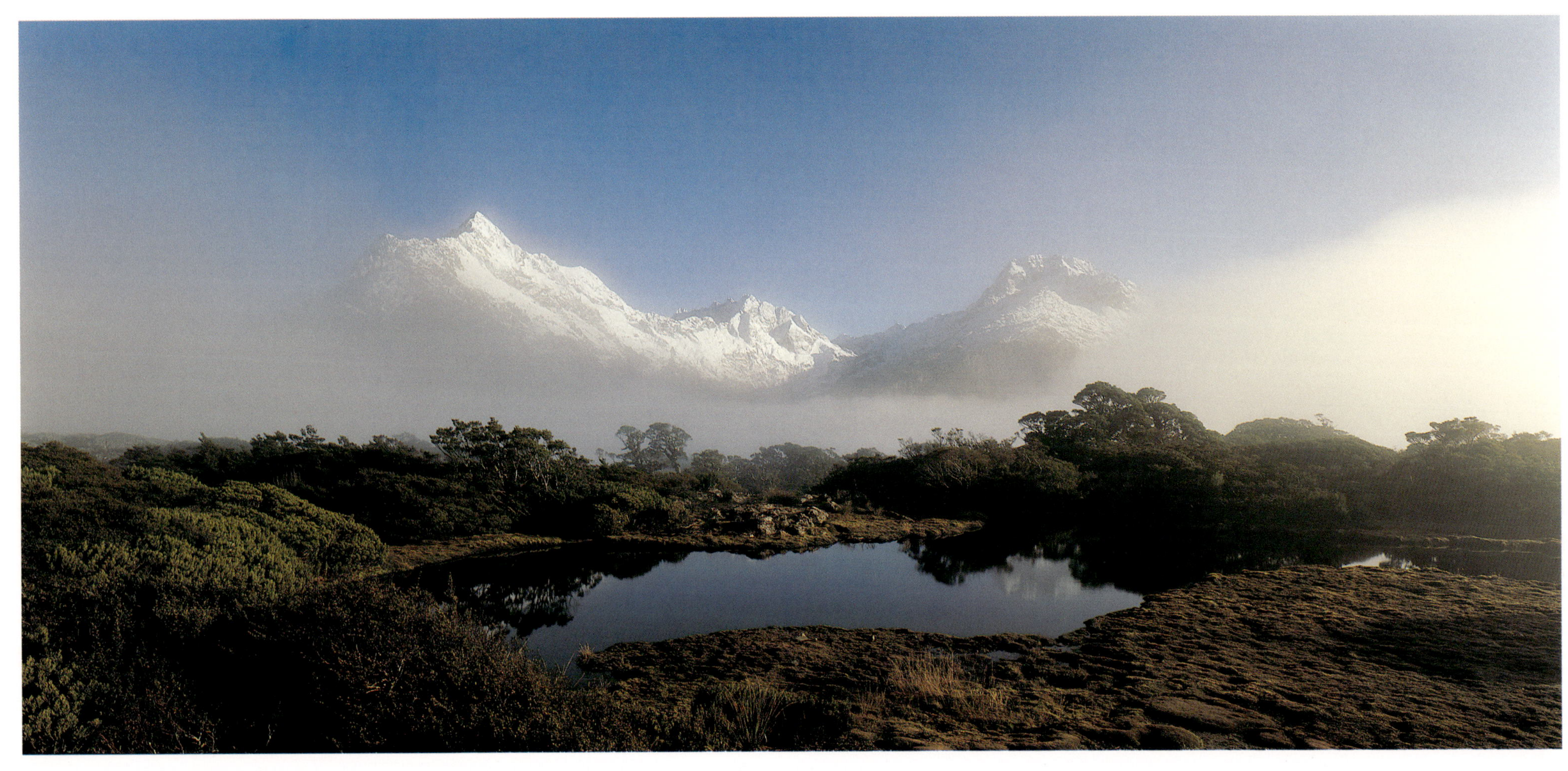

Morning light on peaks at the southern end of the Darran Mountains, photographed from Key Summit near the Fiordland end of the Routeburn Track. The prominent peaks are (from left to right) Mt Christina (2,502 metres), Mt Crosscut (2,230 metres) and Mt Lyttle (1,896 metres).

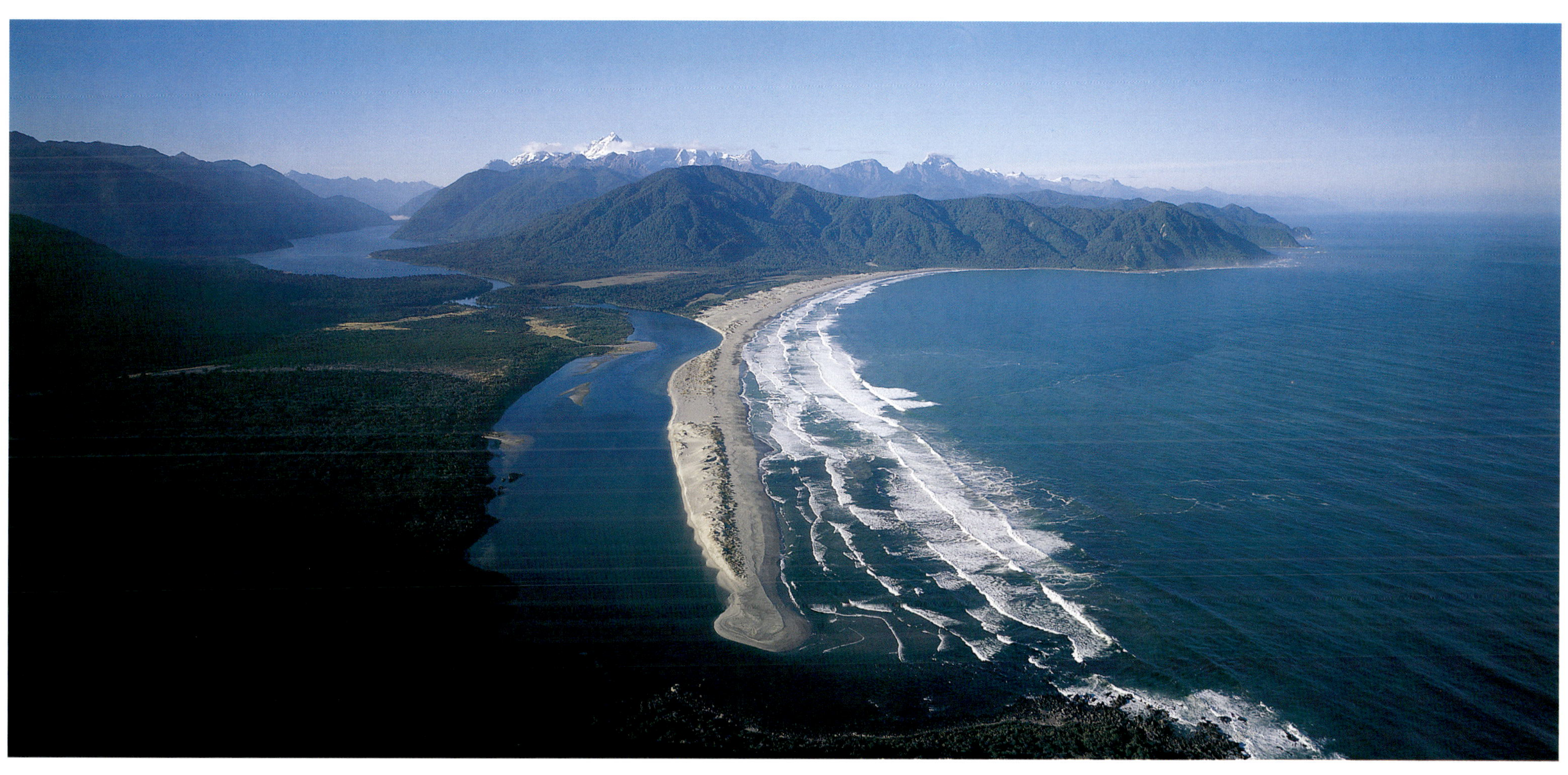

The broad and meandering lower reaches of the Hollyford River meet the sea at Martins Bay, north of Milford Sound. Behind the coastal alluvial plain Lake McKerrow fills the entire lower Hollyford Valley from which the Darran Mountains rise in typically abrupt manner to the south, dominated by the icy summits of Mt Madeline (2,537 metres, left) and Mt Tutoko (2,746 metres).

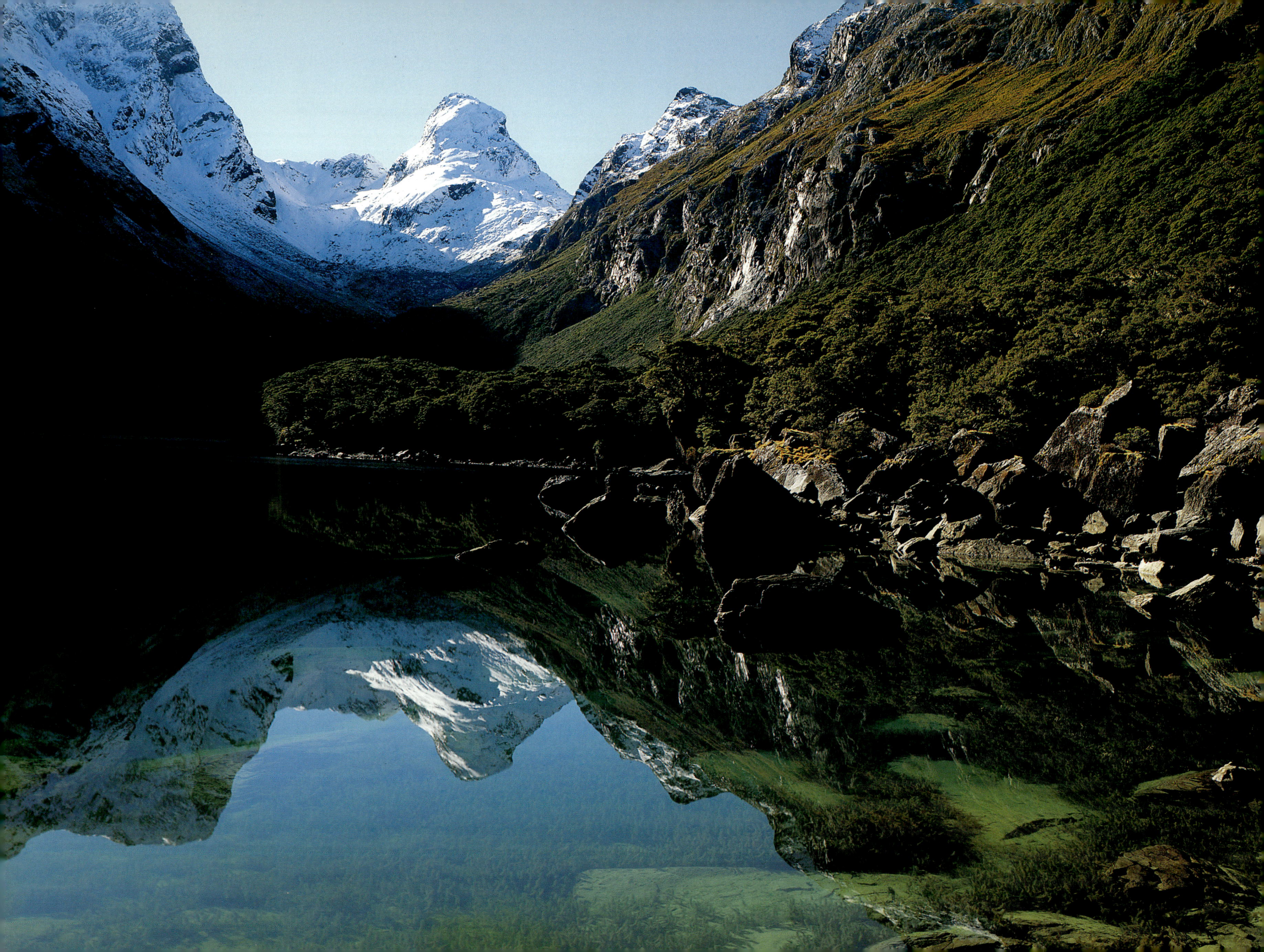

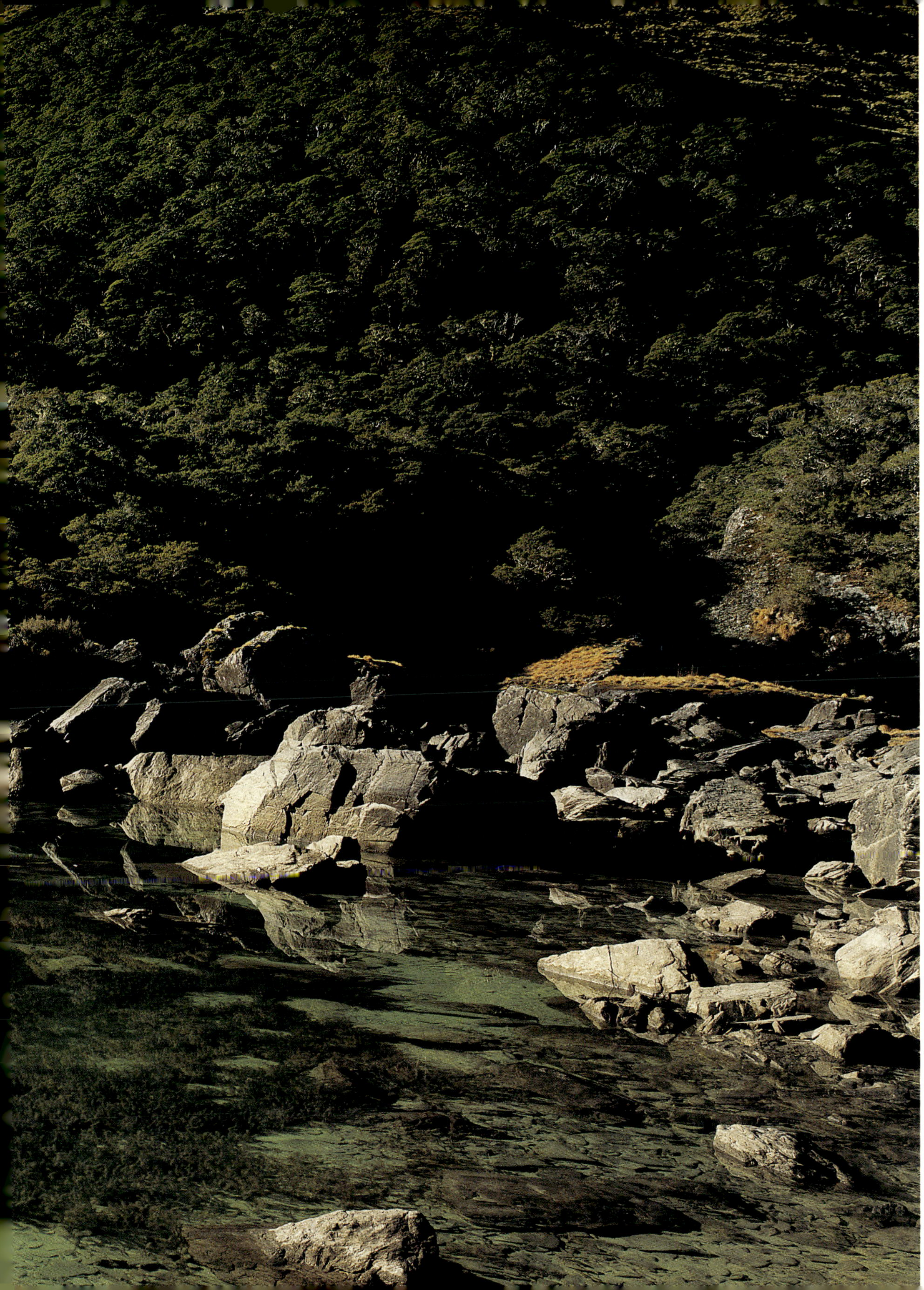

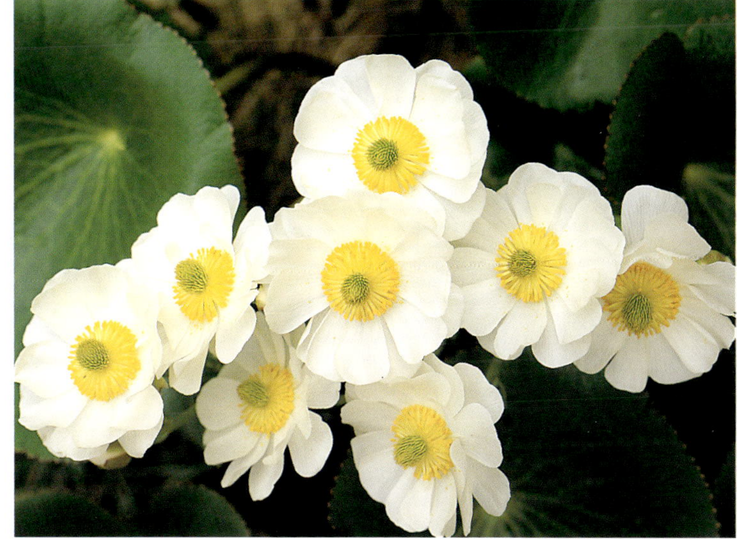

The giant mountain buttercup (or 'Mount Cook lily'), one of the glories of alpine herbfields throughout the wetter parts of the mountains of south-west New Zealand, is renowned for its magnificent displays of exquisite white flowers from November to January. The largest buttercup in the world, it has, along with other alpine herbs, suffered severely in the past from browsing by deer, goats, chamois and thar, but is now recovering well where animal control is effective.

LEFT: Early winter sun on Emily Peak (1,820 metres) reflected in the forest-fringed waters of Lake Mackenzie on the Hollyford valley section of the Routeburn Track.

OVERLEAF: Beech forest in the Eglinton valley east of Lake Te Anau, home to a wide range of native forest birds including threatened mohua (yellowheads), kakariki (yellow-crowned parakeets) and Fiordland brown kiwi. Also present in these forests are threatened native long-tailed bats, one of two species of small forest-dwelling insectivorous bats that prior to the arrival of humans were the only land mammals present in New Zealand.

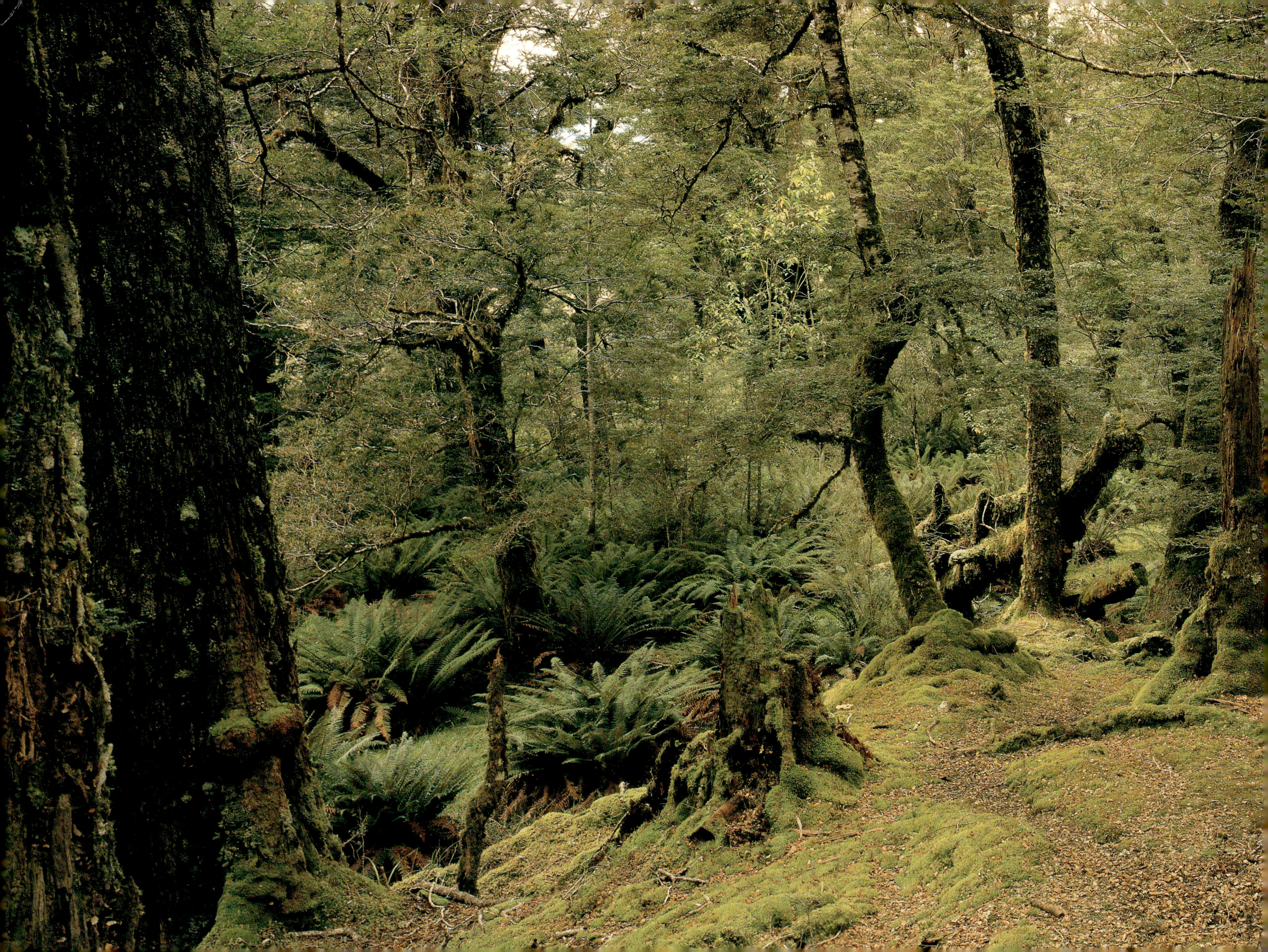

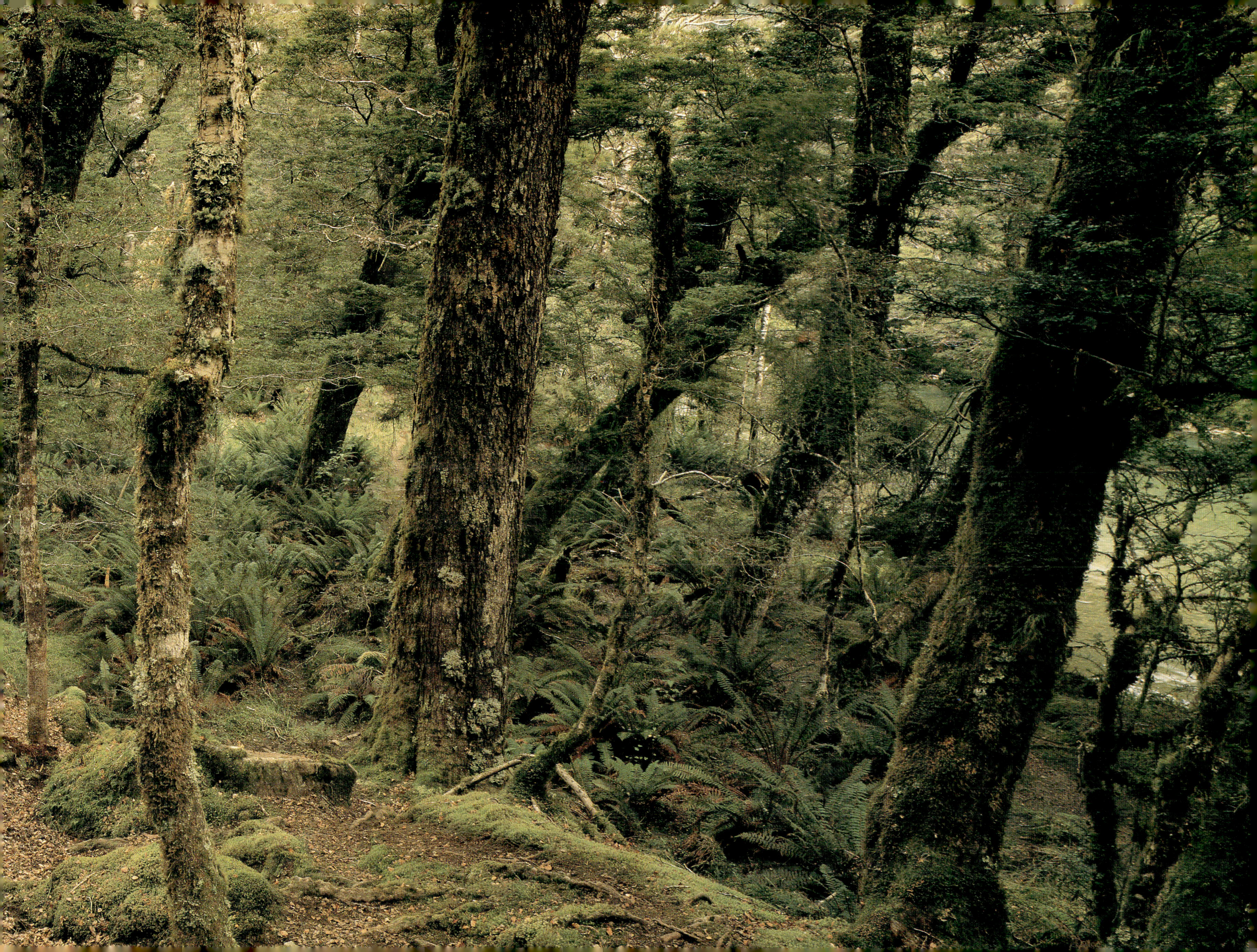

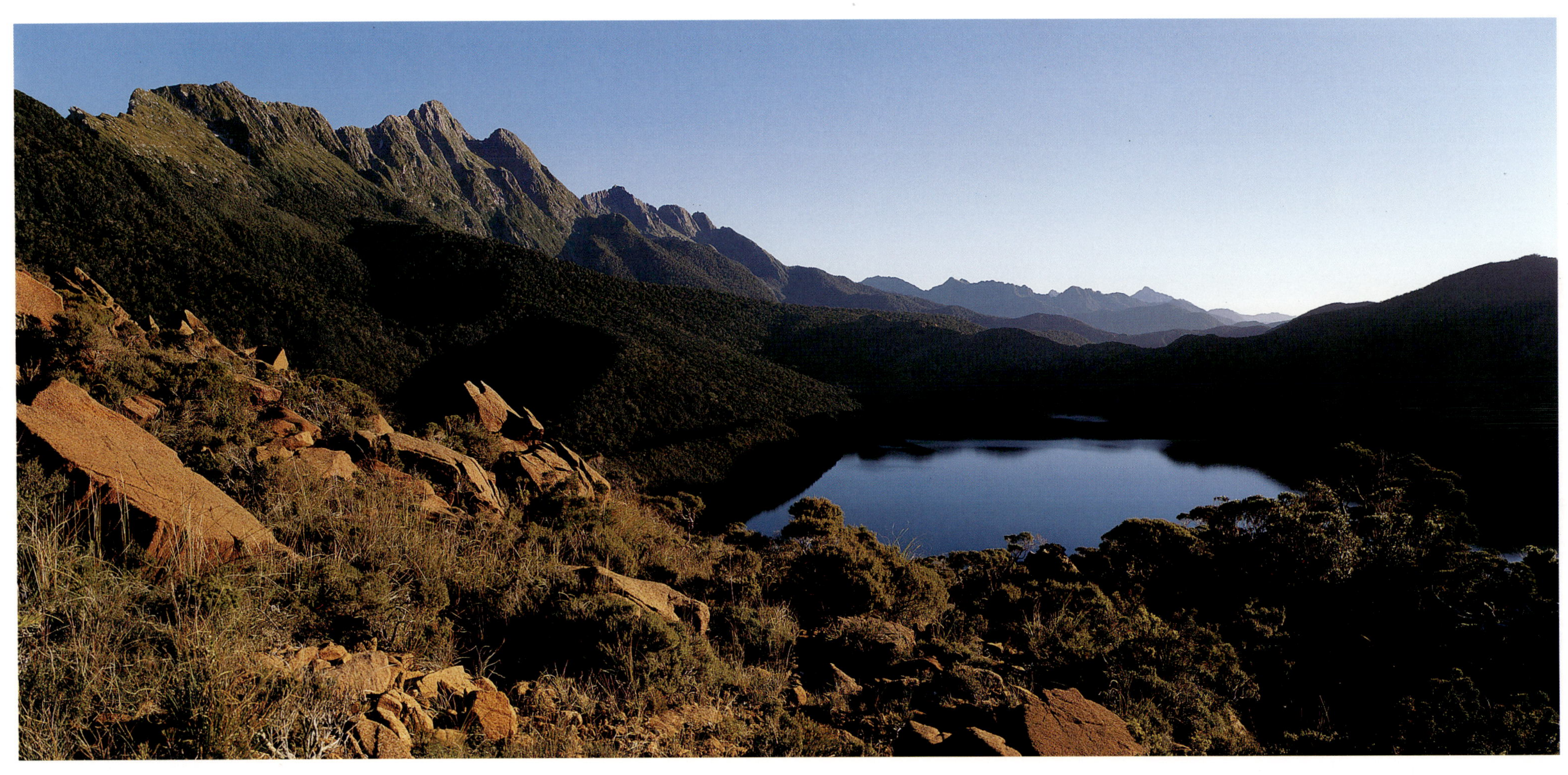

Lake Ronald, south of Milford Sound, marks the southern limit of the russet-coloured ultramafic rocks responsible for the barren topography of the Red Hills Range 150 kilometres north in Mount Aspiring National Park (page 65).

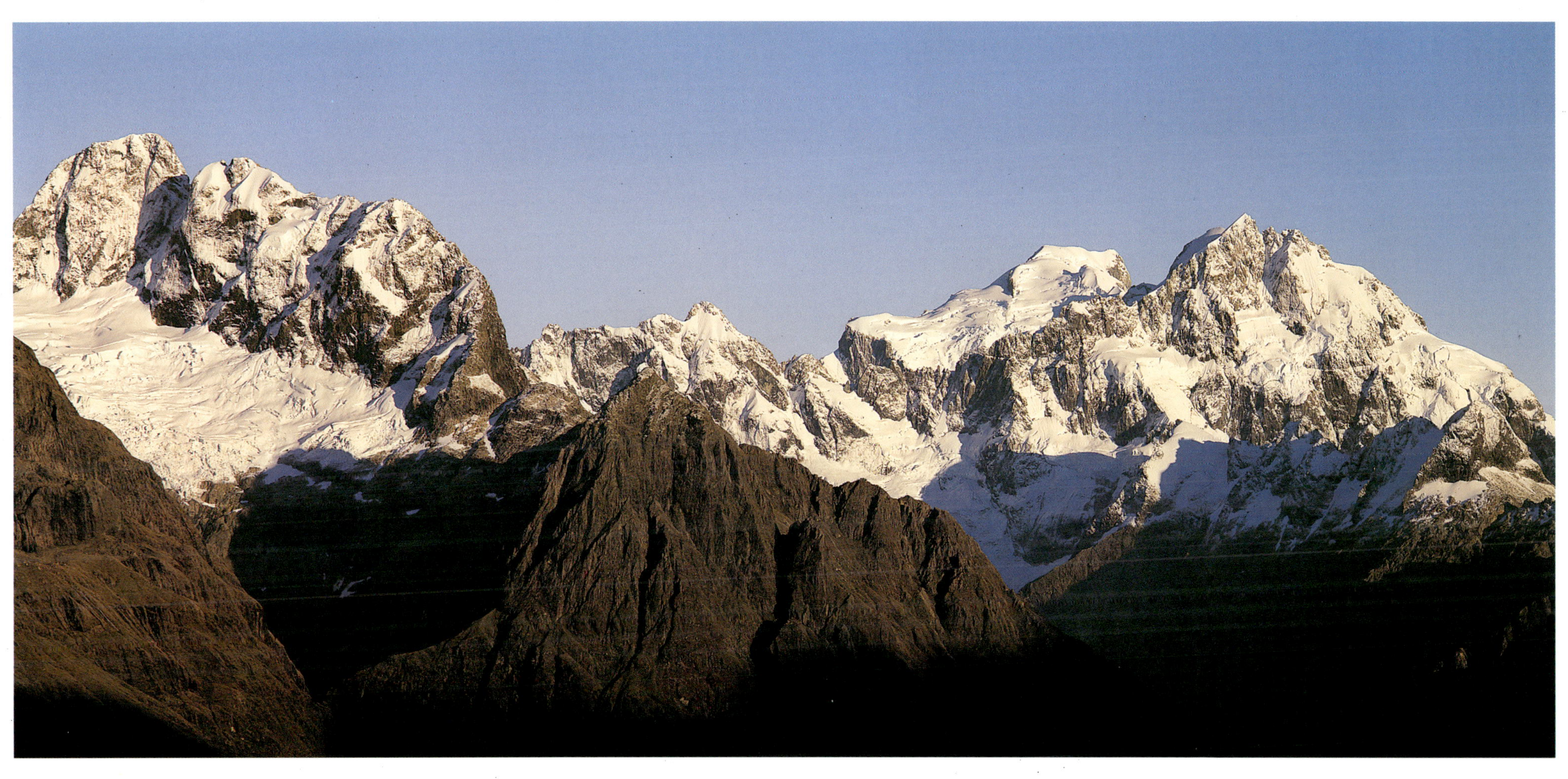

The Darran Mountains photographed across the Hollyford valley at sunrise from near Lake Mackenzie.

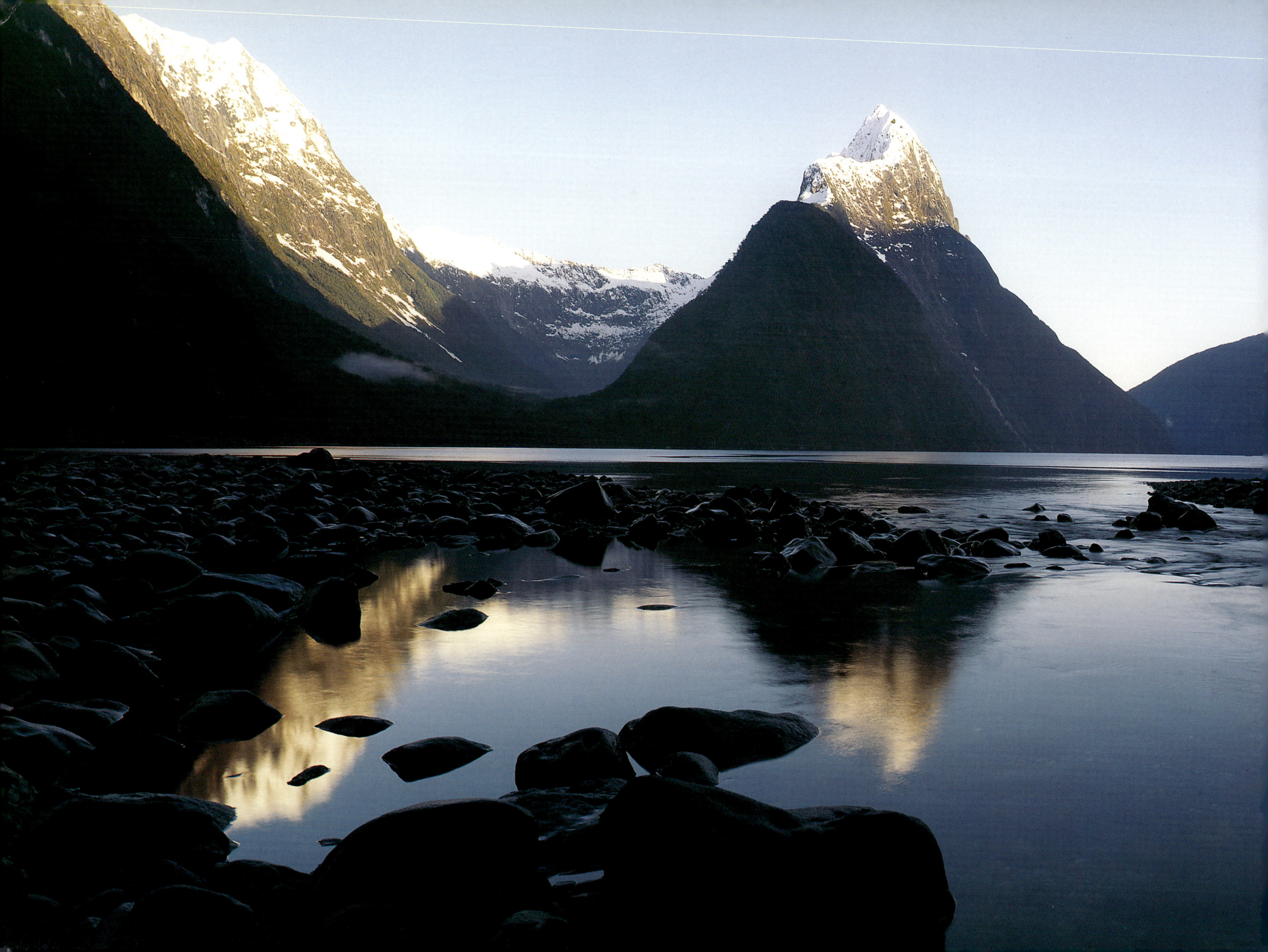

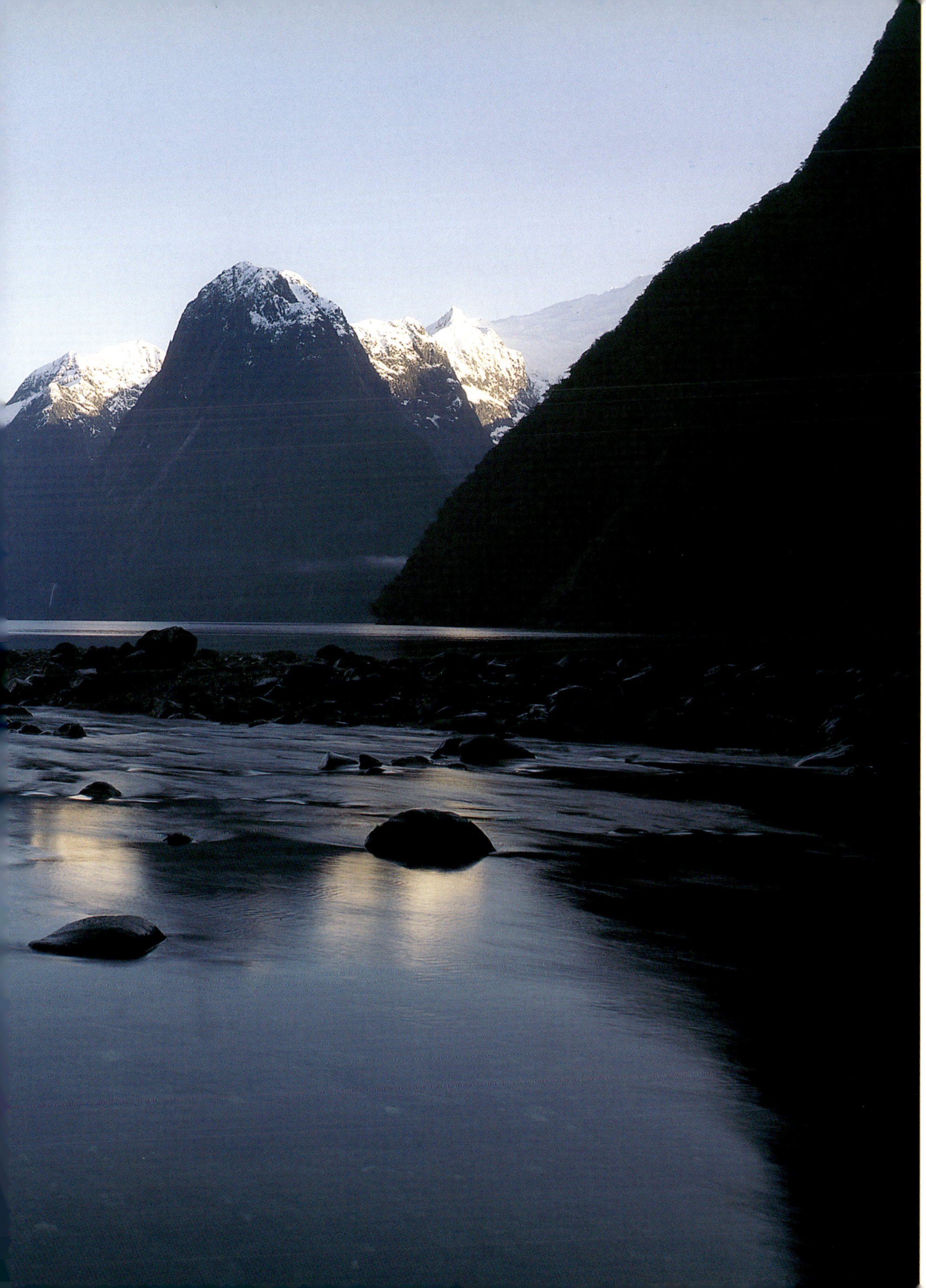

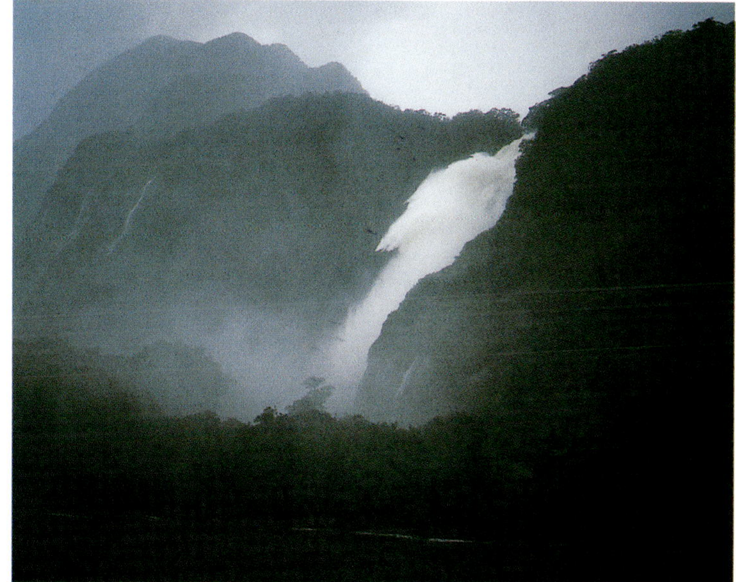

The 160-metre cataract of the Bowen Falls delivers the results of a Fiordland deluge from the hanging valley of the Bowen River into the head of Milford Sound.

LEFT: A winter dawn at Milford Sound, with the early sun catching the summit snows on the upturned wedge of Mitre Peak (1,692 metres). To the left of Mitre Peak is Sinbad Gully, one of three locations in the Milford area from which the last kakapo surviving on mainland New Zealand were transferred to sanctuary islands in the late 1980s.

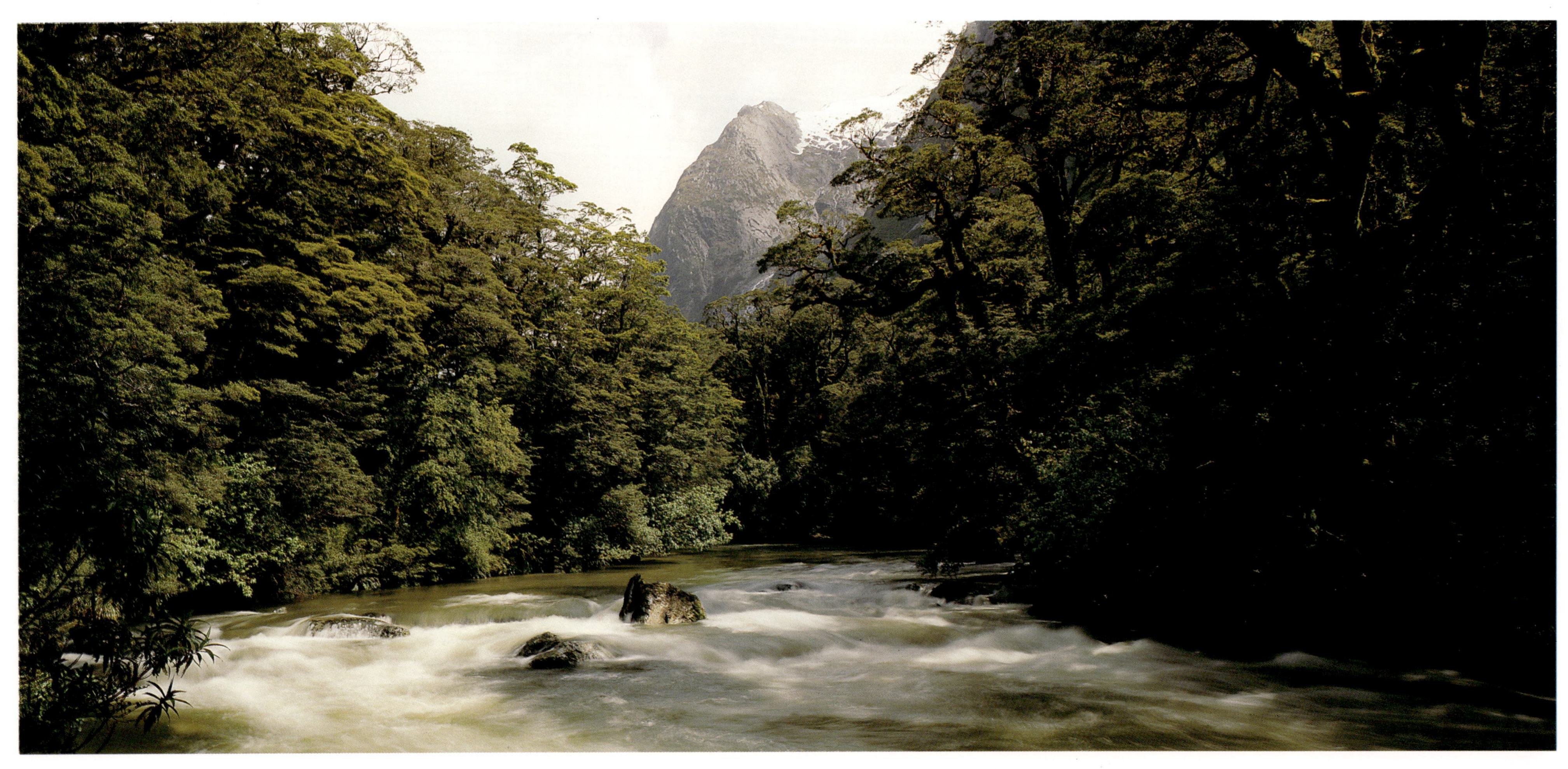

The Milford Track follows the banks of the Clinton River for twenty kilometres from the northern end of Lake Te Anau to the foot of Mackinnon Pass.

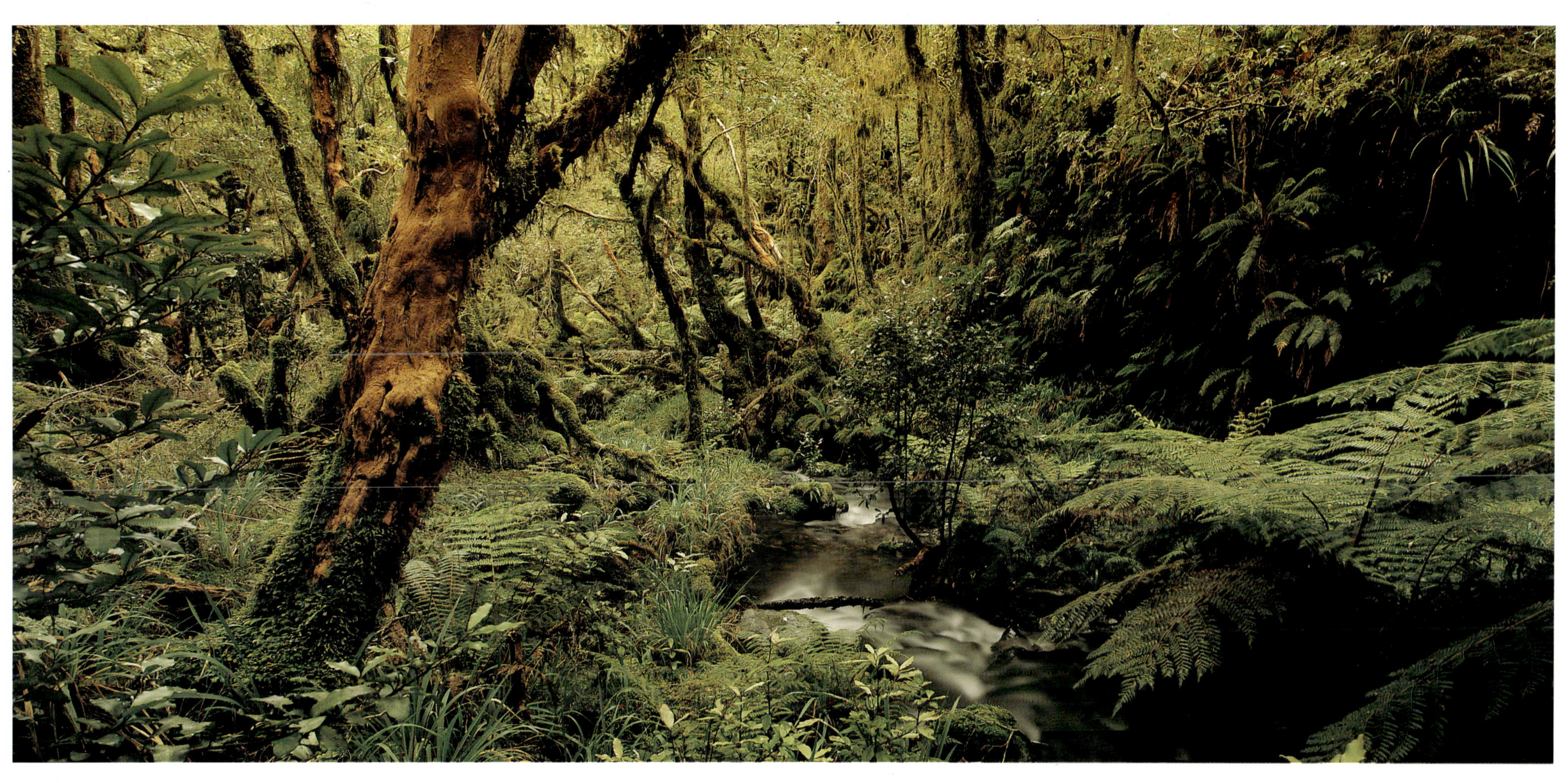

A small, slow-moving stream wends its way through ferny, moss-draped forest in the Kaipo Valley north of Milford Sound. The trees with papery orange bark are kotukutuku, the New Zealand tree fuchsia (*Fuchsia excorticata*), one of only three deciduous native trees in New Zealand.

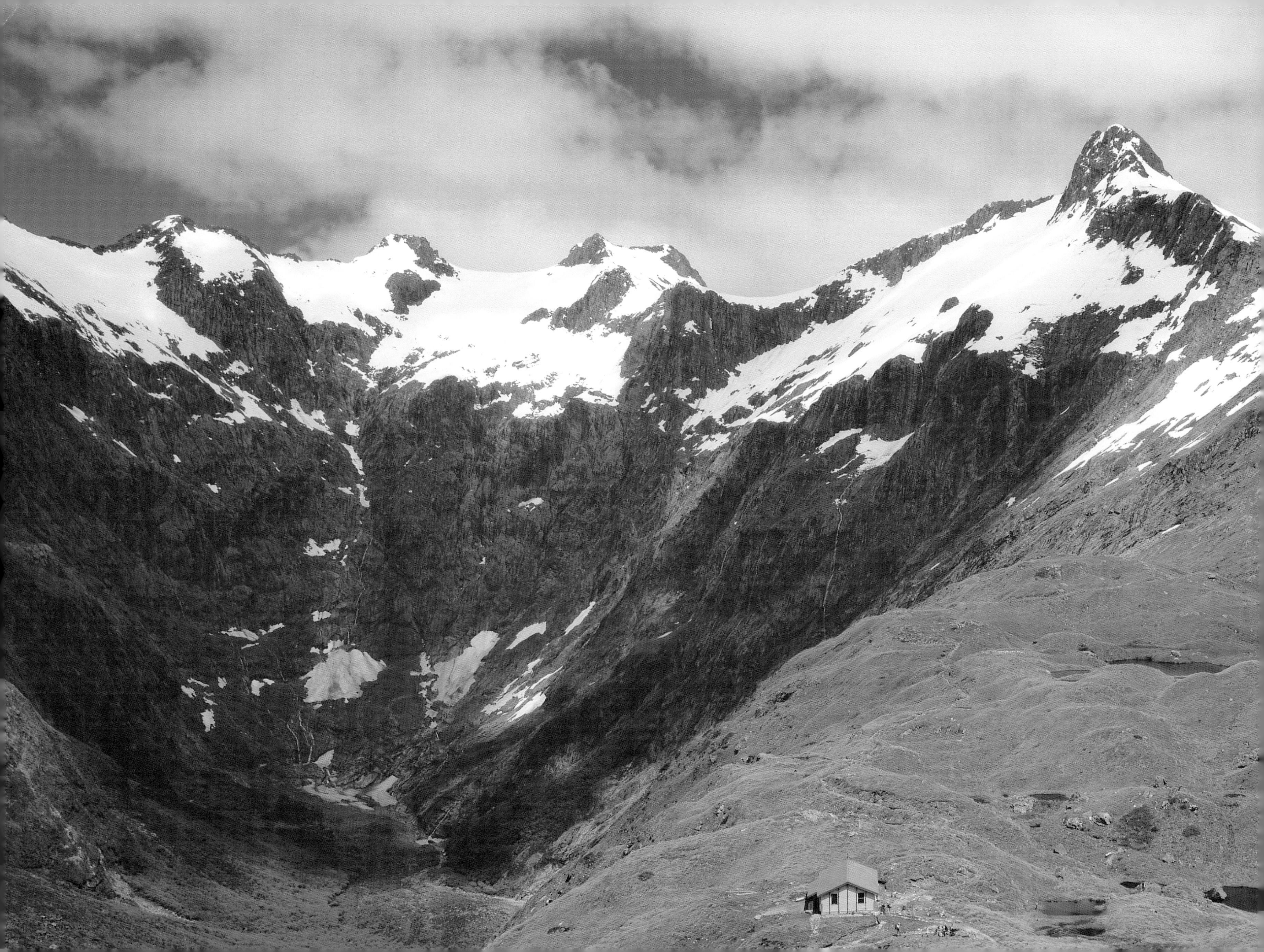

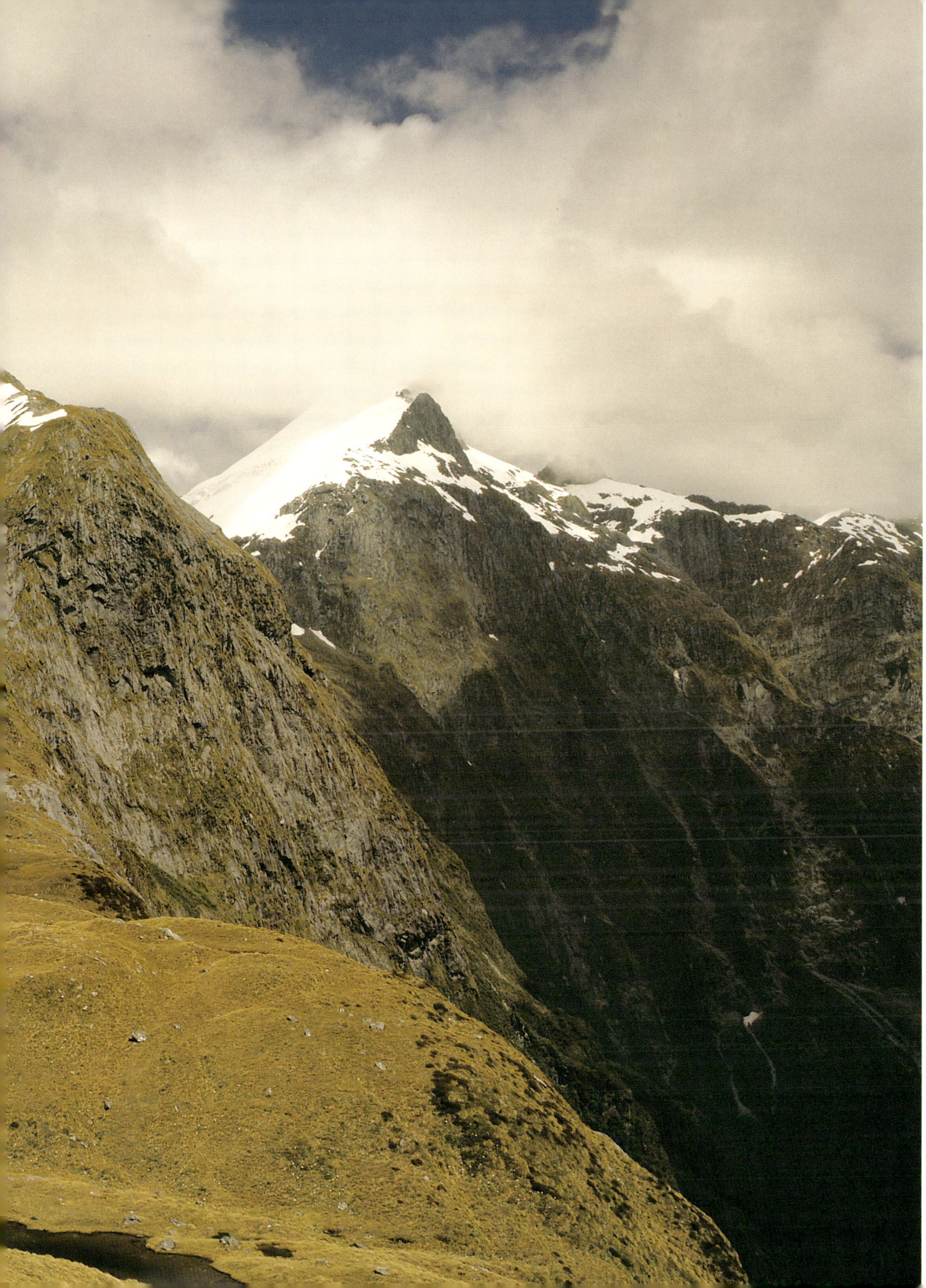

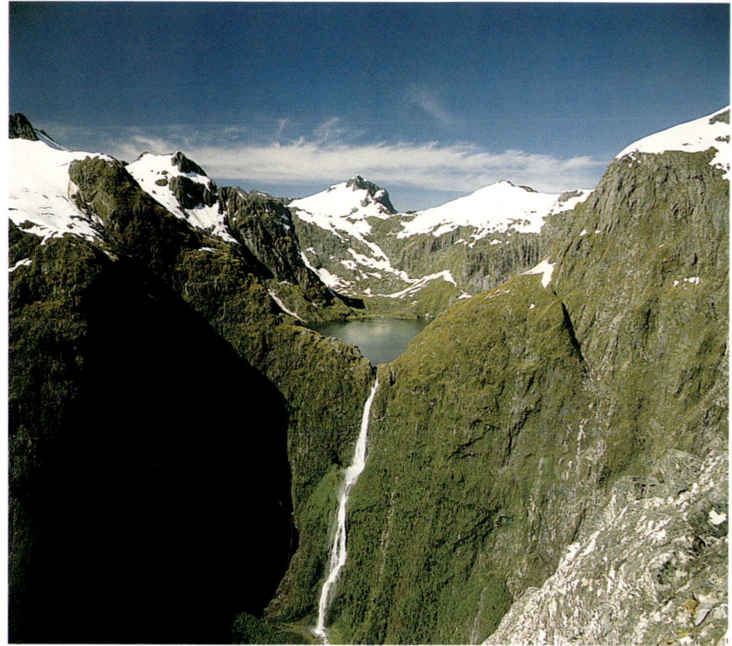

One of the scenic highlights of the four-day Milford Track, Sutherland Falls tumbles 580 metres in three leaps from the high cirque containing Lake Quill into the headwaters of the Arthur River.

LEFT: The high point on the Milford Track—Mackinnon Pass (1,073 metres), with the shelter hut for trampers in the foreground and Mt Hart (1,172 metres) directly beyond the pass. Mackinnon Pass was formerly part of a Maori 'greenstone trail' between Lake Te Anau and the pounamu source at Anita Bay, near the entrance to Milford Sound. From 1889 until the completion of the Milford Road in 1953 the Milford Track was the only land route to and from the Milford region.

OVERLEAF: Jagged Fiordland ridgecrests silhouetted against a shining Tasman Sea, from near Couloir Peak in the mountains surrounding Lake Quill at the head of the Sutherland Falls.

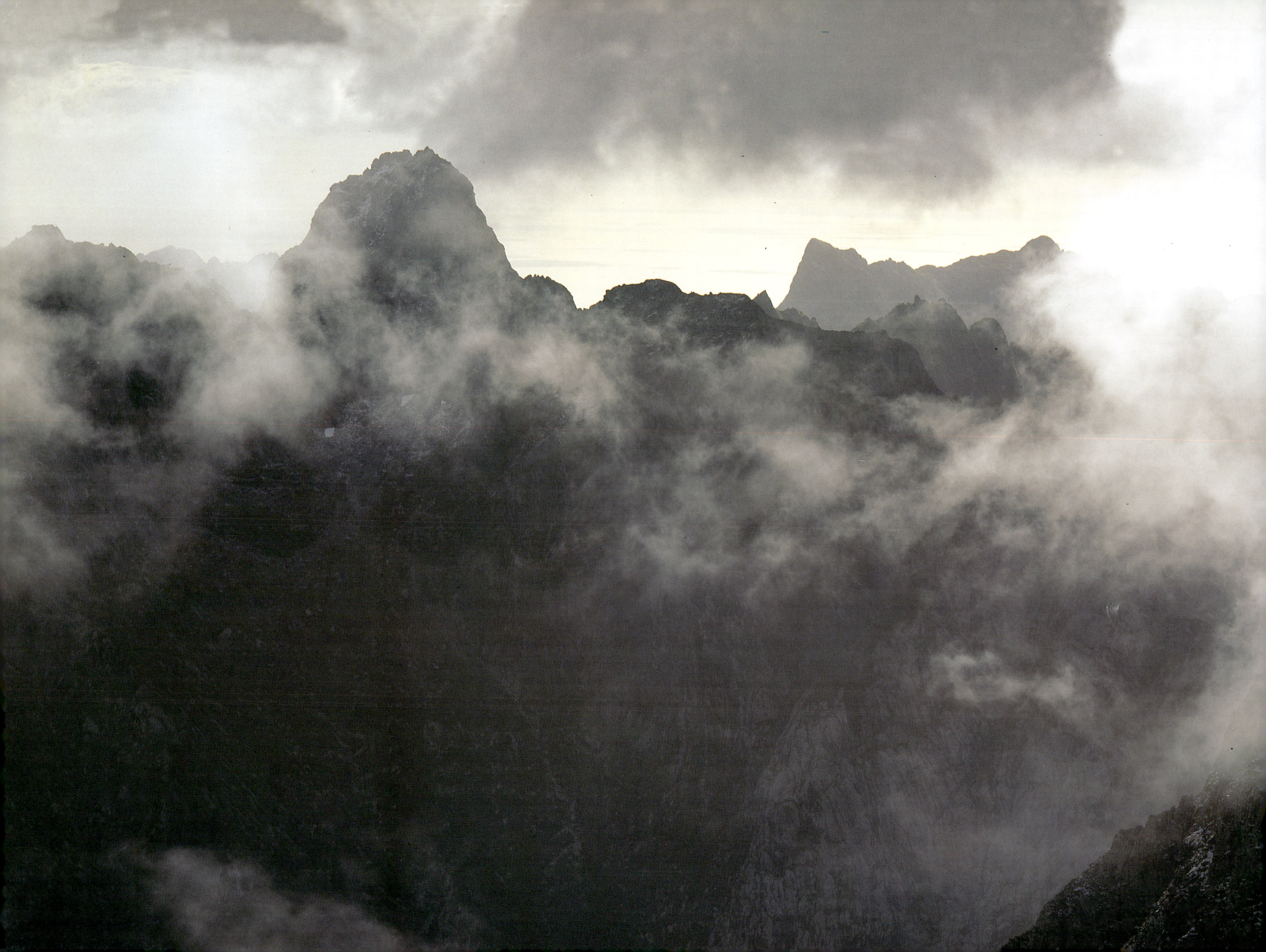

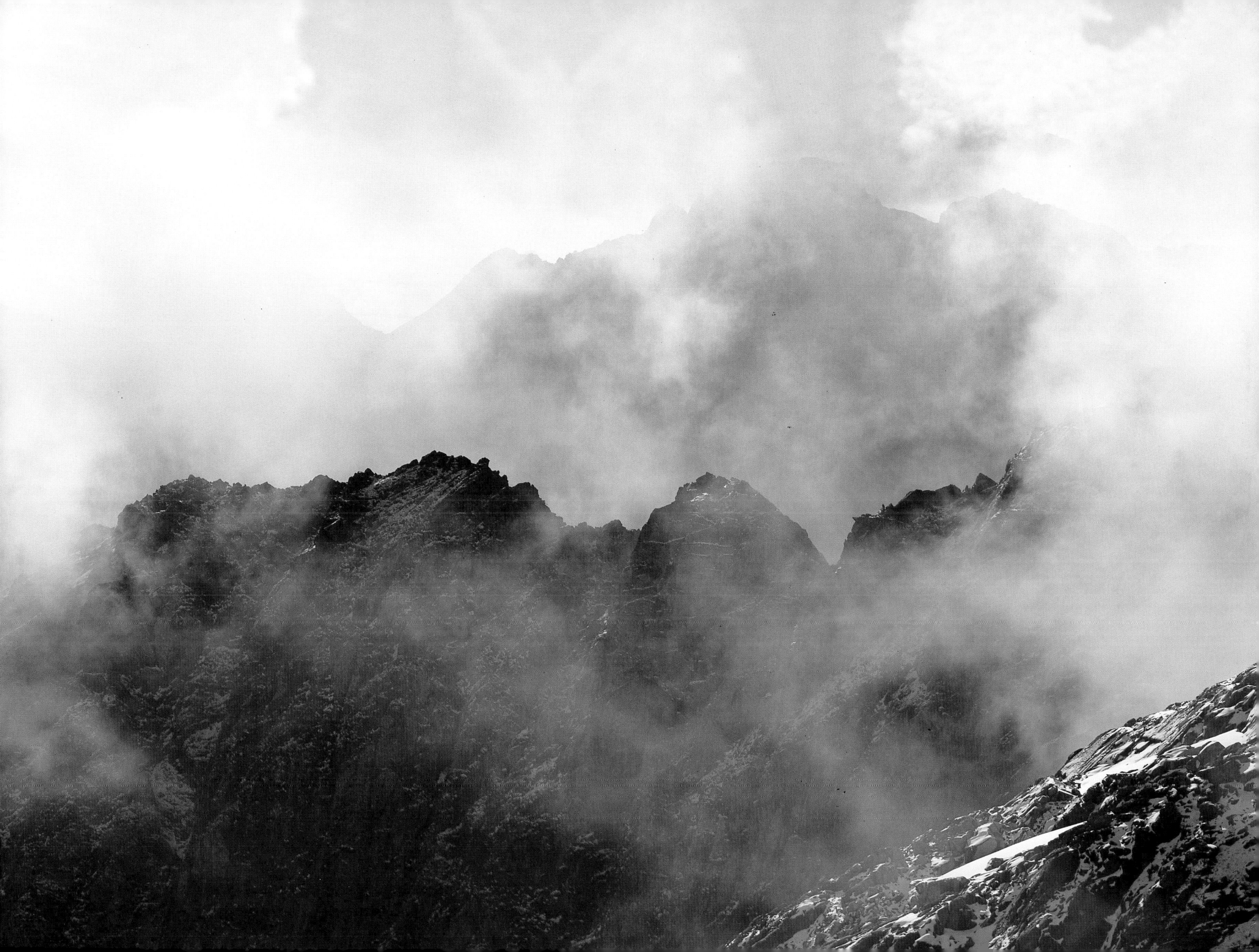

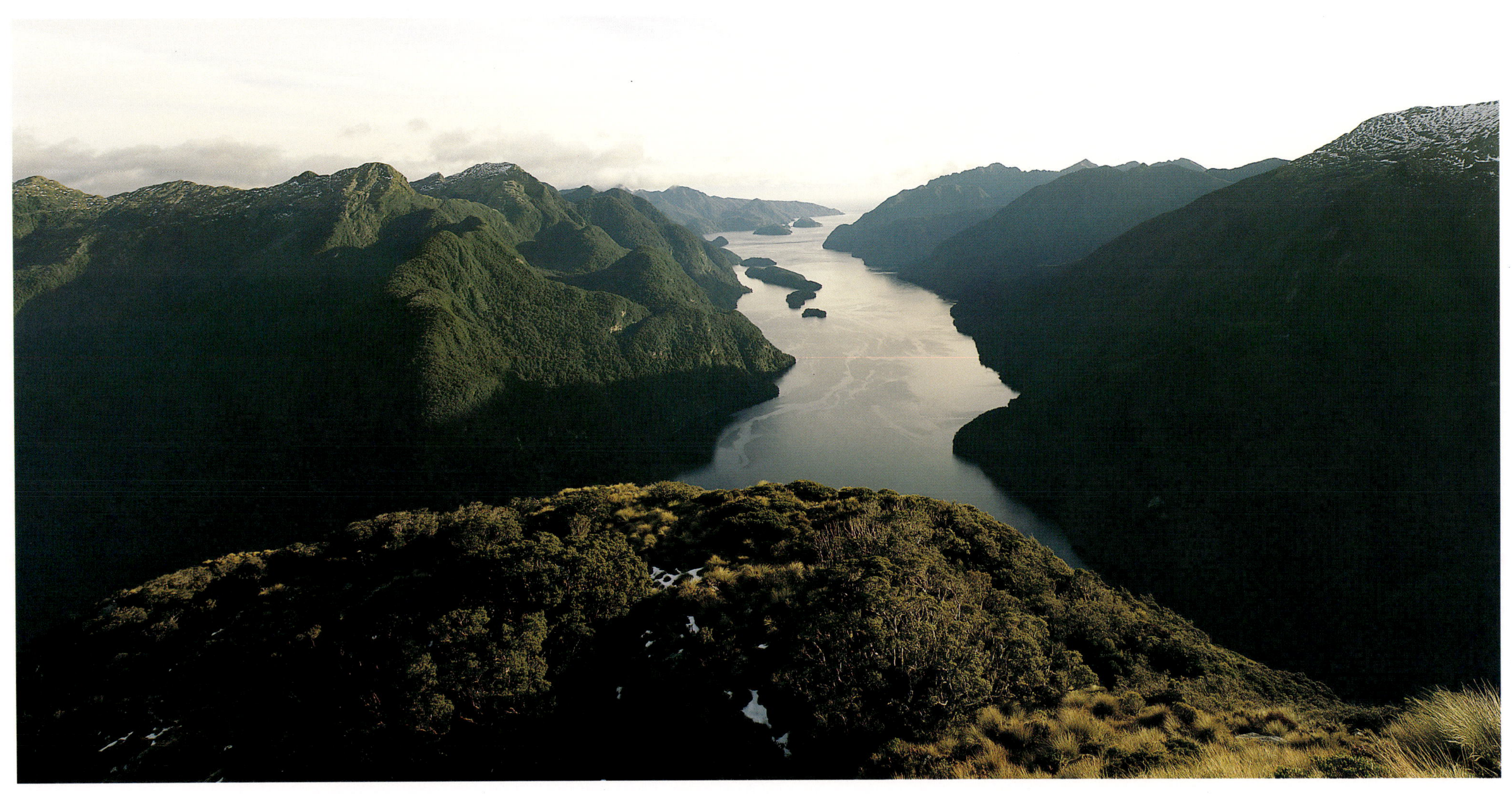

A view westwards over the main section of Breaksea Sound from above Chatham Point, where the fiord divides into two narrow inner arms. The small islands near the mouth of the fiord are important refuge islands for threatened wildlife along with larger Breaksea Island which is concealed behind the ridge at the right of the entrance to the fiord.

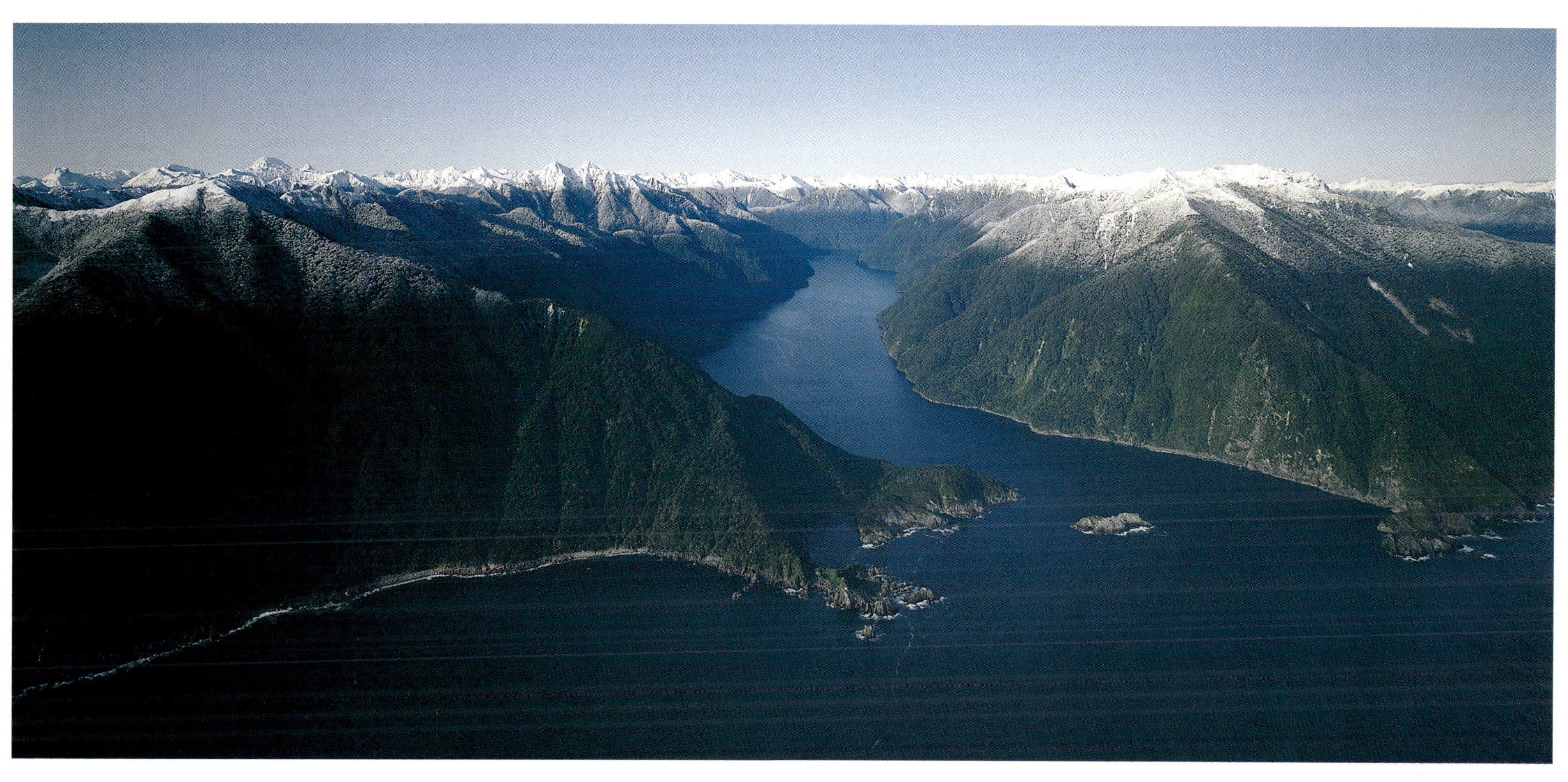

Nancy Sound, sixty kilometres north of Breaksea Sound. The panorama of snowy summits spread across the distant horizon illustrates the remarkably uniform height of mountain ranges throughout much of central and southern Fiordland.

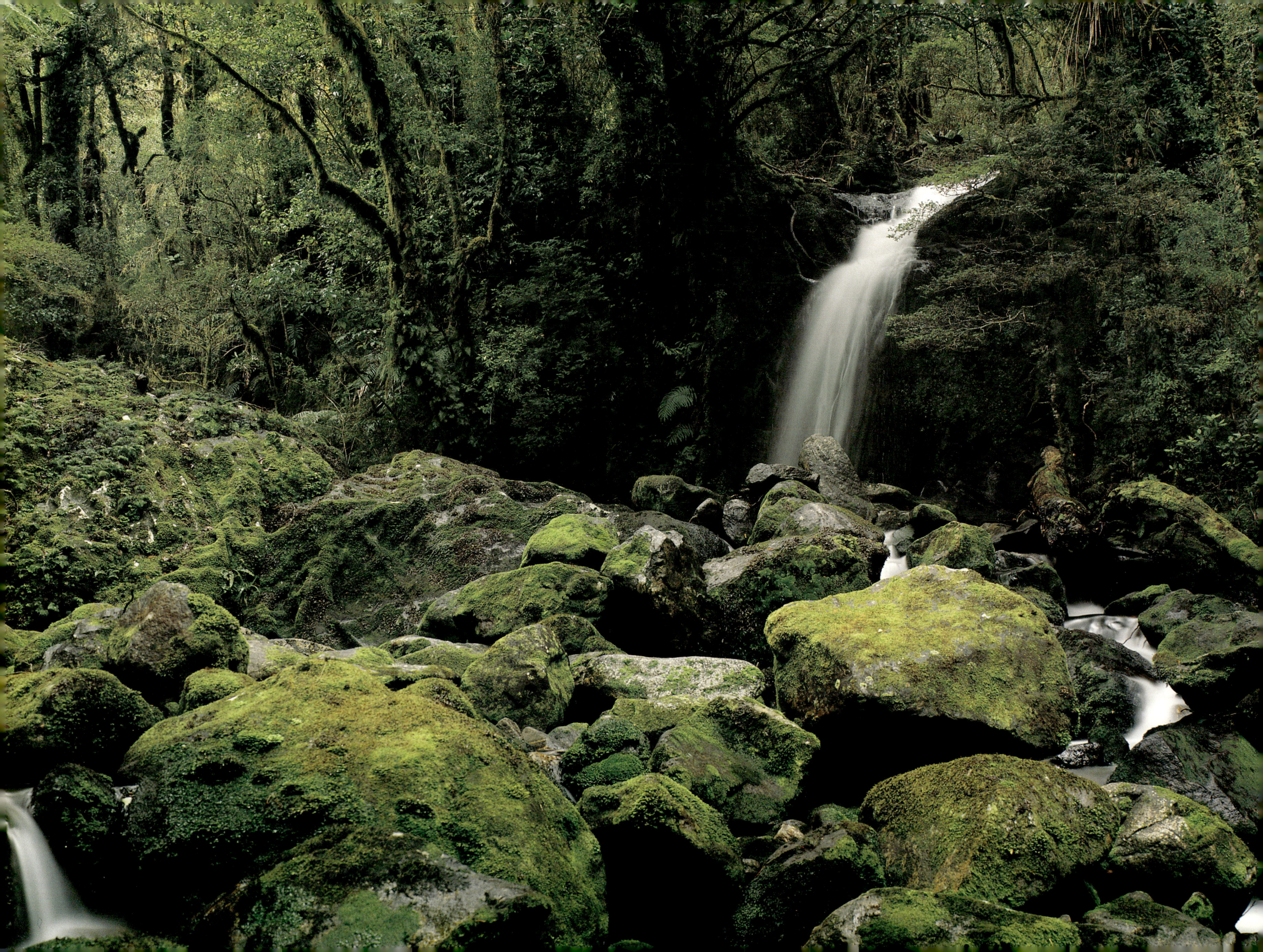

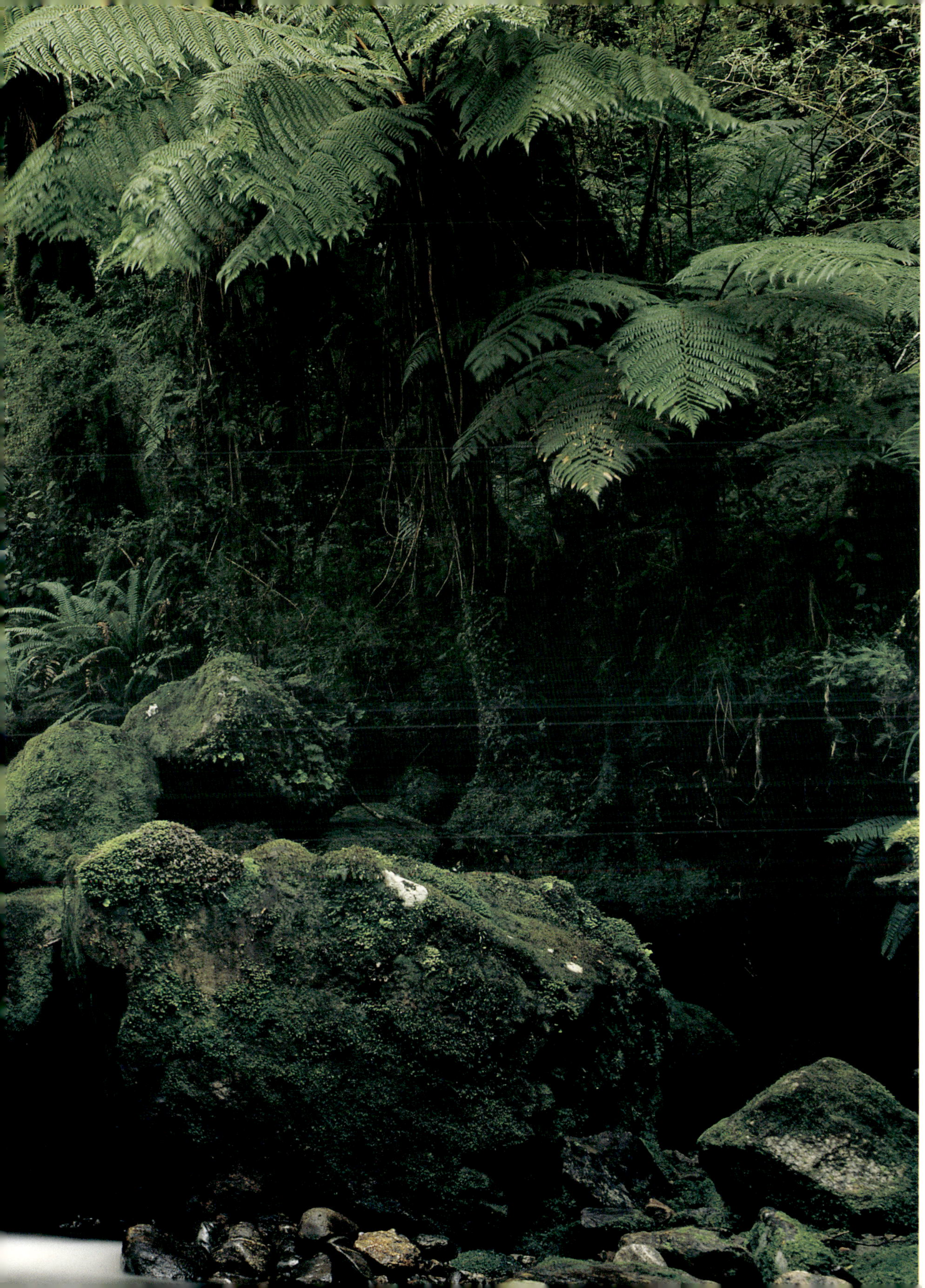

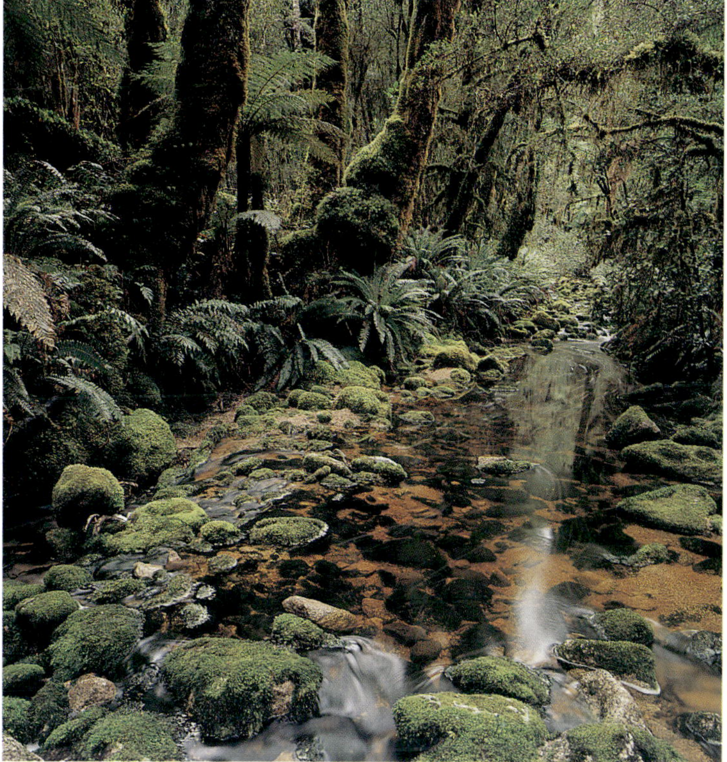

Mossy forest interiors typical of western Fiordland lowlands—the photograph at left was taken near the head of George Sound, while the one above is from Kisbee Bay on the southern side of Preservation Inlet.

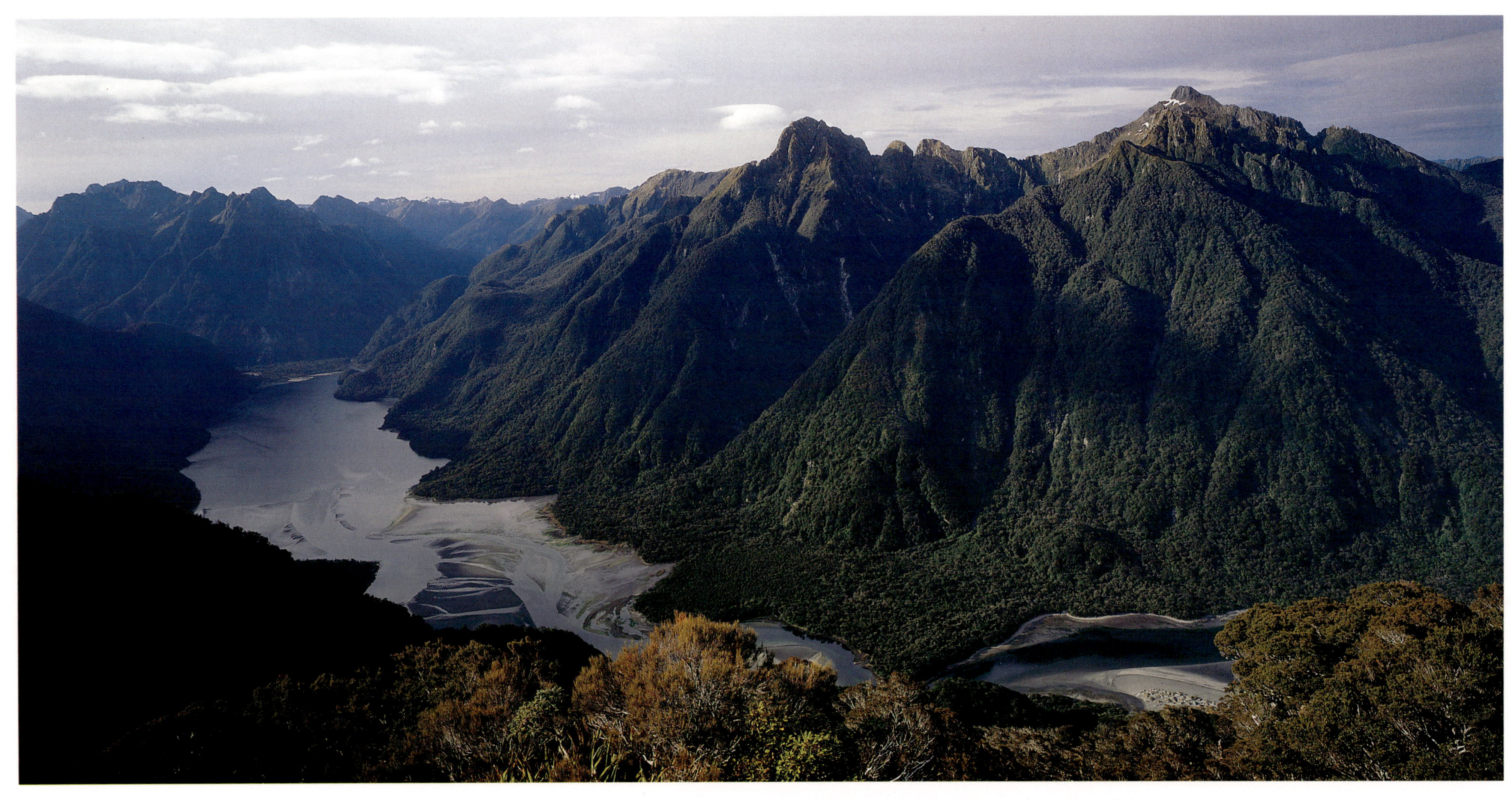

Sutherland Sound, photographed from above the shallow tidal area in the middle section of the fiord.
The peak on the right is Mt Longsight (1,472 metres).

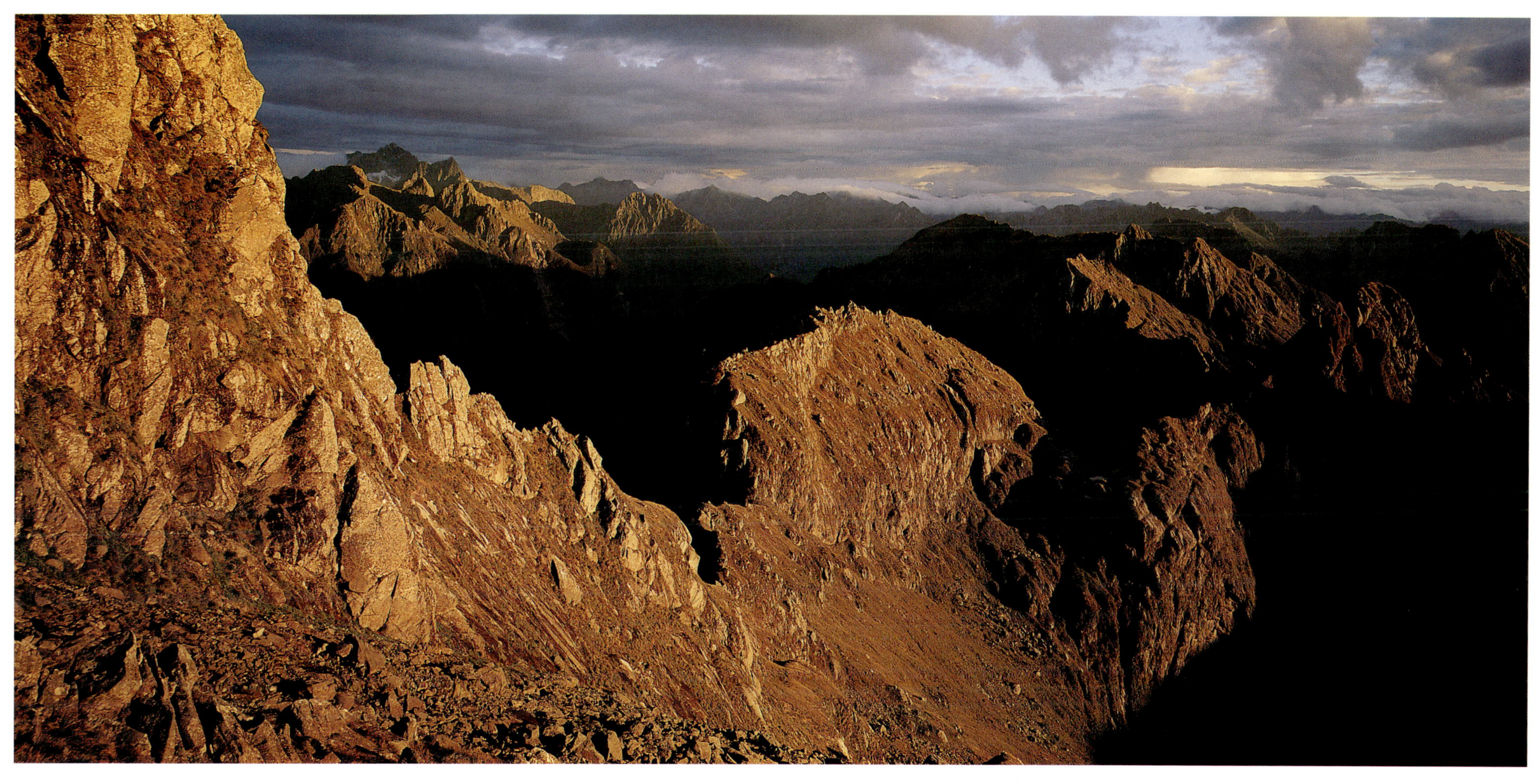

Evening sun illuminates a craggy ridge on Mt Longsight south of Sutherland Sound. In the background are the Franklin Mountains which lie to the west of the northern end of Lake Te Anau.

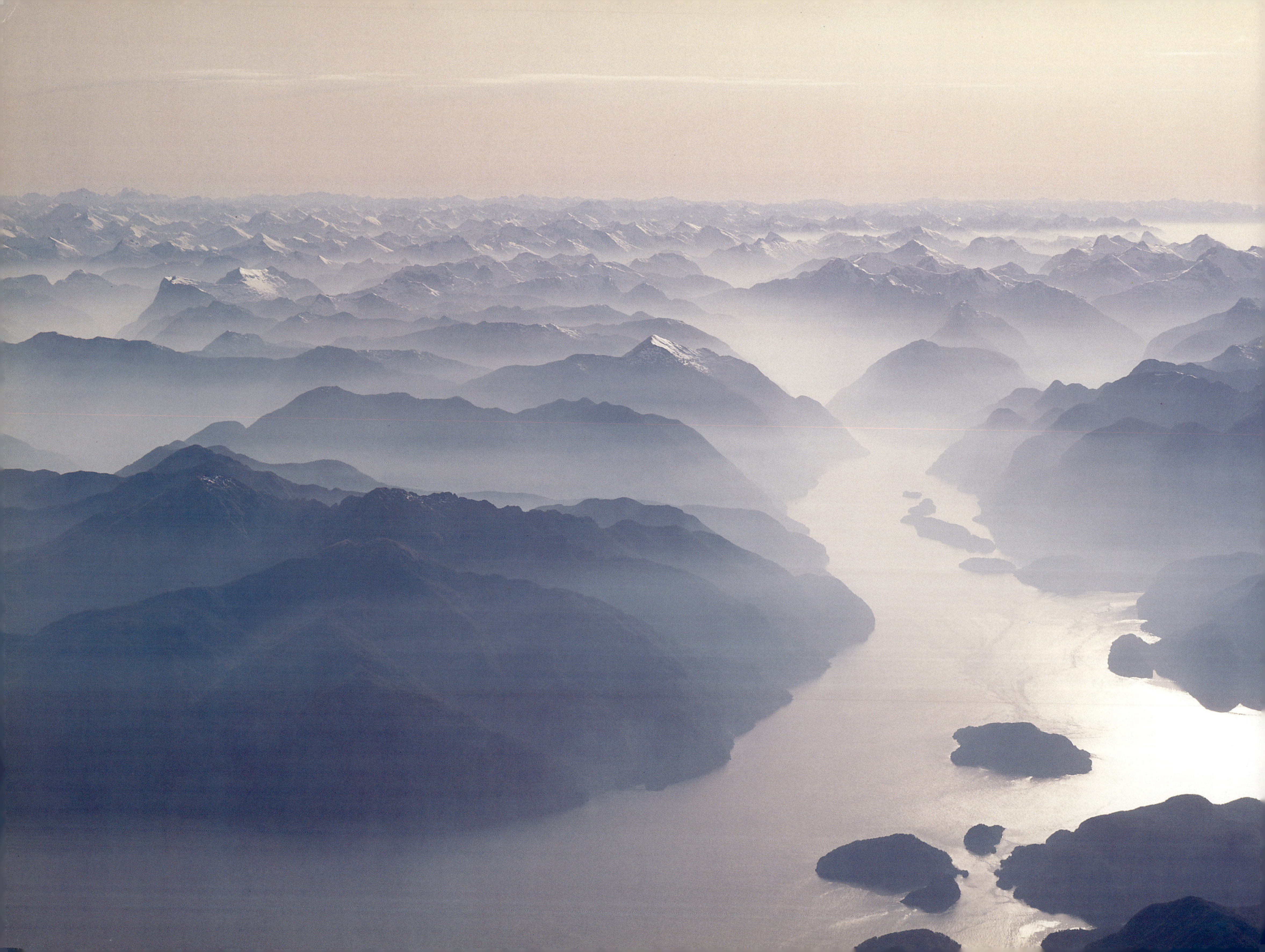

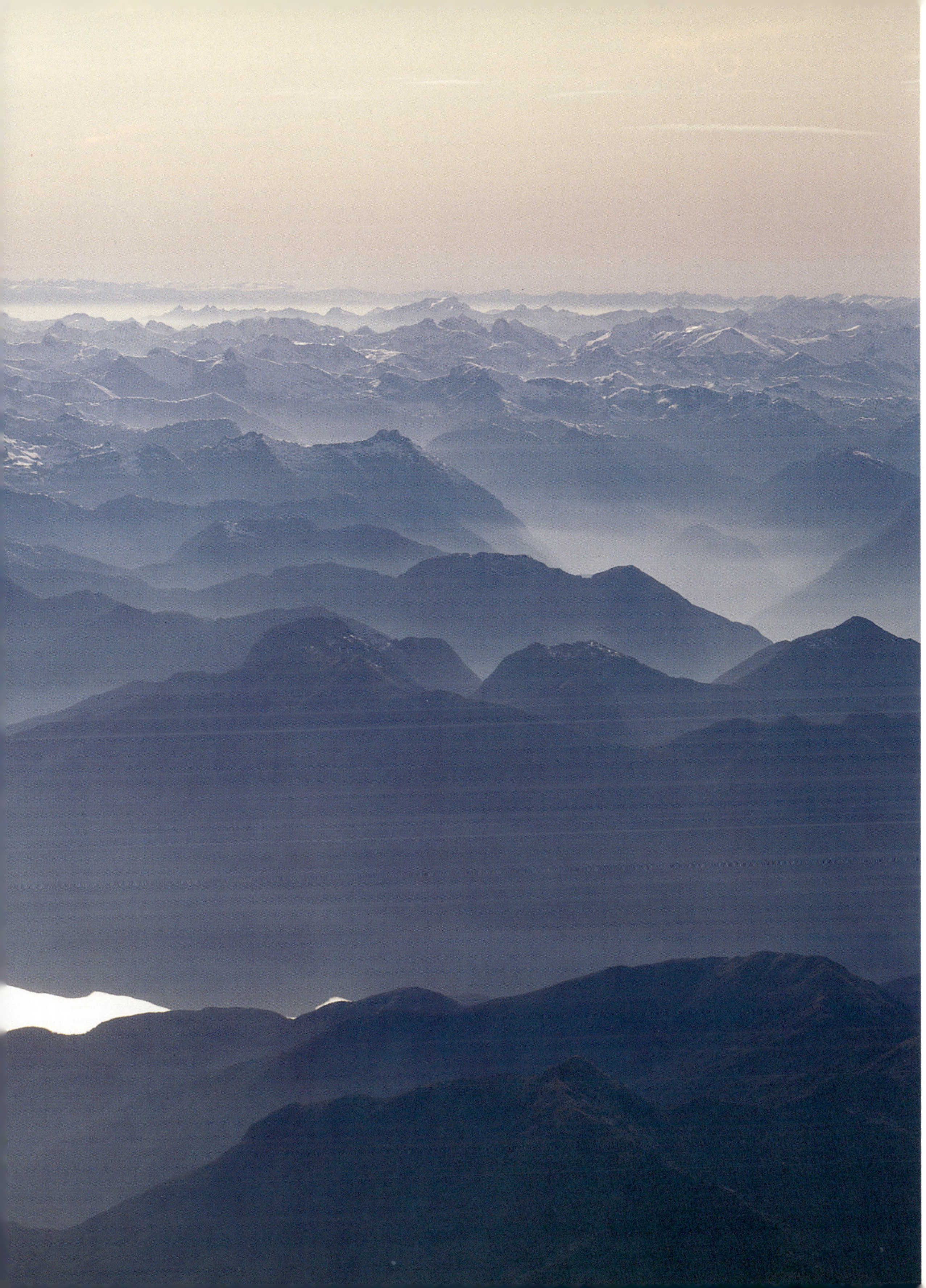

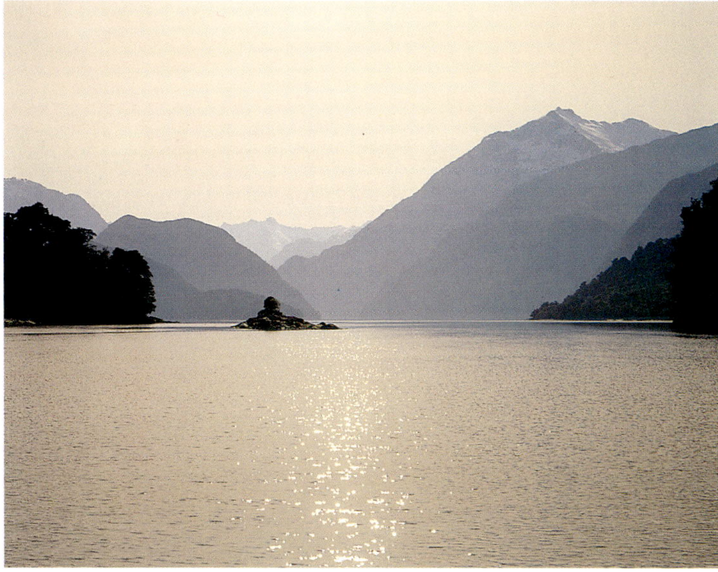

The head of Dusky Sound from Nine Fathoms Passage at the inner end of Cook Channel. The forested ridge at the left is part of Cooper Island and the high peak to the right is Mt Solitary (1,454 metres). Dusky Sound features prominently in the annals of zoological exploration in New Zealand as a result of a six-week sojourn here in 1773 by Captain James Cook and the crew of the Resolution, during which time his scientists (principally Johann and George Forster) set about studying and collecting a wide range plants and animals previously unknown to European science.

LEFT: The remoteness and grandeur that is Fiordland—a boundless sea of mountains and valleys stretching away north-eastwards from Breaksea Sound to the distant ranges of western Otago.

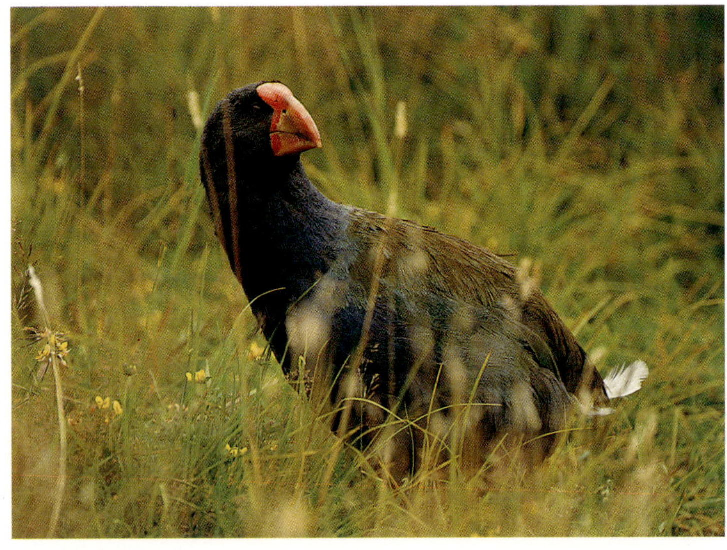

Once widespread throughout the mountains of both the North and South islands, takahe (*Notornis mantelli*) were confined to Fiordland by the time of European colonisation and were believed to have been extinct for fifty years before being rediscovered in 1948 in the Murchison Mountains, west of Lake Te Anau. Hampered by a slow reproduction rate and vulnerable to both predators and harsh winters, this wild population of fewer than 200 birds struggles to survive, although a successful captive breeding programme has made the species somewhat more secure than it was a decade ago.

Right: Beech forest frames a view of Lake Manapouri's Hope Arm, looking out over the tarns and lakes in the swampy lower valley of the Garnock Burn towards Calderwood Peninsula. Prior to the arrival of Europeans the lake was known to Maori not as Manapouri but as Roto-ua ('rainy lake') or Motu-rau ('many islands'), the latter on account of the thirty-four forested islands scattered across its 150 square-kilometre surface.

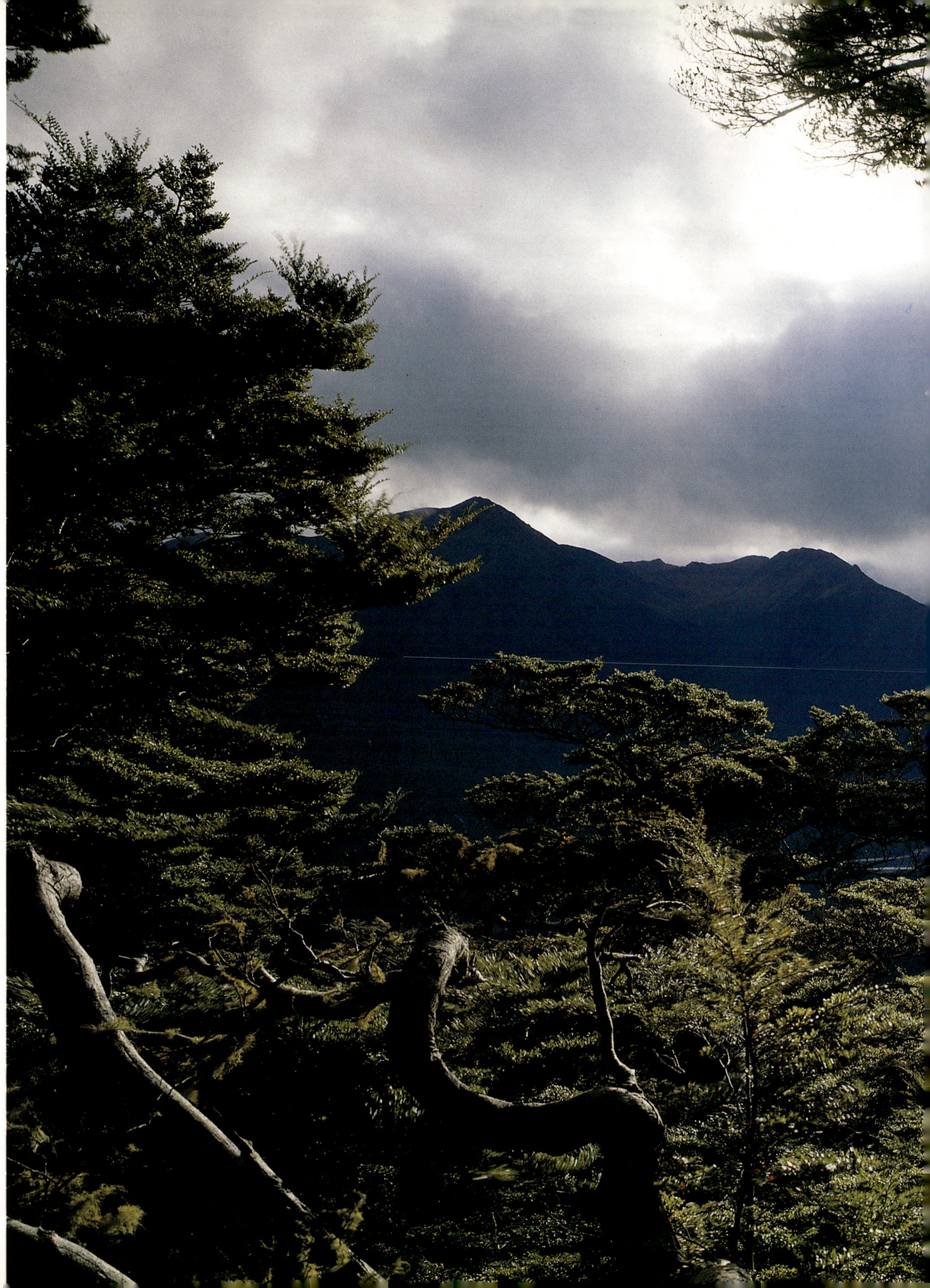

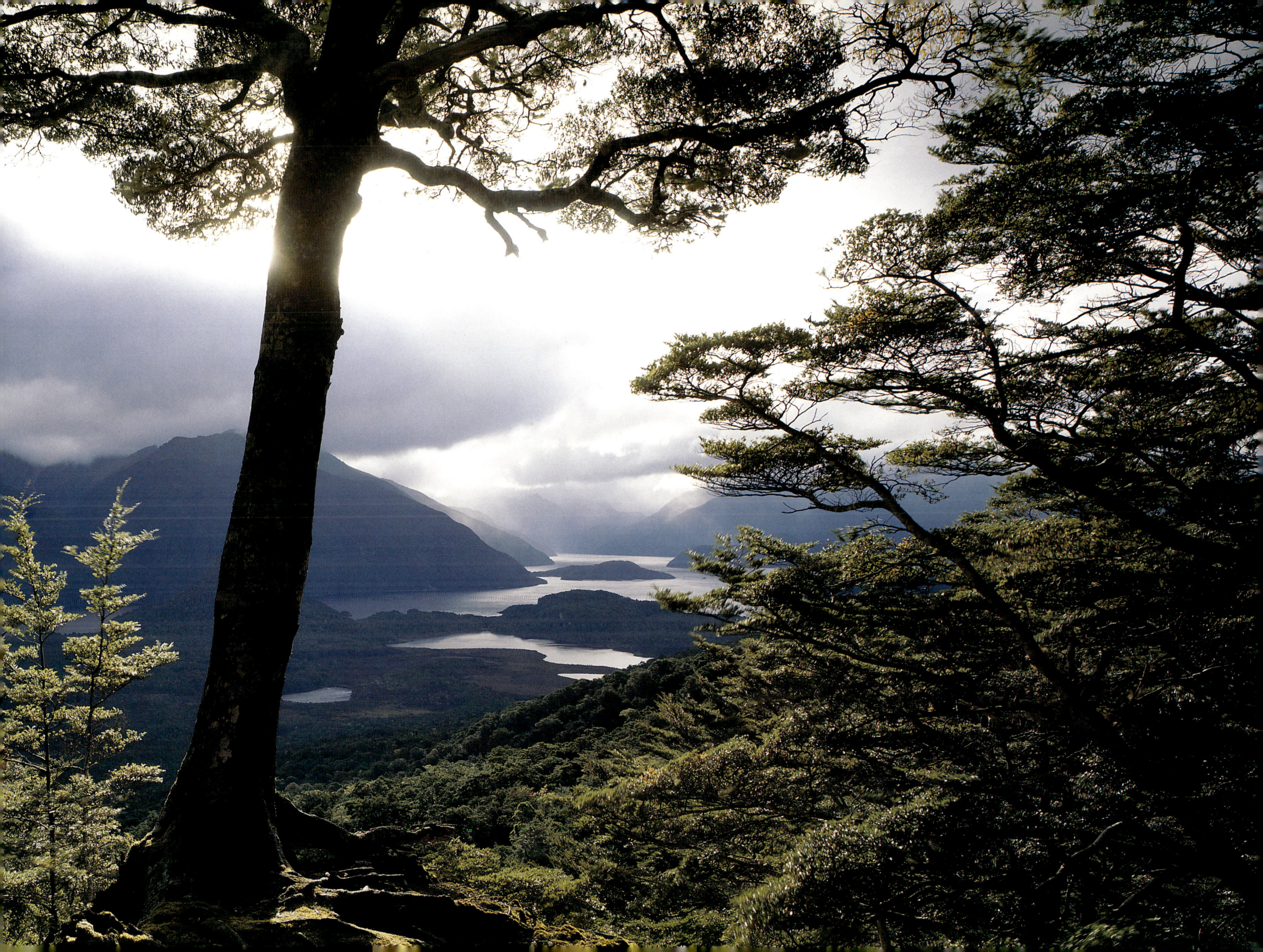

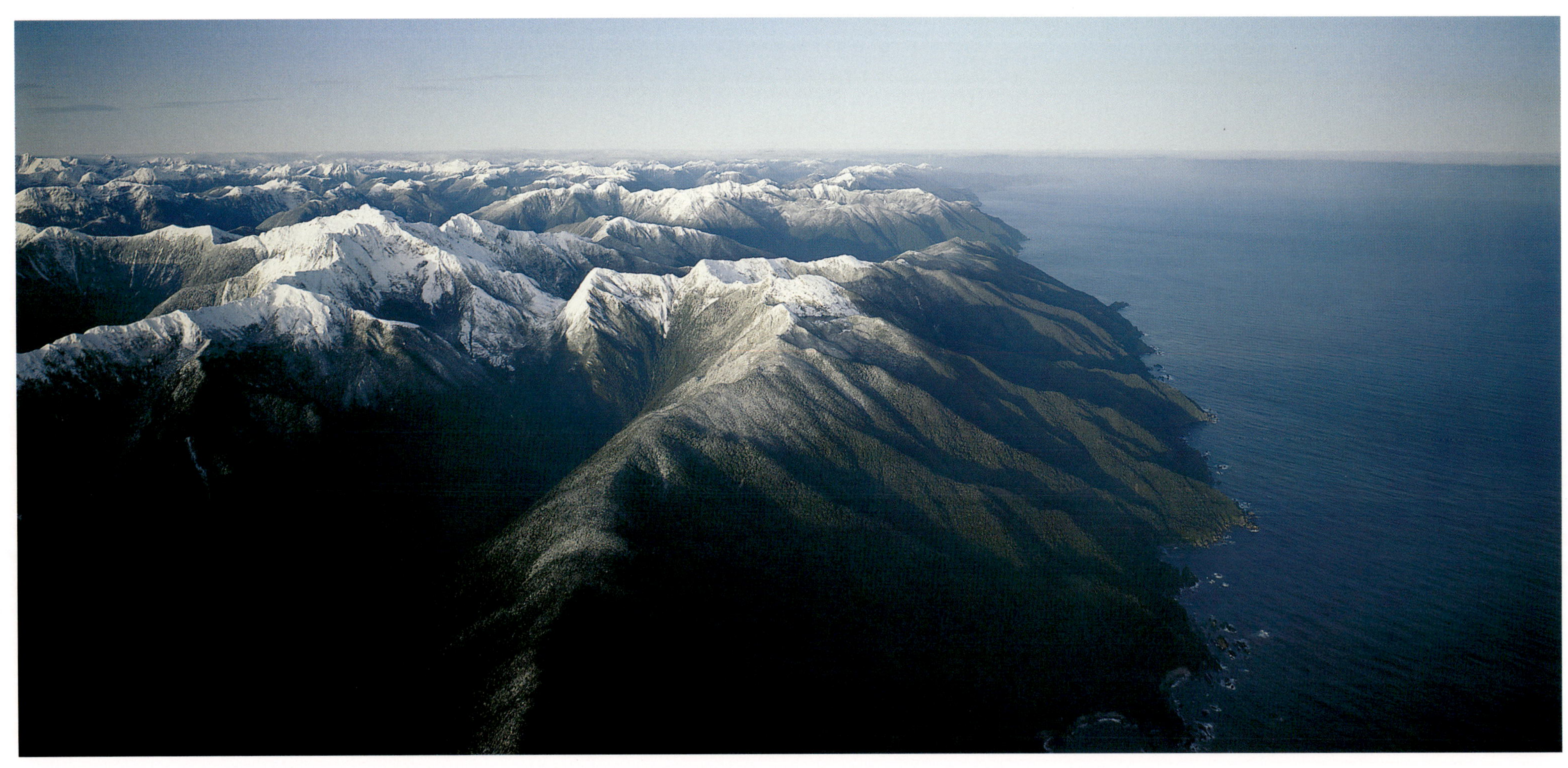

The outer Fiordland coastline between Doubtful and Breaksea sounds drops steeply into the sea, much as it does all the way north to Milford Sound.

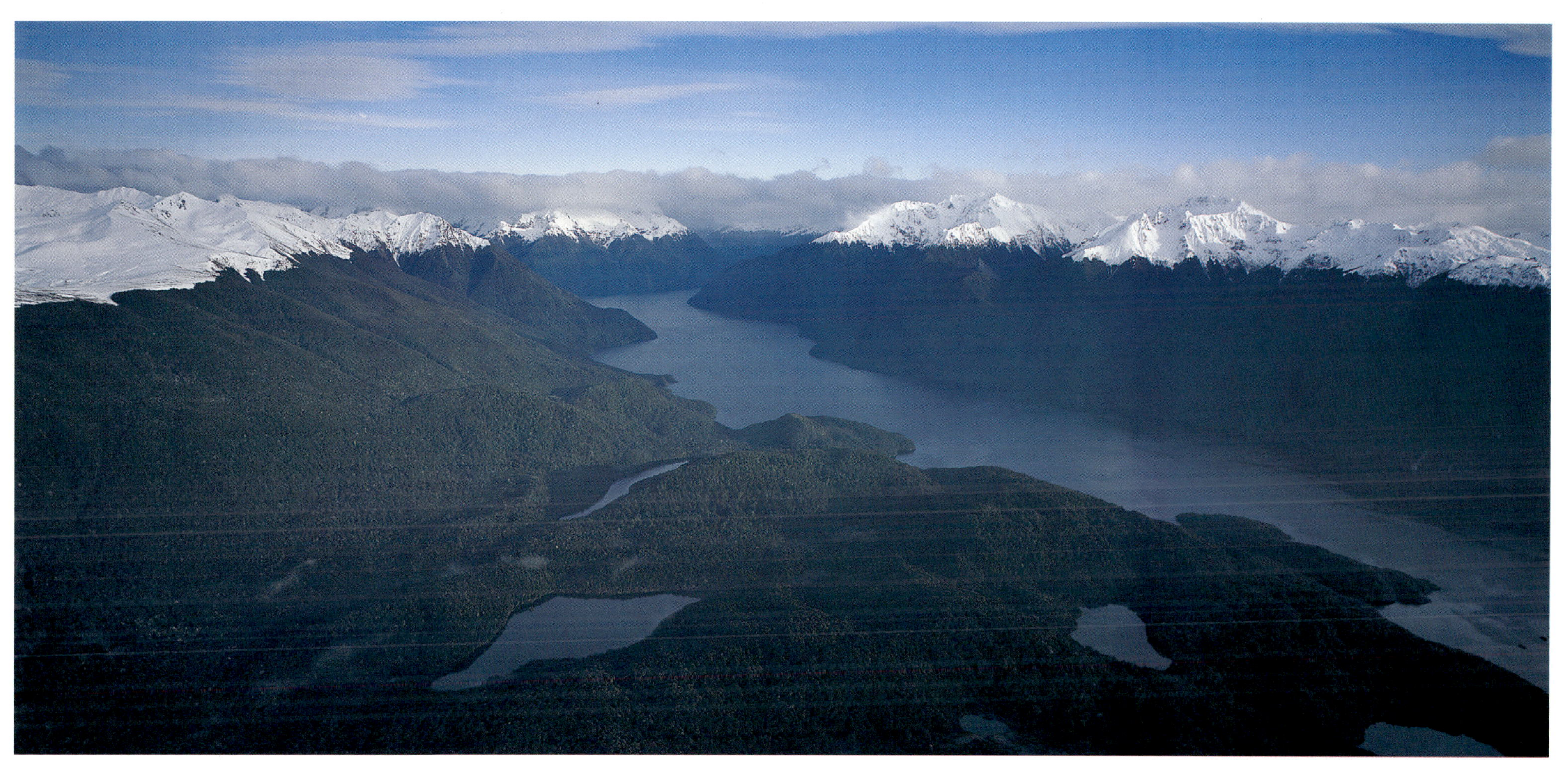

The South Fiord of Lake Te Anau in winter, with the Kepler Mountains to the left and the Murchison Mountains to the right.

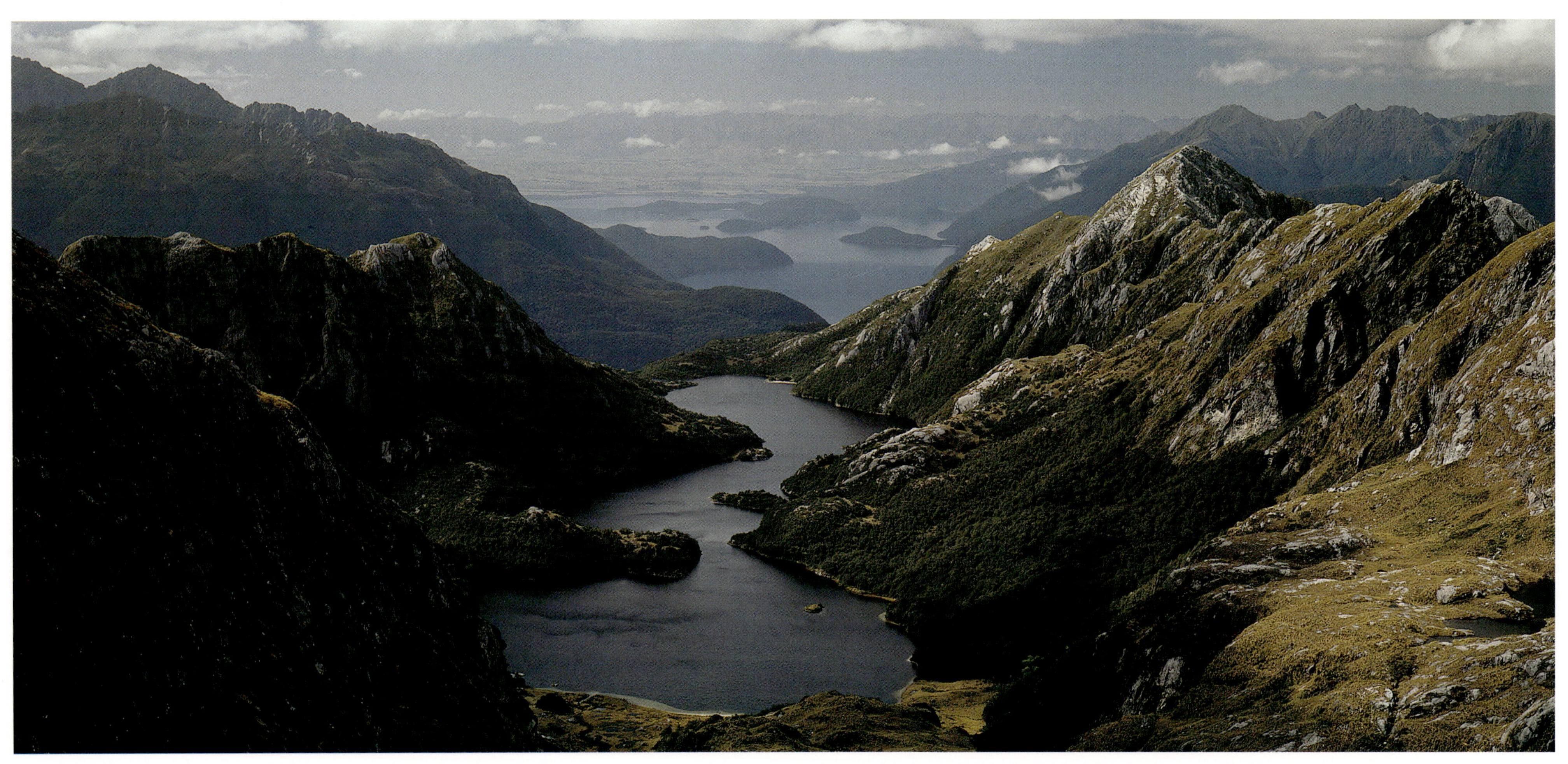

Northwest Lake occupies a glacier-excavated trough (or cirque) overlooking the western end of Lake Manapouri in a classic Fiordland upland landscape of stunted beech forest, tawny alpine grassland, and crags steepened and smoothed by ice age glaciers.

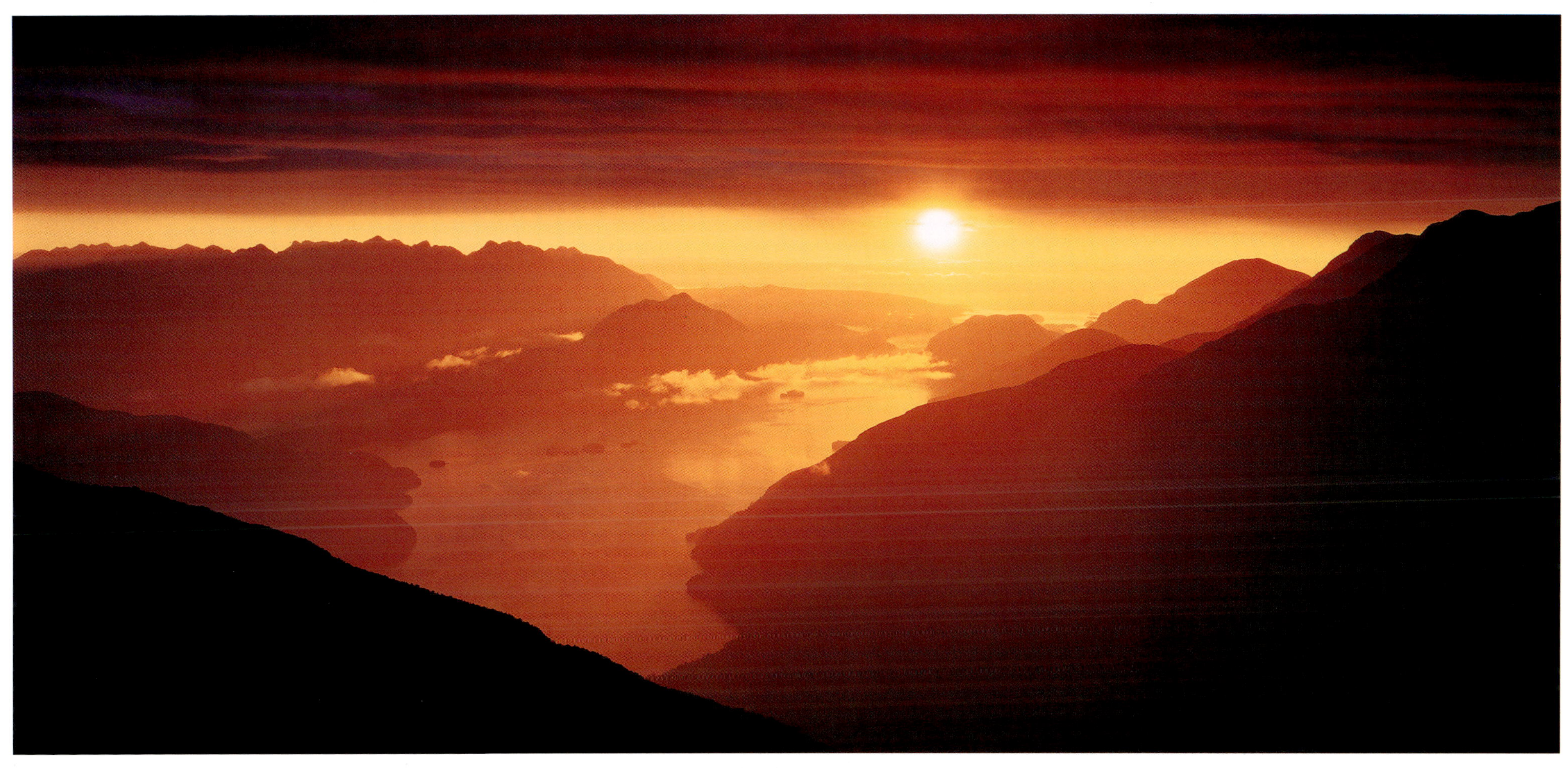

The entrance to Dusky Sound photographed from Mt Pender as the evening sun dips from dense banks of cloud into a clear sea-horizon, spreading ethereal light across a calm Bowen Channel in the centre of the photograph.

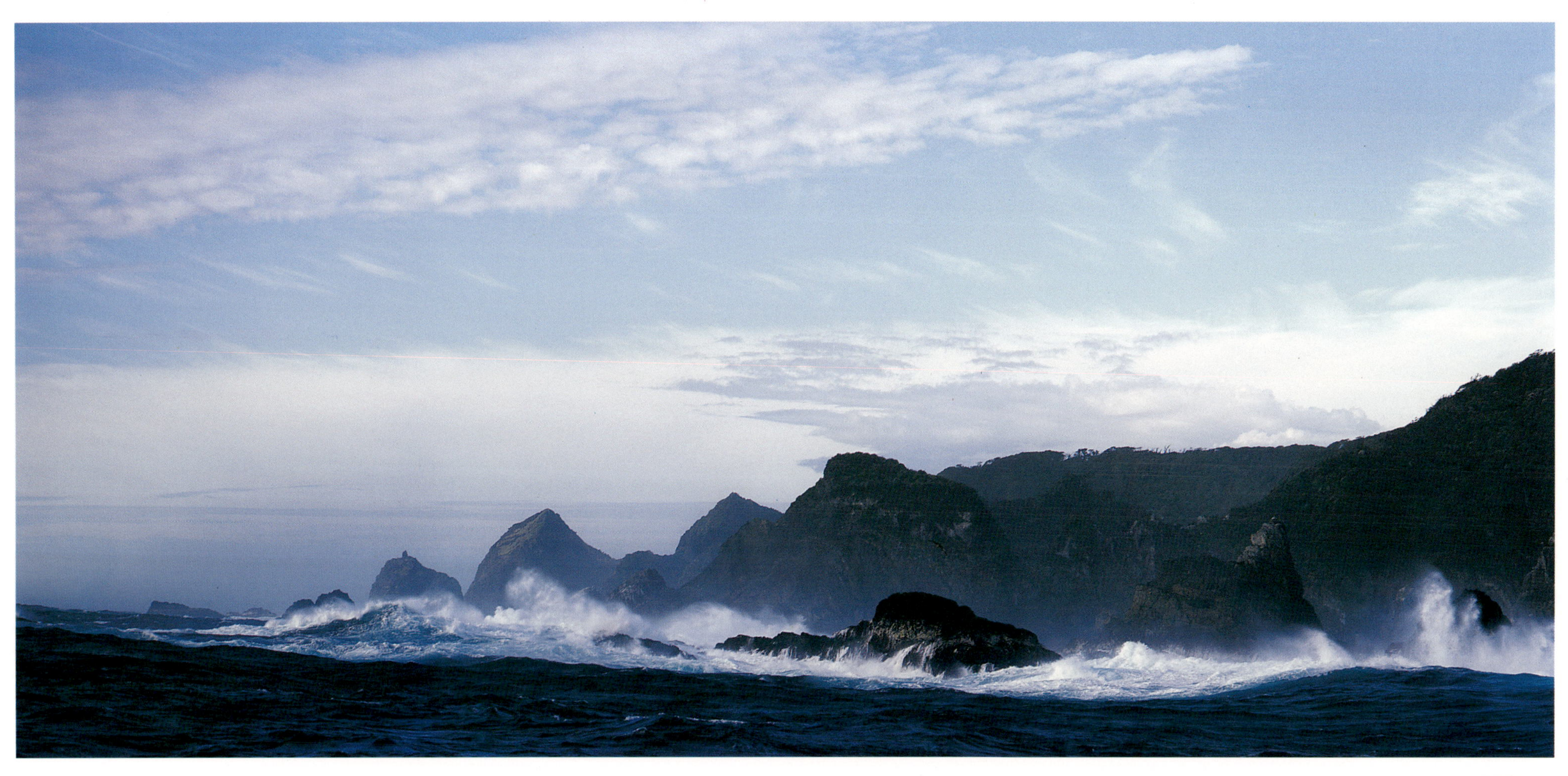

Waves that have begun to gather their momentum thousands of kilometres away in the vast emptiness of the Southern Ocean crash onto Fiordland's rocky outer coast near the entrance to Dusky Sound.

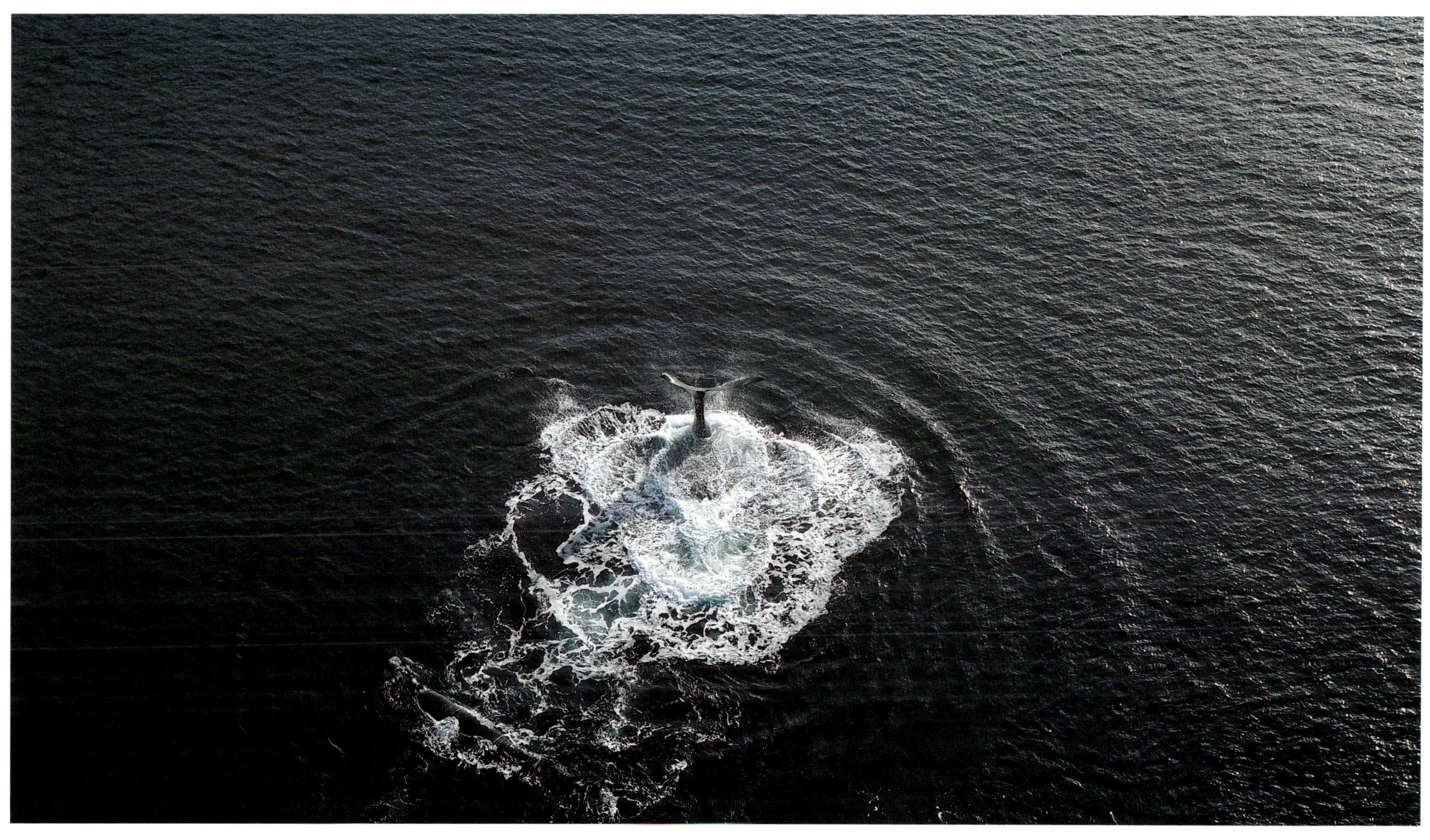

A southern right whale (*Eubalaena australis*) begins a dive in the waters of George Sound, encircled by two of its companions. Right whales were hunted virtually to extinction before being protected in 1936. Today there are only some 200 to 300 in New Zealand and Australian waters.
Overleaf: Sunset on the Dingwall Mountains between the heads of Breaksea and Dusky sounds, photographed from Mt Crowfoot.

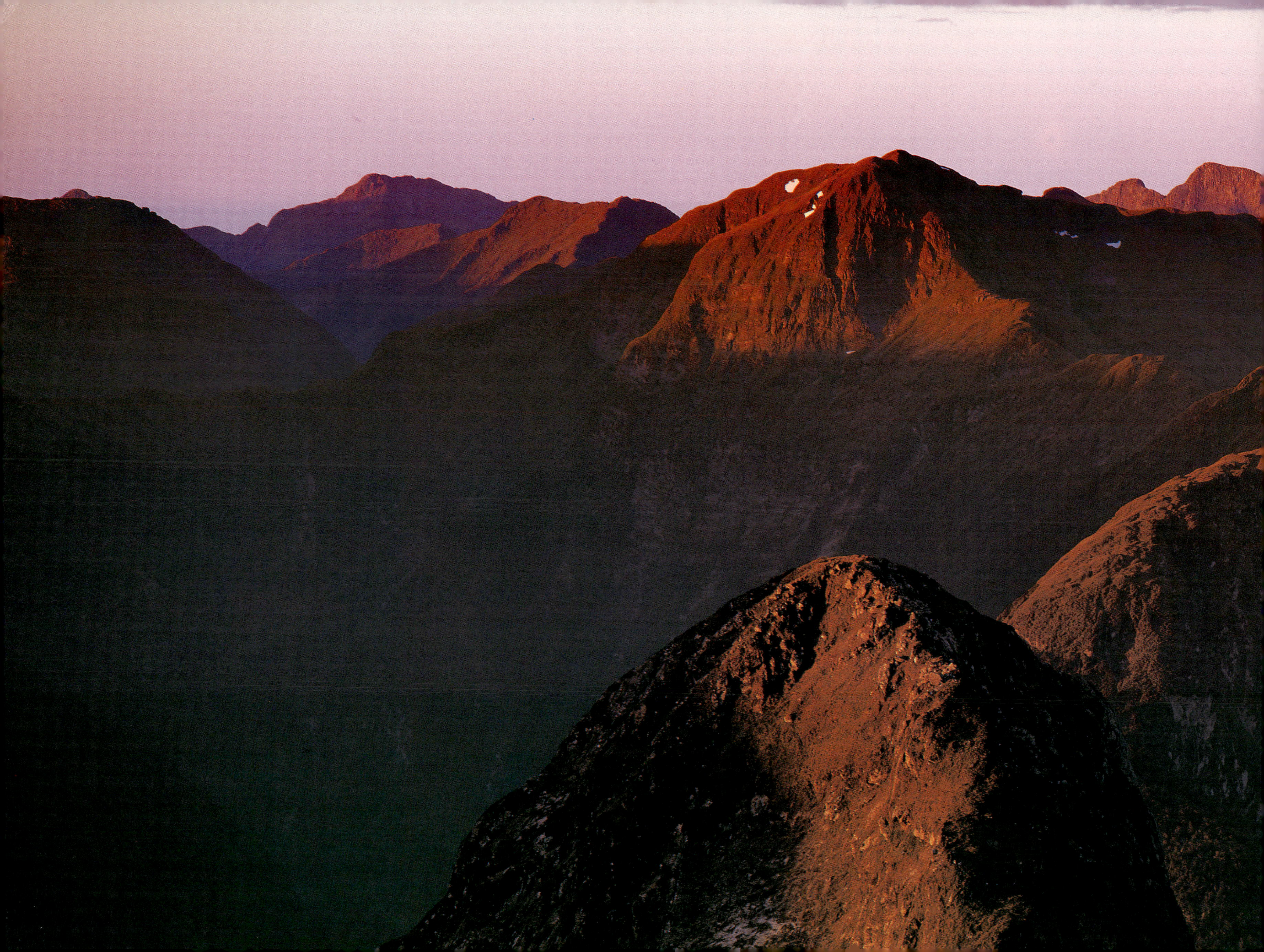

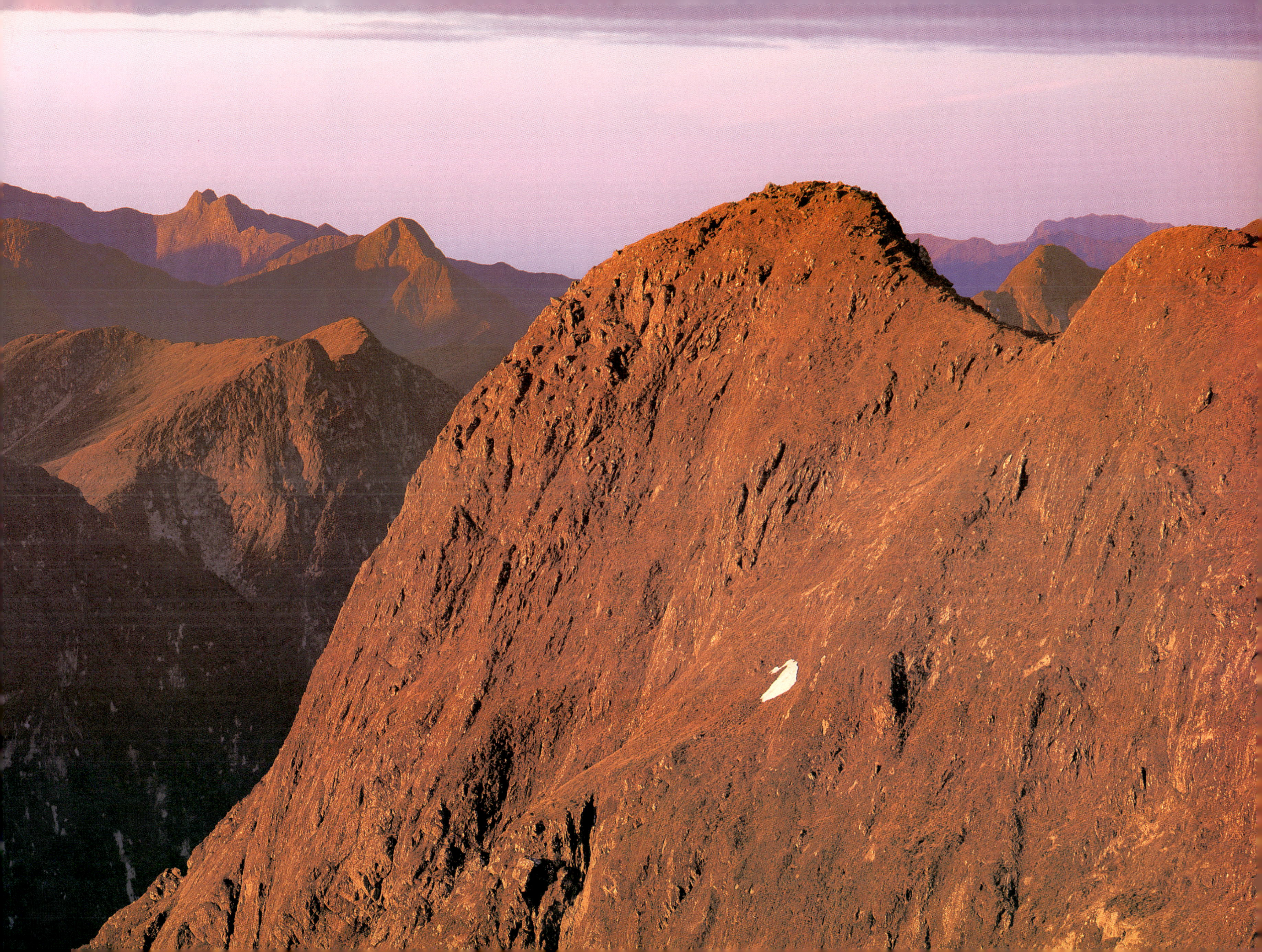

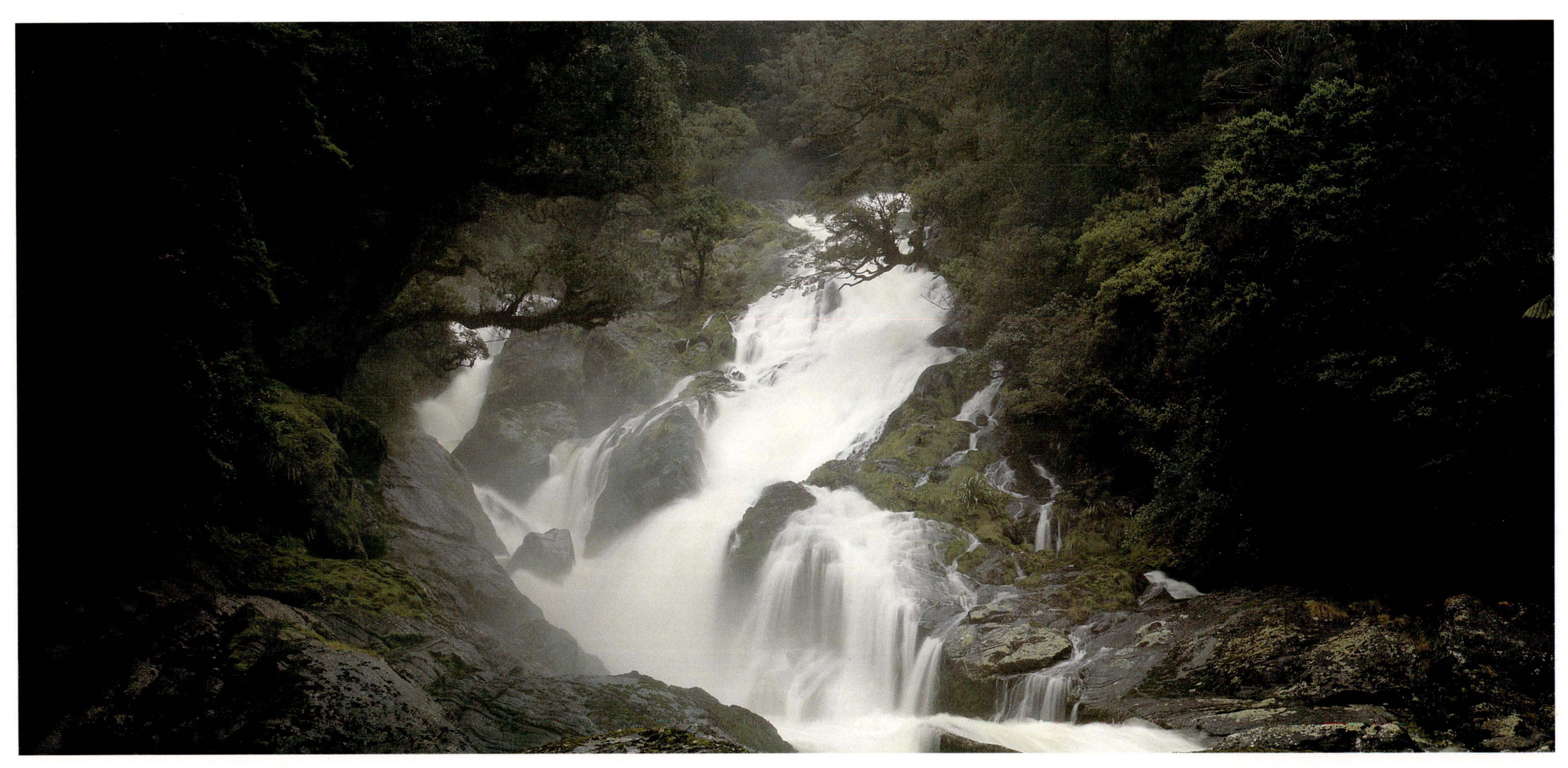

The waters gathered by the Edith River west of the Stuart Mountains empty from Lake Alice and spill down Alice Falls at the head of George Sound.

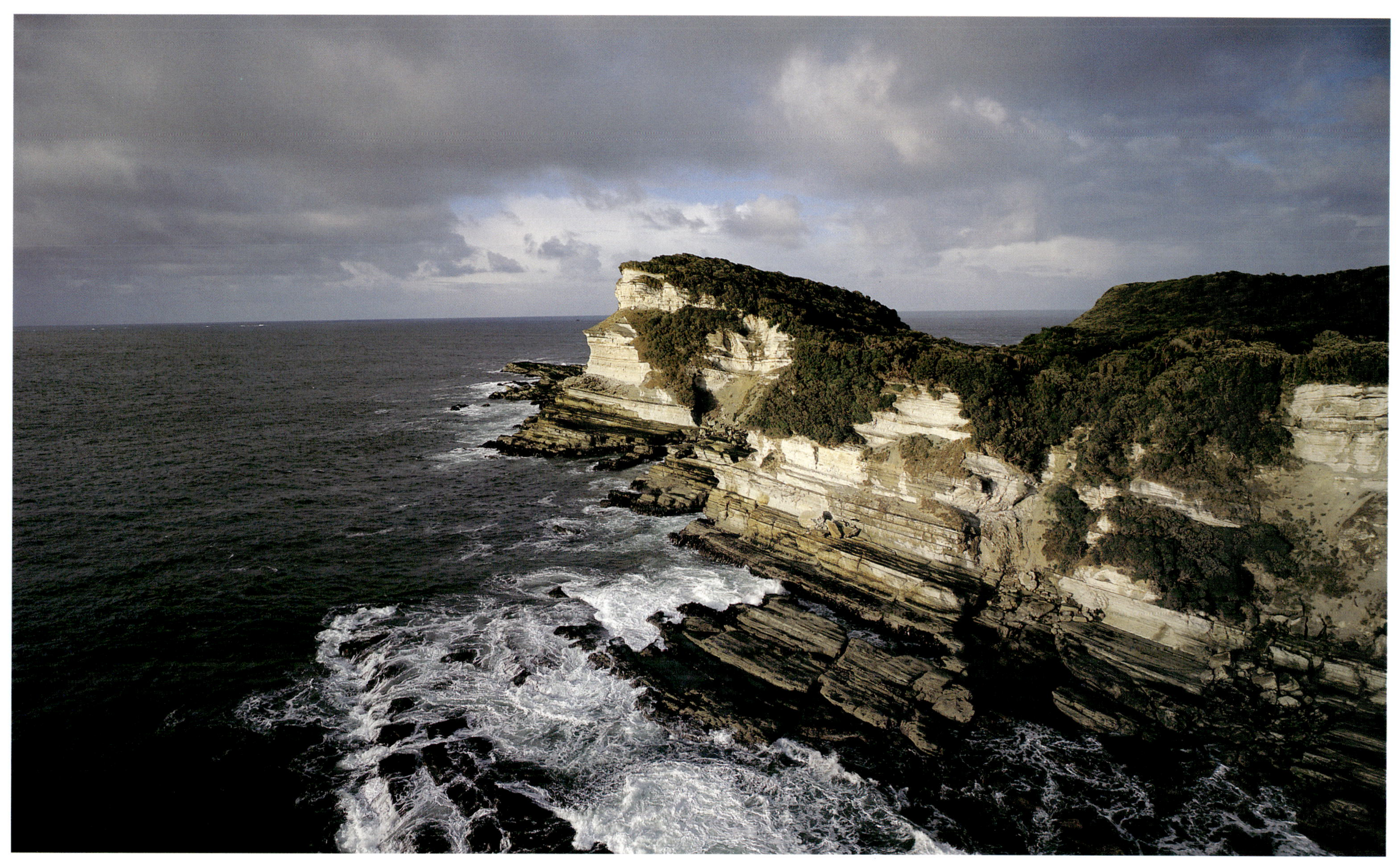

Stratified limestone sea-cliffs on Chalky Island, the outermost of a group of larger islands at the seaward end of Chalky Inlet.

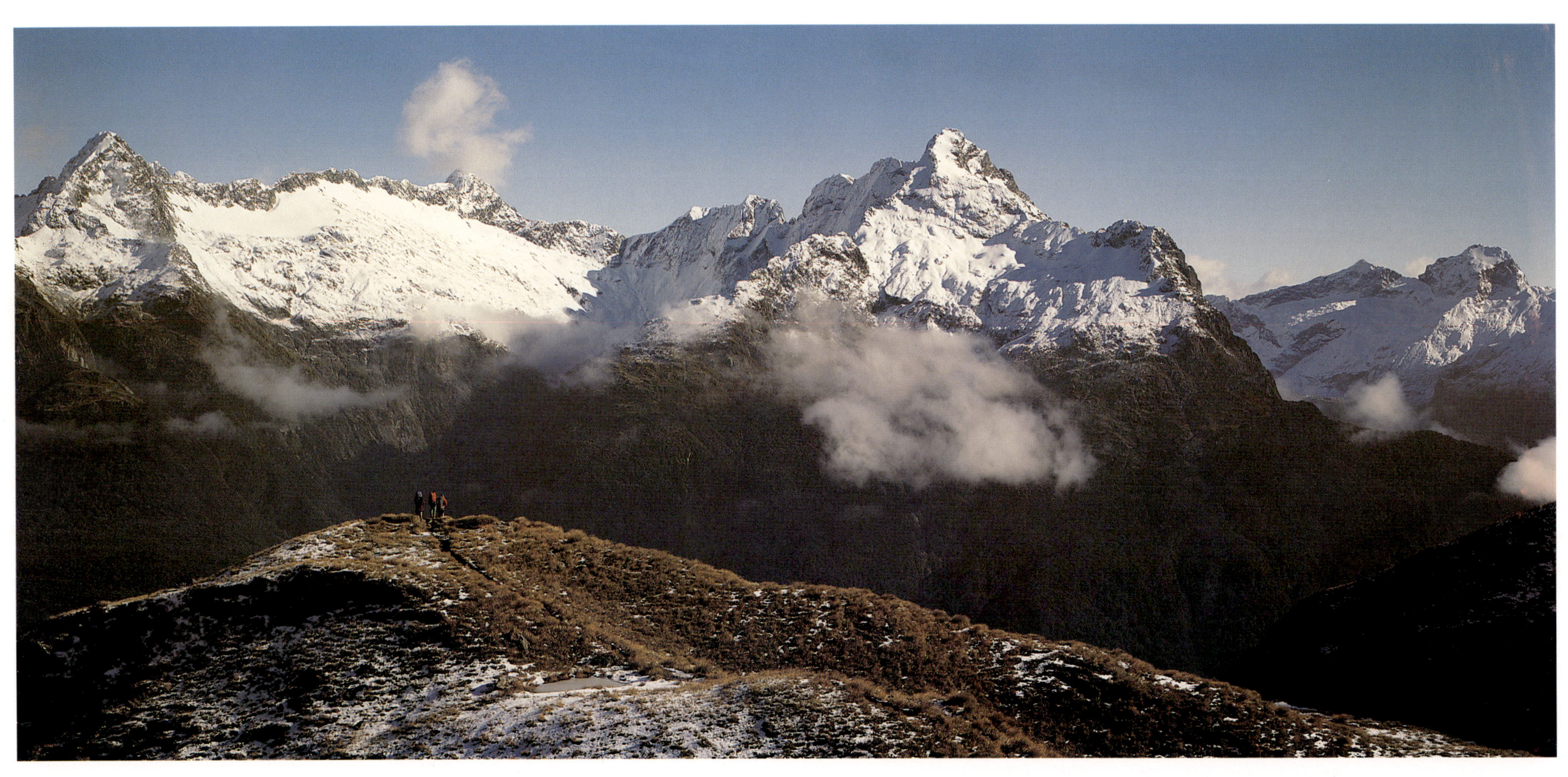

On Harris Saddle, the high point of the Routeburn Track, looking west towards Mt Gunn on the left (2,050 metres) and East Peak (2,158 metres) in the Darran Mountains.

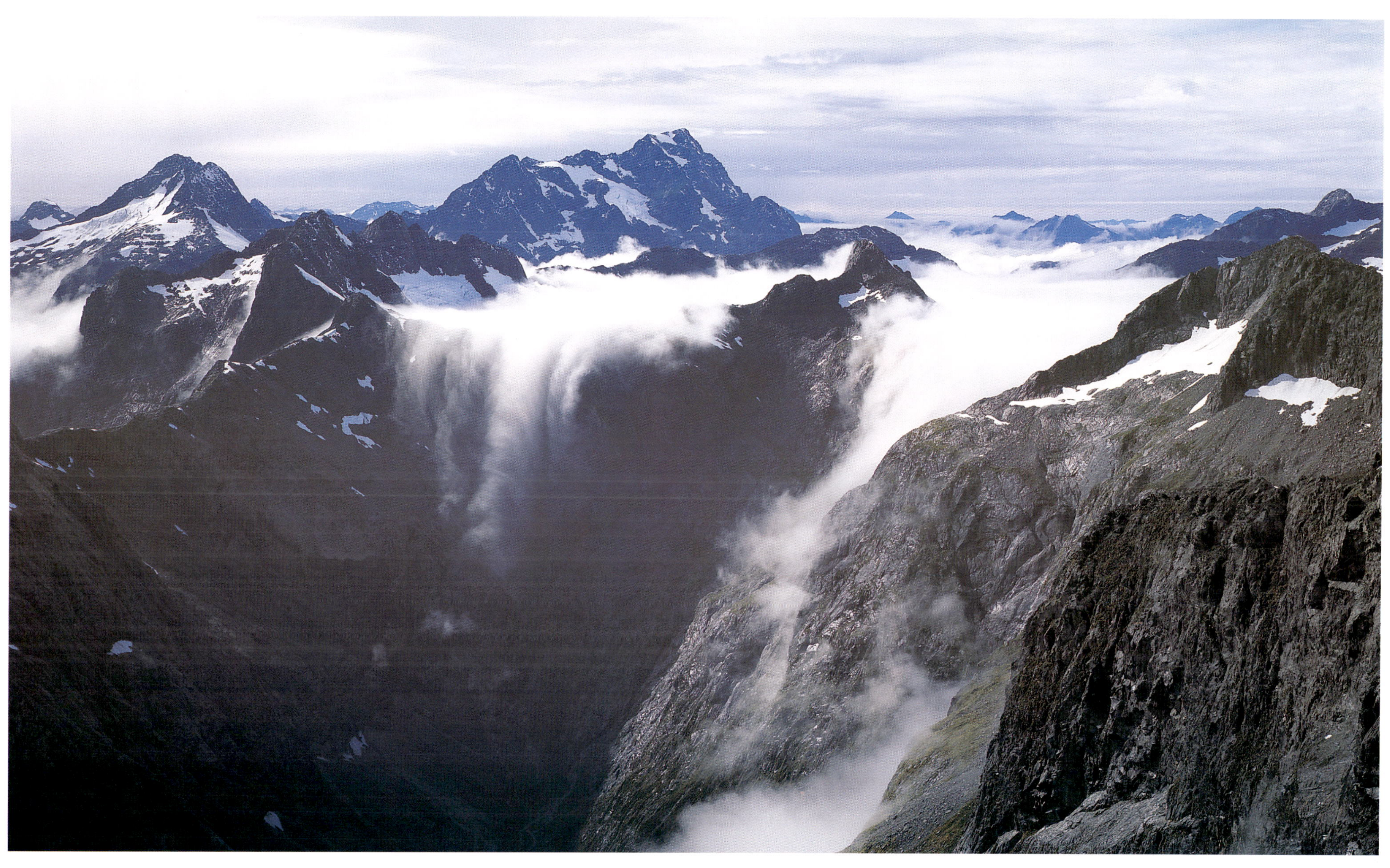

Photographed from Mt Gendarme in the Wick Mountains, the imposing bulk of Mt Christina (2,504 metres), dominates the view east while in the foreground cloud blanketing the head of the Hollyford valley dissipates as it spills over into the valleys on the Milford side of the range.

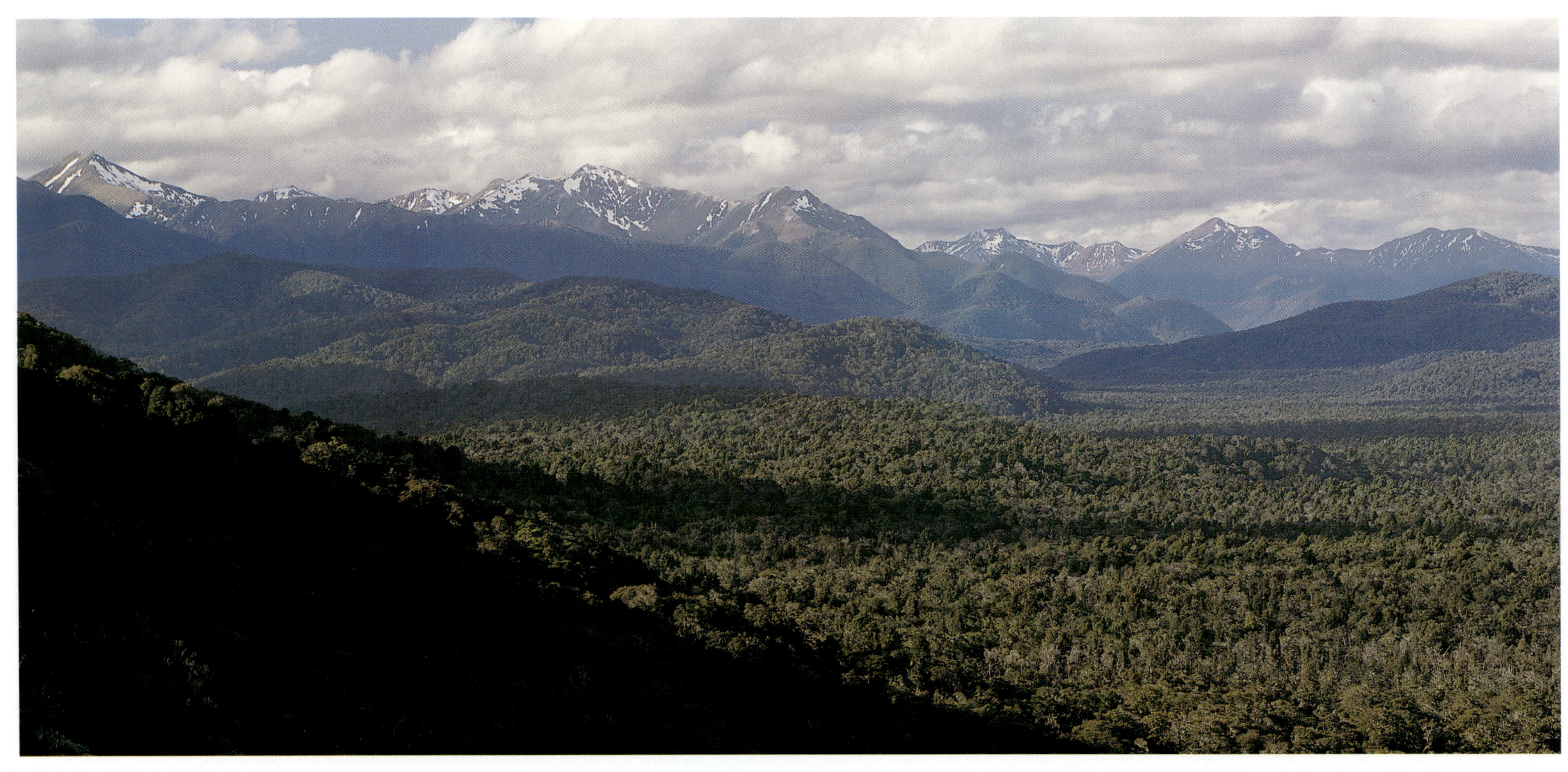

The 45,000-hectare Waitutu Forest west of Hump Ridge (opposite) is one of the largest tracts of unmodified lowland forest left in New Zealand and is of outstanding conservation significance for its unique sequence of marine terraces, superb podocarp forest and diversity of threatened species (which includes all four species of threatened native freshwater fish present in the Southland/Fiordland region).

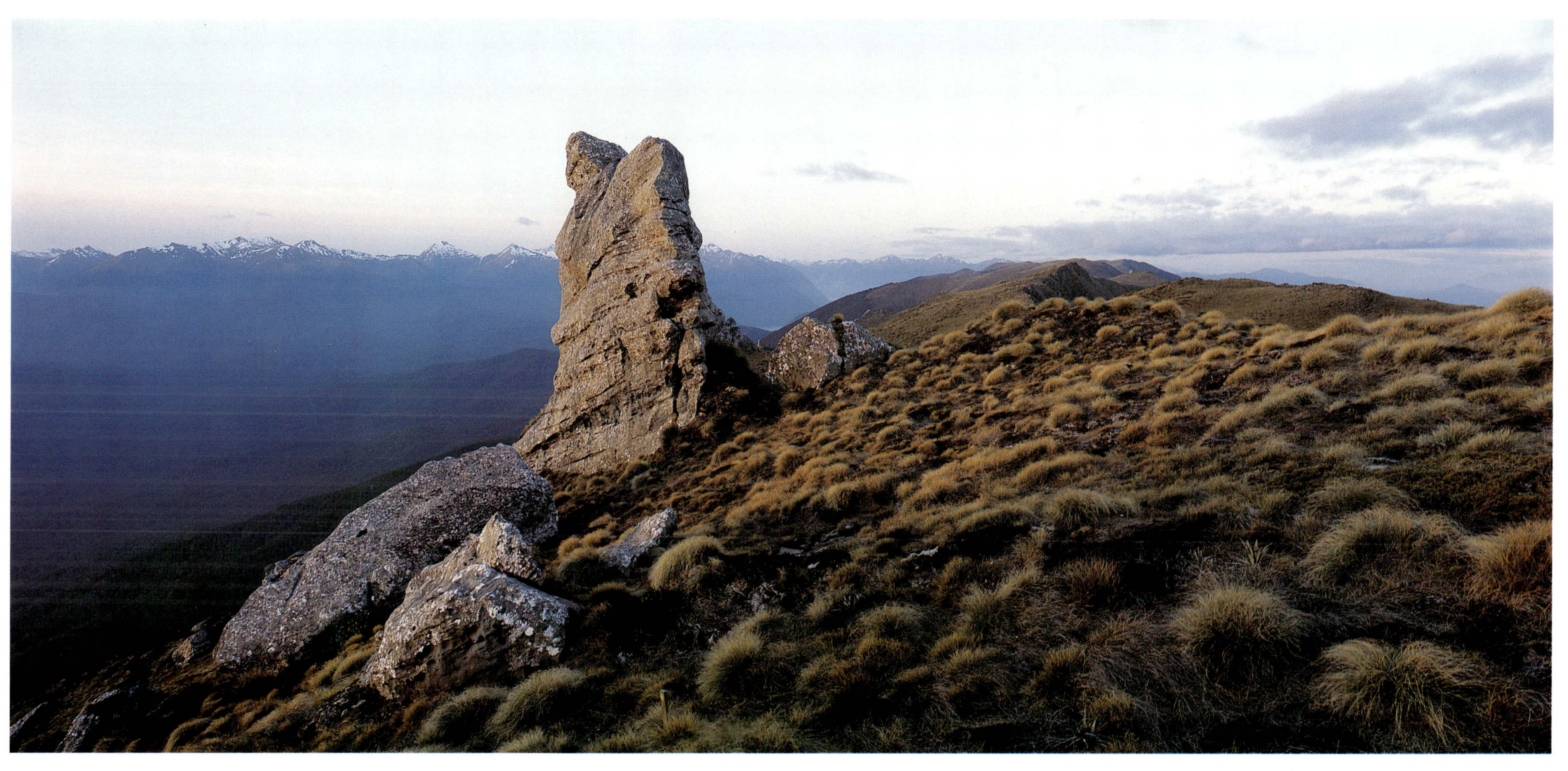

The tussock-covered Hump Ridge lies at the south-eastern extremity of Te Wahipounamu between Lake Hauroko and the south coast. Standing aloof from the ranges to both the north and west it provides superb views of the southern Fiordland coastal region and is also a location of major biological significance, especially for the high level of invertebrates that are unique to the area.

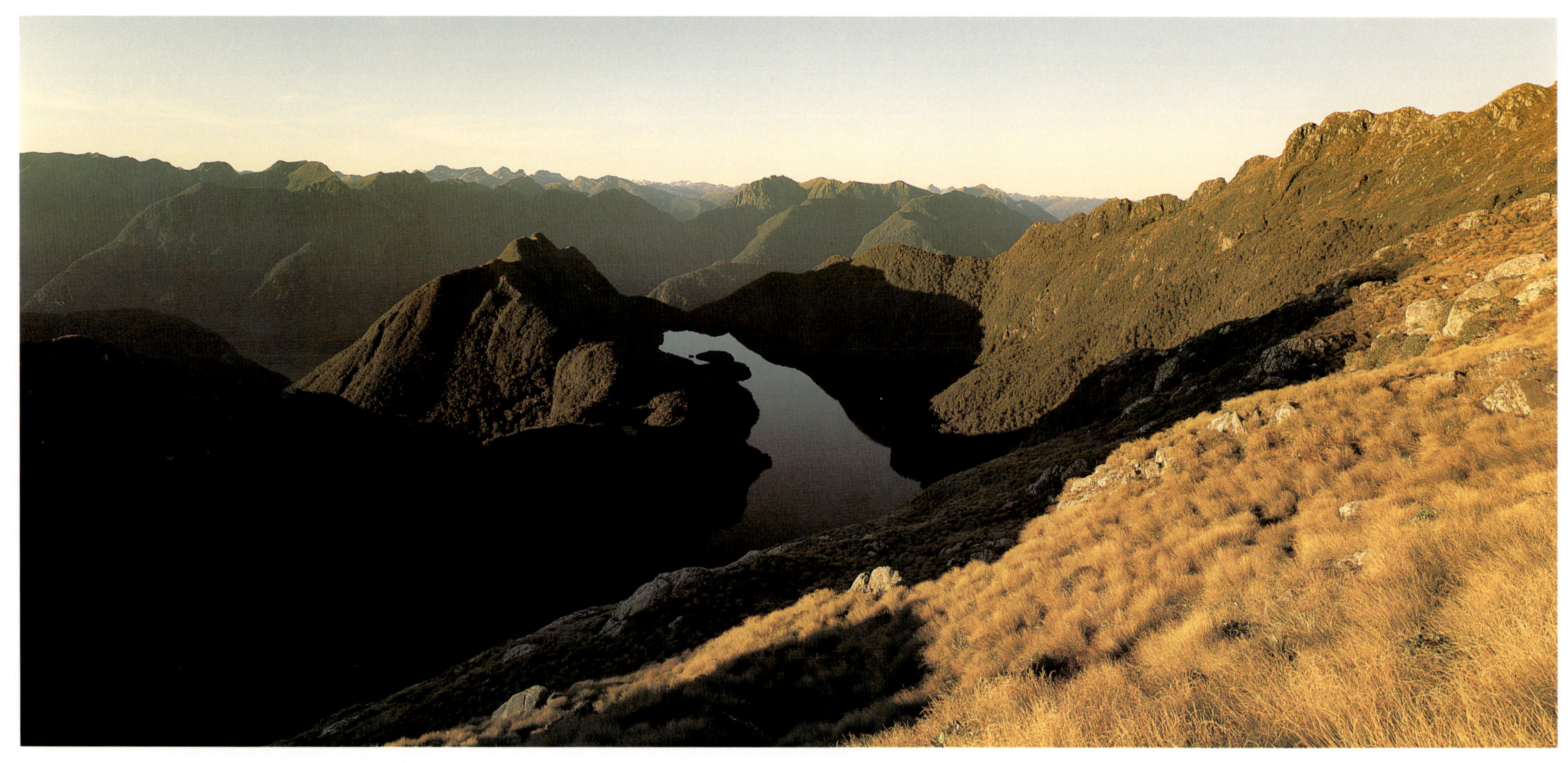

Morning light illuminates alpine tussock grasslands on the upper slopes of Mt Richards just north of the entrance to Breaksea Sound. The photograph looks southwards across a high unnamed lake towards the ranges between Breaksea and Dusky sounds.